Formative Assessment for LITERACY

Grades K–6

Formative Assessment for LITERACY

Grades K–6

Building Reading
and Academic
Language Skills
Across the Curriculum

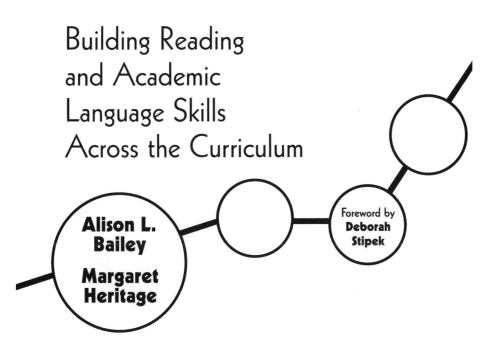

Alison L. Bailey

Margaret Heritage

Foreword by
Deborah Stipek

CORWIN PRESS
A SAGE Company
Thousand Oaks, CA 91320

Figures 2.2, 2.3, 2.4, 2.5, and 2.6 are reprinted from Bailey (Ed.), *The Language Demands of School* (p. 177), New Haven, CT: Yale University Press, by permission of Yale University Press.

For information:

Corwin Press
A SAGE Company
2455 Teller Road
Thousand Oaks, California 91320
www.corwinpress.com

SAGE Pvt. Ltd.
B 1/I 1 Mohan Cooperative
    Industrial Area
Mathura Road, New Delhi 110 044
India

SAGE Ltd.
1 Oliver's Yard
55 City Road
London EC1Y 1SP
United Kingdom

SAGE Asia-Pacific Pte. Ltd.
33 Pekin Street #02–01
Far East Square
Singapore 048763

Printed in the United States of America

Library of Congress Cataloging-in-Publication Data

Bailey, Alison L.
Formative assessment for literacy, grades K-6 : building reading and academic language skills across the curriculum / Alison L. Bailey, Margaret Heritage.
    p. cm.
Includes bibliographical references and index.
ISBN 978-1-4129-4907-1 (cloth)
ISBN 978-1-4129-4908-8 (pbk.)
    1. English language—Study and teaching (Elementary)—United States. 2. Language arts—United States—Evaluation. 3. Educational tests and measurements—United States. 4. Effective teaching—United States. I. Bailey, Alison L. II. Heritage, Margaret. III. Title.

LB1576.B24 2008
372.6'044—dc22   2007050192

This book is printed on acid-free paper.

08   09   10   11   12   10 9 8 7 6 5 4 3 2 1

Acquisitions Editor:	Cathy Hernandez
Editorial Assistant:	Ena Rosen
Production Editor:	Veronica Stapleton
Copy Editor:	Gretchen Treadwell
Typesetter:	C&M Digitals (P) Ltd.
Proofreader:	Dennis Webb
Indexer:	Kirsten Kite
Cover Designer:	Karine Hovsepian

Table of Contents

Foreword

Anyone who thinks it is easy to teach reading needs to read this book. It places in clear relief that reading is a multifaceted activity. Teaching reading requires attention to every facet of reading development, as well as closely assessing how children's skills are evolving to ensure that instruction constantly matches their needs. First, children need to know the basics—that the scribbles on pages represent sounds which add up to words which add up to sentences, that they read from left to right, and so on. They need to develop phonological awareness, decoding, and sight recognition of familiar words.

Reading also requires knowledge and experience. Most of us would have no difficulty reading the words in an article on astrophysics, but few of us would be able to make any sense of what we had "read," just as a child who is unfamiliar with baseball might have difficulty making sense of a story about a baseball team. Vocabulary is also important, as well as an understanding of grammatical structures. Most of us can get the gist of a text, even if we don't know one or two words. But consider the child who is not familiar with many of the words, including words central to the topic of the text. For many children, the problem is not in decoding the words, it is in making sense of them. This is especially true for those children who come to school with English as a second language.

Indeed, language and reading skills are fundamentally related, yet much of what is written on reading has little to say about its connection to language development. This book integrates the two, making clear the importance of developing academic language to enable students to read texts in the disciplines they encounter in school. We now recognize that reading, science, math, novels, and poetry require different kinds of knowledge and vocabulary, and an understanding of different genres of writing and styles of discourse. Like it or not, teachers of all disciplines are reading teachers.

Students also need to develop the *metacognitive* skills required to make sense of text—identifying key concepts and ideas, making appropriate inferences and connections with previous knowledge, assessing comprehension, and so on. These strategies do not come naturally to most children. They need to be taught, and teachers need to know how to teach them.

Effective teachers need knowledge of the processes involved in reading and the academic language in the domain in which they are teaching. Moreover, they have to know how to *teach* all the various aspects of reading. Just as important, they need to know their students' current skills along the various dimensions to select appropriate materials and provide appropriate guidance to enable students to take their skills to the next level. What makes the task particularly challenging is the inevitable range of skills in a classroom of students. Whatever the class, students will vary in their experiences, vocabularies, content knowledge, use of comprehension strategies, and in the early grades, decoding skills.

Assessment, therefore, is a critical part of effective teaching. Indeed, teaching reading or any discipline without continuous assessment makes little sense. Alison Bailey and Margaret Heritage understand the importance of ongoing, formative assessment. In this book, they explain how formative assessment is different from other kinds of assessment and they provide a comprehensive and detailed account of how it can be woven into any instructional program that involves reading. To make concrete the strategies they recommend, they provide many real-life applications of formative assessment, including verbatim exchanges between teachers and students, which illustrate teachers' reasoning and inferences about student learning in oral language and reading.

The book is based on the best research on reading and language development and gives readers an opportunity to see nationally renowned experts' advice in their own words. But rather than a dreary summary of research findings, this book brings alive knowledge from decades of reading research by providing detailed descriptions and illustrations of the practical implications for classroom teaching.

While the book reminds us how difficult teaching is, it comes to our rescue by providing the kind of support teachers need to do it well. In all respects, the authors of this book practice what they preach. They highlight vocabulary that may be new to the reader, and they provide definitions and many examples that illustrate the concepts they introduce. They help make the concepts useful by illustrating them with vivid applications of the strategies being implemented in real classrooms. And they provide tools (e.g., for assessment) that teachers can use in their own classrooms. The authors also reassure readers who might be intimidated by the complexity of the task that they don't have to figure it all out in a day or even alone. Just as teachers slowly and surely lead their children to being proficient readers, this book provides scaffolding and a suggested system of schoolwide support for teachers to develop their skills as reading teachers.

Deborah Stipek
Dean, Stanford School of Education

Preface

ORIGINS OF THE BOOK

The origins of this book are in the chance request made to a university laboratory school by a local school district. In 1999, Margaret Heritage, who at that time was principal of the Corinne A. Seeds University Elementary School (UES) at UCLA, was contacted by the administrators of a local school district. The administrators wanted to get a copy of the classroom assessments that UES used for identifying students who were struggling with learning to read. The staff at the school thought this was an excellent query but had to regretfully inform the district that they had no such set of materials for this vital purpose. However, Margaret and the UES teachers had for some time been considering issues of assessment and interventions for struggling readers and used the request from the school district to join forces with UCLA faculty and research staff, including Alison Bailey, to develop such materials.

Margaret had begun her career as a teacher in an elementary school where the population was 95 percent language minority students. She immediately developed a strong (and indeed necessary) interest in language development. This interest expanded to reading development, which has been a central focus of her work for many years, and has ranged from teaching young children to read to teaching teachers about reading development. Alison started her research career studying verbal input to young children as an undergraduate linguistics major. Her work in graduate school continued the focus on language development in social interaction but added the study of minority language development and literacy to the mix. Her research at UCLA has moved her work squarely into the applied realm where she has worked with teachers in various settings to understand the intersection of language and literacy and how best to assess their development for instruction.

Early on in our collaboration in these domains, a critical decision was made—take what teachers already know about assisting struggling readers and place it into a comprehensive, research-based framework for systematic formative assessment and instruction. The formative assessment approach we created was not only later subjected to a research study, but from its inception was grounded in research. A mantra we adopted then and that you will encounter throughout this book, is that all our work be "rooted in practice" to make it useful, and also "evidence-based" to be responsive to what good research can teach us.

The concerns of the district teachers and administrators and those of us at UES were primarily about the type and quality of assessments that were available to teachers to help them identify children at-risk of reading failure. Their concerns were confirmed by the National Research Council (NRC), which concluded from a review of assessment practices with preschool and kindergarten children that:

> The array of instruments currently used . . . are time-consuming and costly to administer. . . . Such measures need to be refined, extended and, as appropriate, combined into screening batteries that are maximally informative and efficient. (National Research Council, 1998)

In response to this problem, the goal of our practitioner-researcher collaboration was to develop a comprehensive and manageable assessment system that could provide teachers with diagnostic information about the development of both oral language and literacy skills, along with clear procedures for instructional intervention in the classroom with children as early as kindergarten. The result of this collaboration was the Literacy Development Checklist (LDC) and accompanying manual of in-class assessment and intervention suggestions (University Elementary School, 2001).

As Chapter 1 will outline, much impetus for this book came from our development and study of how teachers were using the LDC along with other available tools to gather information and apply it during instructional decision making. We were able put the combination of research and practice that had informed the LDC to use with various summer institutes at UES. Founded as a laboratory elementary school in 1882, UES now serves as a major catalyst for research on education and child development at UCLA, as well as a teacher training site for local public school districts.

Over the years, one of the book contributors and a former UES assistant principal, Norma Silva, has sent the teachers of her new school to the UES institutes to learn from the approaches that combine research and practice. Her current school is the Para Los Niños Charter Elementary School (PLN).

The PLN school is part of the larger community-based organization of Para Los Niños, which was originally founded to serve children in the "Skid Row" area of downtown Los Angeles. The PLN school mission is to develop literacy skills in Spanish while teaching academic English through the content areas of mathematics, science, and social studies. Teachers are trained in creating educational environments that provide experiences that promote language and conceptual knowledge. Founded in 2002, the school now educates 350 students from kindergarten through fifth grade. The PLN teachers who helped with the creation of the practice chapters describe the formative assessment strategies they use on a daily basis to help them formulate evidence of academic language and reading development throughout the curriculum. Other teachers also provided us with the impetus for this book by sharing their own formative assessment practices with us. These teachers teach at various schools, predominantly in Southern California, most with linguistically and ethnically diverse populations of students.

WHO CAN USE THIS BOOK?

Elementary school teachers, both new and experienced, should find the descriptions of others' practices immediately applicable and, we hope, inspiring for further ideas about their own formative assessment. If used as part of a pre-service program, the book can readily integrate the content of courses on language development and reading methods with assessment practices in these areas. In the professional development context, the book can be used to refresh or update in-service teacher content knowledge, as well as provide professional development directors and principals a combined course of study in the areas of language, literacy, and formative assessment.

The teachers of English language learners (ELL students) will undoubtedly find the example practices in this book especially helpful. The fact that ELL students are now a part of many mainstream classrooms due to recent educational policies (No Child Left Behind Act, 2001) makes every teacher and administrator responsible for these students' academic success. The English language learner emphasis is consequently a natural one. Throughout this book we recognize the special issues of language learning and reading for ELL students. However, language and literacy issues presented in this book are salient for *all* students—all students, whether native English speakers or not, may have issues with language in academic contexts as well as struggles with learning to read.

We also see another important purpose for this book. Administrators like Norma Silva find themselves supporting new teachers in their use of reading strategies and methods of assessment each and every year. The comprehensive model that integrates formative reading and academic language assessment for instruction in accessible ways from the practitioner's point of view will be invaluable for administrators who need to offer ongoing training and guidance to novice teachers.

OVERVIEW OF THE CHAPTERS

Chapter 1 outlines the approach we have adopted—that of real-life stories from classroom teachers using formative assessment for literacy instruction. In this chapter, we also describe in more detail our work with the LDC, as well as our vision for formative assessment in the current educational assessment arena.

Chapter 2 presents the ideas underlying the model of formative reading and academic language assessment for instruction. In our view, content knowledge cannot be separated from the linguistic means by which it is understood (Christie, 1985; Schleppegrell & Achugar, 2003). We therefore suggest that teacher domain knowledge and knowledge of academic language are of equal importance, and indeed that academic language should be part of the domain knowledge of a teacher (Heritage, Silva, & Pierce, 2007). Teachers need to invoke both knowledge components simultaneously, and consequently, the approach we have designed explicitly requires teachers to plan for both types of knowledge for their assessment and instruction in reading. While the model can be applied in broad educational settings, it is particularly relevant to assessing and instructing English language learners because of the prominence of language in this model. This chapter includes information about the crucial components of the model, including academic language, teacher domain knowledge, pedagogical content knowledge, and assessment.

In Chapter 3, we join with Mouna Mana, a graduate student of education at UCLA, to provide greater detail about the different kinds of formative assessment. We then introduce the comprehensive model that integrates teacher knowledge bases (e.g., domain knowledge of reading and academic language) with skills needed for implementing formative assessment procedures. In this chapter, we answer the following questions:

- What is formative assessment?
- What do experts have to say about it?
- Why would a teacher use formative assessment?
- How is the model of formative assessment of reading and academic language effectively used within frameworks for assessment and instruction?

Chapters 4 and 5 present the model as it applies to the areas of listening comprehension, oral language, and reading comprehension. The following key questions are addressed using examples of formative assessment being used in K–5 classrooms:

- What constitutes the domain knowledge needed by teachers in these areas?
- What should teachers look for as evidence of progression along developmental continua in these areas?
- How is the formative assessment model implemented to support development in these areas?

Specifically, Chapter 4 with principal Norma Silva, and teachers Gabriela Cardenas and Olivia Lozano of PLN, presents the formative assessment model as it applies to the areas of listening comprehension and speaking skills. This chapter includes the description of the stages of development required for successful listening and speaking abilities (e.g., vocabulary, syntax, event representation, narrative and expository genres, social and academic language, and world knowledge).

Chapter 5 with Barbara Jones, a researcher at the Center for the Study of Evaluation at UCLA, presents the model as it applies to the area of reading comprehension. This chapter includes the stages of reading development in areas such as fluency, word recognition, decoding, academic vocabulary knowledge, and comprehension.

Chapter 6 extends the promise of the model to also include examples of sixth grade English language arts instruction. Specifically, in this chapter we focus on (1) writing in so much as it informs us about student reading comprehension as reading and writing become increasingly interwoven across the curriculum and (2) the implications of the assessment model for English language arts as this content area evolves by the end of the later elementary grades to include more literary uses of language (e.g., creative writing).

In Chapter 7, we conclude the book by looking at the challenges of implementing the formative assessment model schoolwide, particularly in the area of professional development. We make recommendations for how best to prepare teachers to use assessment for instruction, particularly how the formative assessment model can be initiated and sustained by a principal or others in instructional leadership roles.

There are of course often concerns for time and compliance with assessment regulations, which we also hope to dispel with this book. While the standards movement and, more specifically, the No Child Left Behind Act adopted traditional, large-scale, summative assessments for accountability purposes, there can still be a role for formative assessment in the classroom. We, of course, look forward to the day when formative assessment can play an expanded role in the nation's accountability system, but until then, we have chosen to focus on perhaps an even more fundamental challenge to the successful adoption of formative assessment—that of a well-trained faculty. This book was written to do its part in helping to overcome this challenge. Formative assessment implemented effectively needs to be supported by high-quality, ongoing professional development. We hope that the stories told in this book can directly contribute to your knowledge of and enthusiasm for formative assessment for literacy learning.

REFERENCES

Christie, F. (1985). Language and schooling. In S. Tchudi (Ed.), *Language, schooling and society* (pp. 21–40). Upper Montclair, NJ: Boynton/Cook.

Heritage, M., Silva, N., & Pierce, M. (2007). Academic English: A View From the Classroom. In A. L. Bailey (Ed.), *The language demands of school: Putting academic English to the test.* New Haven, CT: Yale University Press.

National Research Council. (1998). *Preventing reading difficulties in young children.* Committee for the Prevention of Reading Difficulties in Young Children. C. E. Snow, M. S. Burns, & P. Griffin (Eds.). Washington, DC: National Academy Press.

No Child Left Behind Act. (2001). Pub. L. No. 107–110, 115 Stat. 1425.

Schleppegrell, M. J., & Achugar, M. (2003). Learning language and learning history: A functional linguistics approach. *TESOL Journal, 12*(2), 21–27.

University Elementary School. (2001). *The Literacy Development Checklist and Manual.* Los Angeles, CA: The Regents of the University of California. Retrieved from http://ldc.gseis.ucla.edu

Acknowledgments

First and foremost, we want to thank all the students and teachers in classrooms across Southern California, and a few other places, who allowed us to share their assessment stories for the chapters in this book. Some of the teachers and students choose to take pseudonyms to protect their anonymity; others choose not to.

We have a special word of thanks for those who agreed to write with us on several of the chapters: Mouna Mana, Norma Silva, Gabby Cardenas, Olivia Lozano, and Barbara Jones. During this process, we cooked up more than just lunch in Margaret's "kitchen" over the summer of 2006. We not only learned about language, literacy and assessment from one another, but also learned about forging truly meaningful collaborations across research and practice. This was an experiment in friendship and professional development for us all.

Next, we thank our colleagues who have encouraged us over the years, given us feedback on our ideas about assessment, or provided support in different ways for the writing that has gone into this book: Ron Gallimore, Joan Herman, Deborah Stipek, Dylan Wiliam, Frances Butler, Eva Baker, Ashley Burdick, Larry Casey, Peter Hayes, Allyssa McCabe, Kristi Smith, Robert Rueda, and Abeer Alwan.

At Corwin Press we thank Cathy Hernandez, Tatiana Richards, Megan Bedell, Phyllis Cappello, Gretchen Treadwell, and Veronica Stapleton and at the beginning, Rachel Livsey, who simply insisted we write this book until we agreed. We also wish to thank the excellent anonymous reviewers of the proposal and drafted manuscript. This book is truly a better one for all the time and effort they dedicated to the reviewing process.

Our families and all our friends are gratefully acknowledged for their continued love, support, and enthusiasm. Florence and Michael Rex Bailey remain as always the "Prof's PAs," for Alison. Philippa has been a source of encouragement to Margaret.

The book was a consummate collaboration. Neither one of us feels that we could have written the book without the other's expertise, dedication of purpose, and friendship.

Finally, we thank Nicholas Ziolkowski, John Heritage, and Frank Ziolkowski. Each of their contributions holds very special meaning for us.

PUBLISHER'S ACKNOWLEDGMENTS

Corwin Press gratefully acknowledges the contributions of the following reviewers:

Jacie Maslyk
Principal, Crafton Elementary School
Pittsburgh, PA

Carin Ong
National Board Certified Teacher
Oceanside, CA

Michael A. Power
Assistant Superintendent, Tacoma Public Schools
Tacoma, WA

Ronald L. Russell
Associate Director, Loess Hills Area Education Agency 13
Shenandoah, IA

Jeffrey Smith
Professor, College of Education
University of Otago, Dunedin, New Zealand

Brenda Vatthauer
AYP Support Coordinator, Northwest Service Cooperative
Thief River Falls, MN

About the Authors

 **Alison L. Bailey** is Associate Professor in the Psychological Studies in Education Program of the Department of Education, University of California, Los Angeles, in addition to being a faculty associate researcher for the National Center for Research on Evaluation, Standards, and Student Testing (CRESST). A graduate of Harvard University, Dr. Bailey's research focuses primarily on language and literacy development, English language development in second language learners, and language assessment. At CRESST, her work focuses on researching the empirical basis of academic language for assessment, curriculum, and teacher professional development. Dr. Bailey serves on the advisory boards of numerous states and commercial publishers developing language and literacy assessments for English language learners. Dr. Bailey is also coauthor of the new *IPT Assessment of English Language Development, Pre-Kindergarten-Kindergarten* (Ballard and Tighe Publishers, 2005), editor and contributing author to *The Language Demands of School: Putting Academic English to the Test* (Yale University Press, 2007), and coeditor and contributing author (with Allyssa McCabe and Gigliana Melzi) of *Spanish-Language Narration and Literacy: Cognition, Culture and Emotion* (Cambridge University Press, forthcoming, 2008).

 **Margaret Heritage** is Assistant Director for Professional Development at the National Center for Research on Evaluation, Standards, and Student Testing (CRESST) at UCLA, and also leads the Data Use Program of the Accountability and Assessment Comprehensive Center. Prior to joining CRESST, she had many years experience in schools as a teacher and administrator in the United Kingdom and the United States, including a period as a County Inspector of Education in the United Kingdom, and as Principal of the University Elementary School, the laboratory school of the Department

of Education at UCLA. Heritage has extensive experience in teaching reading development at the University of Warwick, England, and at UCLA. Currently, she is a member of the advisory group for the Chief Council of State School Officers' initiative on formative assessment and of the Teaching and Learning Subgroup of the National Forum on Education Statistics Data Model Task Force.

Heritage has made numerous conference presentations and published extensively on topics including literacy, data use, and assessment. Her current work focuses on data use for school improvement, including formative assessment, the development of literacy assessment tools, and the measurement of teachers' mathematics knowledge.

This artwork was produced by a group of second grade students at Para Los Niños Charter Elementary School, Los Angeles, as a response to their science study on force and motion.

Used with permission.

1

Formative Assessment

*Stories of Language
and Literacy Learning*

> Craft knowledge is the collection of wisdom and insights one accumulates by showing up on the job. If ways can be found to unlock, celebrate, and exchange craft knowledge, how much better each of us can perform our work. Storytelling is one way.
>
> —Roland Barth (2003, p. 2)

This is a book of storytelling—stories from and about teachers using work-a-day assessments for effective teaching. We take to heart Roland Barth's suggestion that storytelling can be a vital instrument in the professional development toolkit (Barth, 2003). Storytelling has both cognitive and cultural appeal to us as authors and as educators. The purposeful recounting of events in our lives may be a basic human trait—a way to make meaning out of the apparent mayhem and chaos of day-to-day happenings (Bruner, 1990). And storytelling, while favoring different norms for style and content in different cultures, is a form of interaction found in most, if not all, human societies (Pinker, 2002).

In a series of real-life stories, this book reveals how to successfully implement an integrated model of language and literacy with assessment for instruction. Specifically, the formative assessments we describe in the chapters of this book provide teachers with the kind of information they need for effective language and literacy instruction. By formative assessment we mean the types of tasks, tests, activities, and observations that give teachers a steady stream of information and feedback on their teaching and their students' learning. In short, the stories this book contains are stories of how teachers have made order out of the chaos of teaching and assessment so that they might share their "craft knowledge" with other teachers.

The chapters devoted to practice describe the use of assessment for instruction in the oral language skills of the classroom context (academic language) and in literacy, primarily reading. Each chapter contains stories of formative assessment used by real classroom teachers. Many of these teachers teach at the Para Los Niños (PLN) Charter Elementary School in Los Angeles, California. Implementation of the model of reading and academic language assessment for instruction with ELL students is at the very core of teaching at PLN Charter Elementary School. The fact that the book includes an emphasis on this population of students is a decision which deserves some attention.

The English language learner population is large and growing. By the last official count, there are 5.1 million English language learners enrolled in U.S. public schools (U.S. Department of Education, 2005a). These large numbers alone should warrant the attention of educational researchers and teachers alike; however, ELL students are also not doing well in our schools. Among these children, reading performance on the National

Assessment of Educational Progress (NAEP) at fourth and eighth grade levels is alarming; 73 percent of fourth graders and 71 percent of eighth graders who are ELL students cannot read at or above the basic level (U.S. Department of Education, 2005b). As Diane August, the principal investigator of the recent Report of the National Literacy Panel urges us:

> Rapid increases in the numbers of language-minority children and youth, as well as their low levels of literacy attainment and its consequences—high dropout rates, poor job prospects, and poverty—create an imperative to attend to the literacy development of these students. (August & Shanahan, 2006, p. xiii)

The narration of events unfolding in these teachers' and other teachers' classrooms illuminates how teachers can focus on both the language skills and the reading development that has to take place for school success. Knowledge of both domains by teachers is incomplete without the wherewithal to assess and interpret the results of assessment for instruction. This is where we propose an integrated model of formative reading and academic language assessment for instruction. The model is described in Chapters 2 and 3 and can be viewed in two halves. The first half is made up of the knowledge that teachers will need in order to make any kind of judgment of a student's progress or development in reading or academic language. This knowledge includes the domain knowledge of reading and academic language, as well as pedagogical content knowledge of instructional and formative assessment strategies. The second half of the model includes the skills that teachers will need to competently implement different kinds of formative assessment (e.g., observations, analysis of student responses, planned-for interactions, and so on) and interpret the evidence of learning (or not learning) that formative assessments generate.

As we capture in Chapter 7, the implementation of the formative assessment model is best done with the help of peers, instructional leaders, and principals so that a culture of support and positive attitude is built up around the use of formative assessment. Some of our own recent research findings and those of our colleagues have shown that these three components—*knowledge, skills,* and *attitude*—are important teacher characteristics and thus need to be central to professional development:

> First, teacher knowledge is emphasized for an effective understanding of content-area concepts, processes (big ideas and connections between and among them), and facts and their organization, as well as an understanding of how formative assessment is conducted. Then, teacher skills are stressed for the competent execution of learning activities and the proficient interpretation and translation

of assessment information into instructional action. Finally, teacher attitude is acknowledged . . . as the appreciation for the pivotal role of formative assessment in instruction; namely the understanding that formative assessment is worthwhile, that it yields sound information about student learning, and could have value in a comprehensive accountability system. . . . (Heritage & Bailey, 2006, p. 147)

ROOTED IN PRACTICE—RESPONSIVE TO RESEARCH

The book is rooted in practice. It is also responsive to research. While teachers write about their practice, they also make links to a variety of studies that have, for example, investigated the effectiveness of certain instructional techniques, or researched certain language and reading measures for their abilities to predict later reading success. Throughout the book, we report on the details of studies in separate "What the Experts Say" text boxes for ease of reference. The two chapters that review language and literacy development and formative assessment are also informed by research. In these foundational chapters, we explain findings from research studies to provide the rationale for the integration of a wide array of academic language and reading skills in assessment and instructional practices. We also provide definitions and further examples of "Key Terminology" in separate text boxes that are meant to function primarily as refresher material rather than be in-depth descriptions of new concepts or knowledge.

LEARNING TO "SEE" THE RIGHT STUDENT NEEDS

The Literacy Development Checklist (LDC) was developed at the University Elementary School (UES) between 1999–2002. The research and development team of teachers and researchers collated and field tested a wide range of available and newly created assessments and interventions in the classrooms of UES and local school district teachers. The checklist was then further refined during a Governor's Reading Professional Development Institute for teachers in California, which was held at UES. The UES laboratory setting allowed for a unique component: the institute participants spent time working one-on-one with students whom they had identified as at-risk for reading difficulties using assessment and interventions provided by the LDC.

In 2000, the National Science Foundation provided a grant to study teacher use of the LDC (University Elementary School, 2001). This small-scale study found that the students who were identified as struggling readers were, as a group, below the norm on many standardized measures of literacy—suggesting that the teachers, using their formative assessments, were indeed focusing on the "right" group of students. We concluded that teachers had readily learned to "see" the strengths and weaknesses of their students through a research-based lens (Bailey & Drummond, 2006; Bailey & Gallimore, 2001/2). By research-based lens, we mean making judgments of student performance in the language and literacy domains proven related to successful reading outcomes by research studies. What this and other work demonstrated to us is that classroom-based assessments of reading, by providing ongoing information to guide instruction in response to students' specific needs, appear key to improving students' reading success.

A VISION FOR A READING ASSESSMENT SYSTEM

In *Knowing What Students Know (KWSK)*, a committee of the National Research Council (NRC) described an ambitious vision for a coordinated system of assessment that includes assessments to give teachers the day-to-day information they need to guide instruction and assessments to provide evidence of student achievement needed by the public and policy makers (NRC, 2001).

The committee outlined three characteristics of such a system:

1. *Comprehensiveness.* A system that includes a range of ways to assess students to provide the evidence needed for educational decision making

2. *Coherence.* A system that combines large-scale and classroom-based assessments built on the same underlying models of student progression in learning with assessments providing information that maps back to the progression

3. *Continuity.* A system that includes measures of students' progress over time (more like a video than a snapshot) to provide a continuous stream of evidence about performance

Although we remain at quite a distance from the *KWSK* vision, there are a number of ways in which teachers can move toward realizing at least part of this vision to benefit their students' reading development (NRC, 2001).

First, while most existing standards emphasize what levels of performance students should reach at specific points, in the main, they do not set out a clear progression in learning. To better support teaching and assessment, teachers can use their reading content knowledge to create collectively a detailed progression of learning to read, or in other words, a road map to reading proficiency. Many teachers in schools and districts have already begun this work and have a clearly defined progression in reading skills along the sequence in which they typically develop. A similar progression of academic language skills would help teachers know what the sequence in syntactic development, for example, might look like. Moreover, if the academic language pathway were linked to the reading pathway, teachers would have information about both academic language and reading skills that they could profitably use in instruction. We will examine in more detail in Chapters 4, 5, and 6 how teachers can establish academic language demands in conjunction with a learning progression of reading development.

The benefits of such learning progressions are that, in addition to enabling systematic planning, they also permit teachers to connect a range of formative assessment opportunities to a continuum of learning along which students are expected to progress. The information from the assessments maps back onto the progression and assists teachers to identify where students are in their learning and, additionally, to pinpoint what they need to do next with each child.

These practices all relate to the three *Cs* in the *KWSK* vision (NRC, 2001). Employing a range of formative assessment strategies provides teachers with a *comprehensive* system of assessing their students. Assessments connected to a progression of proficiency in reading present a *coherent* view of student achievement, and also provide teachers with *continuous* evidence about performance in reading.

Where do summative, interim benchmark, and diagnostic assessments fit into this picture? Although these assessments are not constructed from a progression of learning like the one described above, they directly reflect (or should reflect) the standards that students are expected to reach. Learning progressions should articulate, in terms of a pathway, how to meet state and other desired standards. For example, one of Wisconsin's English language arts–reading standards at fourth grade is expressed as:

---

1. Use effective reading strategies to achieve their purposes in reading

   A component of the standard is described as:

   - Uses a variety of strategies and word recognition skills, including rereading, finding context clues, applying knowledge of letter-sound relationships, and analyzing word structures (Wisconsin Department of Public Instruction, 2005).

Figure 1.1   Fourth Grade English Language Arts–Reading Standard from Wisconsin

To effectively plan instruction, teachers will need to build a learning progression that outlines the enabling skills required to "use a variety of strategies and word recognition skills" expressed in this standard. The learning progression will serve to focus formative assessments so that instruction can be targeted to students' needs as they are developing the necessary enabling skills. Thus, there will be clear links between formative assessments and summative and benchmark assessments.

NEXT STEPS

Essentially, this book is an outgrowth of the LDC and our own continued study of assessment, language, and literacy. The book aims to assist teachers, through a range of formative assessment strategies, to collect evidence of their students' strengths and weaknesses in critical aspects of language and reading development. From the outset, our work on the development of the LDC was framed by theory and grounded in classroom practice. We have adopted a similar approach in writing this book. Together with the vision of assessment we have outlined and a theoretical framework to be described in Chapters 2 and 3, we can point to what teachers should look for as evidence of aspects of academic language and reading development. The stories of classroom practice at UES, PLN Charter Elementary School, and many other schools will serve as guides for using this evidence to plan instruction. As we move to the next chapter, we are reminded of Roland Barth's words at the beginning of this chapter—the stories told in this book are a form of exchange of knowledge from which all teachers can benefit.

REFERENCES

August, D., & Shanahan, T. (2006). *Developing literacy in second language learners: Report of the National Literacy Panel on language minority children and youth.* Mahwah, NJ: Lawrence Erlbaum Associates.

Bailey, A. L., & Drummond, K. V. (2006). Who's at risk and why? Teachers' understanding of early literacy and their rationale for the selection of students for targeted intervention. *Educational Assessment, 11*(3 & 4), 149–178.

Bailey, A. L., & Gallimore, R. (2001/2). *Building bridges to student and teacher learning: Early literacy assessment and intervention project: Year one & year two.* Annual Reports to IERI/NSF. Grant No. 0089302. University of California, Los Angeles.

Barth, R. (2003). *Lessons learned.* Thousand Oaks, CA: Corwin Press.

Bruner, J. (1990). *Acts of meaning.* Cambridge, MA: Harvard University Press.

Heritage, M., & Bailey, A. L. (2006). Assessing to teach: An introduction. *Educational Assessment, 11*(3 & 4), 145–148.

National Research Council. (2001). *Knowing what students know: The science and design of educational assessment.* Committee on the Foundations of Assessment. J. Pellegrino, N. Chudowsky, & R. Glaser (Eds.). Washington, DC: National Academies Press.

Pinker, S. (2002). *The blank slate.* New York, NY: Penguin Group, Inc.

University Elementary School. (2001). *The Literacy Development Checklist and Manual.* Los Angeles, CA: The Regents of the University of California. Retrieved from http://ldc.gseis.ucla.edu

U.S. Department of Education. (2005a). *Public Elementary and Secondary Students, Staff, Schools, and School Districts: School Year 2002-03.* National Center for Education Statistics. Retrieved October 12, 2006, from http://nces.ed.gov/pubsearch/pubsinfo.asp?pubid=2005314

U.S. Department of Education. (2005b). *Investigating the Potential Effects of Exclusion Rates on Assessment Results.* National Center for Education Statistics. Retrieved November 6, 2006, from http://nces.ed.gov/nationsreportcard/about/2005_effect_exclusion.asp

Wisconsin Department of Public Instruction. (2005). *Wisconsin's Model Academic Standards for English Language Arts.* Retrieved October 2, 2006, from http://www.dpi.state.wi.us/standards/elaa4.html

2

Making Reading Instruction and Assessment Work for Students and Teachers

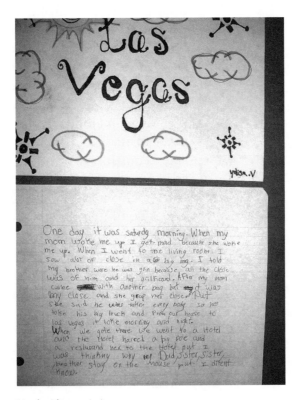

Used with permission.

INTRODUCTION

Reading is a complex linguistic achievement, and teaching children to read is a complex activity requiring a great deal of knowledge and skill.

Let us consider some of the knowledge and skills that we need in order to be effective teachers of reading. First, we must have knowledge about the content of reading and what children need to learn in order to become successful readers. The National Reading Panel (NRP, 2000) identified five core areas of learning for reading proficiency: phoneme awareness, phonics, vocabulary, comprehension, and fluency. We need to have detailed knowledge of all of these areas and their subcomponents. Second, we need to know about the development of reading. This means that in addition to knowledge of what skills to teach, we need to know when to teach them, what level of texts are appropriate for which stage of development, and what differentiates a strong reader from a weaker reader. Third, we must have knowledge about how to teach the range of skills children need for reading competence, how to select the most appropriate method for each child, and how to ensure that these methods motivate children to learn to read and to find reading enjoyable. Fourth, we need to know how to assess students and how to use a range of assessment information to plan for the next steps in children's reading development. Finally, we must have the skills to actually apply all this knowledge in the classroom.

As if all this were not enough, in addition to all the knowledge and skills we have already described, we include academic language as an important aspect in the teaching of reading. What is academic language and why do we include it? To answer this question, first we need to

KEY TERMINOLOGY

Phonological Awareness: The ability to focus on and manipulate phonemes in spoken words. Phonemes are the smallest units of sound in spoken language.

Decoding: The process of identifying unknown words by using knowledge of letter-sound correspondences.

Sight Recognition: Words recognized immediately on sight without need for deliberate decoding.

Receptive Vocabulary: The words comprehended but not necessarily produced spontaneously in speech.

Expressive Vocabulary: The words known and produced in spontaneous speech.

Grammatical Structure (Syntax): The grammar of the language—divided into simple and complex. Simple syntax includes declarative (e.g., "John saw Mary"), interrogative (e.g., "Did John see Mary?"), and imperative (e.g., "John, sit quietly!") sentences. Complex syntax includes subordinate clauses (e.g., "I went yesterday *to see the show*") and embedded clauses (e.g., "John, *who wore a yellow raincoat,* ran for the last bus").

Discourse: The use of language for extended verbal interaction (e.g., conversation, storytelling, exposition.)

Genres: A category of artistic composition, as in music or literature, marked by a distinctive style, form, or content. Dominant literacy genres include storytelling or narrative and factual or expository.

review what we mean by reading and then we will discuss what we mean by academic language and how it is integral to reading.

What Is Reading?

Hollis Scarborough (2001) has catalogued the skills that need to be coordinated for reading to occur. These include *phonological awareness, decoding* skills, *sight recognition* of familiar words, background knowledge of the subject of the text, *receptive* and *expressive vocabulary*, knowledge of *grammatical structures,* inferential skills, and knowledge of different styles of *discourse,* including different *genres* (e.g., narrative, expository).

While reading requires the skillful coordination of many cognitive and linguistic abilities, at its essence it comes down to the recognition of arbitrary symbols on a page or screen that are known to convey meaning. The fluent decoding of combinations of symbols as *words* and of combinations of words as *sentences,* allows us to comprehend the meaning intended by the author. In this book, we pay close attention to the oral language (listening and speaking) antecedents of reading, as well as the often hard to assess and teach meaning-making goal of reading—comprehension.

Teachers anticipate that long before children are taught to read in school, they have been exposed to a rich base of oral language, have heard countless storybooks, and have comics and print-bearing toys in their homes or preschools. These *emergent literacy* experiences along with opportunities to listen to and use oral language extensively prepare students for taking language to the next level—deciphering and encoding it in print—themselves. However, due to differences in sociocultural contexts, not all children will have had such opportunities in English for many different reasons;

> **KEY TERMINOLOGY**
>
> **Emergent Literacy:** Reading-related behavior and activities prior to a child's acquisition of independent reading that demonstrate an understanding of the nature of reading and writing (e.g., looking at books, pretend reading/writing, telling a story from pictures).

English may not be the language of the home, they may not have attended a preschool that focuses on emergent literacy activities, or their families may not be in a position to provide such emergent literacy experiences themselves (Goldenberg, Rueda, & August, 2006). For many students, English is a second or, more accurately, an additional language, because students may learn English after they have already acquired both an indigenous language (e.g., Zapotec) and a national language (e.g., Spanish). English language learners (ELLs) acquire some reading skills (e.g., decoding) in English in much the same manner as native English-speaking students.

KEY TERMINOLOGY

Pragmatics: The culturally appropriate use of language (e.g., politeness routines).

Language Functions: The uses to which language is put, or what we do with language, including explaining, describing, comparing, and summarizing.

Lexicon: The entire vocabulary knowledge of an individual or a thematic subset of words (e.g., mathematics lexicon).

Morpheme: The smallest unit of language that carries meaning. This is often a word, but also derivational affixes, such as "un-" to form an opposite meaning of a word (e.g., *un+likely*), and "-ness" to form a noun from an adjective (e.g., *good+ness*).

Academic Vocabulary: The words used in school settings; can be either general vocabulary that cuts across subject matter (e.g., *describe, create*), or specialized vocabulary that is often prominent in one subject (e.g., *subtraction, water cycle*).

Register: Knowing what to say and how to say it to fit the situation (e.g., formal language used to talk with a teacher versus informal language used to talk with friends).

Context-Embedded (Contextualized): Language used in ways that meaning can be inferred from the immediate surrounding often in the "here and now" (e.g., pointing to a door and saying "Can you close that?" is only comprehended in the context in which it is uttered).

Context-Reduced (De-Contextualized): Language used in ways that do not depend on information about the surroundings at the point it was uttered or written. (e.g., using full nouns for objects or people the first time that they are introduced rather than pronouns *he* or *it* to allow an interlocutor or future reader to comprehend without the aid of the "here and now."

However, other aspects of their oral English skills (e.g., knowledge of syntax) may not be as well-developed as the oral language skills of native English-speaking children and thus not as predictive of their reading outcomes (Chiappe & Siegel, 1999; Chiappe, Siegel, & Wade-Woolley, 2002).

In this book, we devote chapters to the formative assessment of various language and literacy components as each impacts successful reading development—listening comprehension and oral language production, and fluent decoding and reading comprehension.

Now let's consider what we mean by academic language.

What Is Academic Language?

Most often, we learn to speak our native language in the home with a familiar caregiver (Snow, 1977). We learn the *pragmatics* of language so we can use it in a variety of meaningful ways. One very important way we must come to use language is in order to access and engage with the school curriculum. While social uses of language are still important for interaction with peers and teachers in school (Hicks, 1994), often the language of the classroom and of textbooks is characterized by a more formal *register:* a specific way of talking (e.g., use of *academic vocabulary* and specific syntactic structures), for a particular *language function*, or in a particular context—in this case all for acquiring new knowledge in school. This is what we mean by academic language (Schleppegrell, 2004).

Each child will have a different experience of the acquisition of academic language development. Some children will have exposure to academic language through concept and word building activities inside and outside the home (e.g., museum visits) prior to starting school. Still other students will acquire most of their academic understanding and use of language in the school context. For example, ELL students may acquire much of their English language in school. Thus, academic language can in one sense be usefully defined as the unique interaction between language and the personal linguistic experiences of each child.

However, we can still attempt to characterize the language demands that most students face in school on three linguistic levels:

Word level: Demands include the development of different types of word knowledge. This includes general academic word knowledge (also referred to as "mortar" words) that cuts across several content areas (e.g., *progress, measure, report*) and specialized word knowledge for the different content areas such as the technical terminology used in disciplines like math and science (e.g., *base-ten; magma; water cycle*), as well as the words from everyday vocabulary that are used in different senses in a math or science context for instance (e.g., *by* or *goes into* to mean *to divide*). This vocabulary is learned alongside the continued acquisition of a social domain *lexicon*, or the everyday words of home and the playground.

Sentence level: The development of increasingly complex syntax or grammatical structures is necessary to convey precise relationships between ideas, facts, or objects. For example, to express comparisons such as *"town X is larger than town Y"*, the productive use of the *morpheme "-er"* is added to the end of adjectives in English along with the necessary grammatical structure "x than y."

What the Experts Say About Academic Language

Cummins (1981) distinguishes between *Cognitive Academic Language Proficiency* (CALP) and everyday language, which he called *Basic Interpersonal Communicative Skills* (BICS). CALP is thought to be both cognitively demanding and *context-reduced (decontextualized)*, whereas BICS is claimed to be cognitively undemanding and *context-embedded (contextualized)*.

More recently there has been an emphasis on the functions of language in the classroom (Bailey, Butler, Stevens, & Lord, 2007; Chamat & O'Malley, 1994; Cummins, 2000; Phillips, 1972; Schleppegrell, 2001; Schleppegrell, 2004). These *language functions* are the purposes we have for language, and in a school context these include labeling, explaining, describing, summarizing, and hypothesizing.

(Continued)

(Continued)

> The difference between the features of language in school and language in the home can be substantial because different speech communities (e.g., Los Angeles Chicano English) may adopt the following: (1) distinct *lexicons*, (2) non-conventional grammatical structures for the *syntax* of sentences, and (3) distinct *discourse* styles that become the hallmark of membership in the speech community (Delpit, 1995; Goldenberg, 1993; Heath, 1982; Heath, 1983; Philips; 1972; Wells, 1985).

Text (Discourse) Level: Language used in written texts or speech (oral discourse) in ways to convey meaning to others. Oral language and the language of texts often have different syntactic characteristics (Bailey, Butler, Stevens, & Lord, 2007; Reppen, 2001; Schleppegrell, 2001). For example, take this sentence from a Houghton Mifflin first grade text "A chilly wind shook the doors and windows of Miss Hen's House" (McVeigh, 2004). While many first graders will have the social language skills to talk about a cold wind blowing hard, it is quite unlikely that they would use the vocabulary and syntactic structures of this text in every day conversation. Children need to learn that the language of texts is different from spoken language, and to make meaning of what they read, they need to acquire knowledge of the lexical, syntactic, and discourse features of printed language.

In the school setting, we require students to organize their written texts and oral discourse in very specific ways, for example, the creation of a lab report, a book review, a persuasive argument to defend their ideas, or a story retelling typically follow specific organizational patterns particular to each. These are ways of organizing language beyond the level of the sentence that teachers come to expect of their students.

CONTENT AREA LANGUAGE

Beginning in the middle elementary years and throughout the rest of their schooling, students will spend much of their time reading and learning information from texts (Stevens, Slavin, & Farnish, 1991). In other words, in the early grades of school, children learn to read, and in the later grades, they read to learn. Reading to learn means that, in addition to reading skills like word recognition and fluency, children need to have the academic language skills to be able to extract information when they read their content area texts. Susanna Dutro (2003) well illustrates the need for academic language skills by this example of science text: "If we had provided the soil with essential nutrients, the plant would have grown larger" (p. 4). She notes it is much more likely that in oral language the students (and probably their teachers) will express the relationship between essential nutrients and plant growth in a less complex sentence structure than in this text, for example "the plant didn't grow larger because we didn't give the soil enough nutrients." This example nicely underscores the difference between oral language and the language of texts, especially the language of content texts. Assuming that the students had the necessary background knowledge and vocabulary about plants to use the words *nutrients* and *soil*, the syntax of the printed text is more complex than the spoken language example. As Dutro points out, to understand this text students would need knowledge of conditional mood (*if . . . would have*), knowledge of the past perfect (*had grown*), knowledge of the comparative form of the word large (*larger*), and background knowledge and vocabulary about plants to understand the words *nutrients* and *soil*. Without this linguistic knowledge, students will likely not be able to access the meaning of the text.

SCHOOL NAVIGATIONAL LANGUAGE (SNL) AND CURRICULUM CONTENT LANGUAGE (CCL)

We can break academic language down still further into *School Navigational Language* (SNL) and *Curriculum Content Language* (CCL). SNL is the language needed to communicate with teachers and peers in the school setting in a very broad sense. CCL is more narrowly defined as the language used in the process of teaching and learning content material. The distinction that Cummins (1981) made between the everyday, social uses of language, *Basic Interpersonal Communication Skills* (BICS), and the language used for learning in school, *Cognitive Academic Language Proficiency* (CALP), has been criticized for equating BICS with simplicity and CALP with complexity (e.g., Bailey, 2007). Social uses of language can be cognitively demanding and take place outside the immediate context or the "here and now" as well. Because we have found the contextual and cognitive demand distinction to inadequately distinguish between definitions of social language (SL) and academic language, we have attempted to contrast these uses of language in other ways.

Figure 2.1 contrasts SL, SNL, and CCL on the purposes to which these language varieties are put, their degree of formality, the context of their uses, the context of their acquisition, the predominant modalities they utilize (e.g., listening, speaking, reading, writing), teacher expectations for language abilities across the three varieties, and grade level expectations (e.g., those set by standards, instructional materials, administrators). None of the features in the schema is exempt from being used in one or other of the language varieties. However, there is a higher probability that a given feature is used in one of the varieties rather than the others. That is, a word can function as academic in one context (*product* = a result of mathematical multiplication) and as an everyday word in another context (*product* = purchasable consumer goods). We expect words, structures, and discourse features acquired as CCL to show up in SL and SNL once they enter a student's linguistic repertoire (e.g., specialized academic vocabulary words such as *olfactory* may be added to a student's general lexicon to be subsequently used in everyday smelly situations!).

	Social Language (SL)	Academic Language (AL)	
		School Navigational Language (SNL)	Curriculum Content Language (CCL)
Purpose	To communicate with family, friends, and others in everyday, social situations.	To communicate to teachers and peers in a broad school setting (including classroom management).	To communicate to teachers and peers about the content of instruction (including lesson materials, textbooks, tests, etc).
Formality	Informal. Hallmarks: incomplete sentences, use of contractions, restricted vocabulary, contextualized language, restricted variety of genre (mainly narrative).	Informal and formal. Hallmarks: combination of both contextualized and decontextualized language.	Formal. Hallmarks: precise use of language/terminology, complete and complex sentences, lexical diversity, decontextualized referents, variety of genres (narrative and expository).
Context of use (setting)	Home. Peer group. Out-of-school activities.	School noninstructional time (including homeroom, lunch room, and playground). School instructional time (focused on classroom management; personal relationships).	School instructional time (focused on concept learning). Note: some out-of-school activities, including those at home or with peers, may focus on concept learning and thus may include hallmarks of CCL (including the preschool level).

	Social Language (SL)	Academic Language (AL)	
		School Navigational Language (SNL)	Curriculum Content Language (CCL)
Examples	*I took it [= the trash] out before [= before dinner]; Where's the shop at?*	*I need you all to be facing this way before we begin; where is your third period English class located?*	*First, the stamen forms at the center of the flower; Describe the traits of the main characters.*
Context of acquisition	Acquired without explicit instruction.	Largely acquired without explicit instruction, unless student is an ELL student.	Acquired with and without explicit instruction. ELL students, especially, may need explicit instruction.
Modality	Predominantly oral language.	Predominantly oral language.	Both oral and written language.
Teacher expectations	Students will come to school already proficient unless the student is an ELL student.	Students will readily learn language skills unless the student is an ELL student.	*All* students will need to acquire linguistic and pragmatic skills for both general use (cutting across disciplines) and specialized within a discipline. Some teachers will hold students accountable for use of "precise" CCL; others and even the same teachers at different times will allow informal/imprecise uses.
Grade level expectations	More sophisticated uses of language to solve disputes and participate as "good citizens." For ELL students, including ELD levels should be taken into account (e.g., new to the U.S. and at the beginning level will differ from a student who may be younger but at a higher ELD level).	More sophisticated uses of language. Teachers assume prior grades have prepared student to acquire the language (including reading and writing) necessary to take notes, read directions, etc. Redesignated ELL students are expected to be able to manage language demands of the classroom interaction.	More sophisticated uses of language. Higher grades rely on students having learned CCL of prior grades and rely on their reading ability to access and engage with the curriculum and on their writing ability to display or assess their learning. Redesignated ELL students are expected to be able to manage language demands of instruction.

Figure 2.1   Distinguishing Features of Social and Academic Varieties of English

So far, we have described what reading and academic languages are. Now we consider the importance of academic language to reading development.

Academic Language and Reading

Consider these excerpts from the first grade reading standards established by the National Center on Education and the Economy and the University of Pittsburgh in 1999 (New Standards Primary Literacy Standards Committee. 1999/2004, p. 104).

By the end of the year we expect students to:

1. independently read aloud from Level 1 books that have been previewed for them, using intonation, pauses, and emphasis that signal the structure of the sentence and the meaning of the text (p. 100);

2. solve reading problems and self-correct through strategies that include using syntax and word-meaning clues (p. 101);

3. retell the story in correct sequence (p. 104); and

4. from books read to students (more complex conceptual and grammatical structures), make predictions for what might happen next and why, and describe the causes and effects of specific events.

Meeting these standards (and many of the standards established by states across the nation) is not only dependent on the skills within the traditional purview of reading instruction (e.g., word recognition skills), it is equally dependent and based upon students' knowledge of grammatical structures and vocabulary. In Chapter 4, we provide continua of both the listening comprehension and speaking skills students will need to develop over the course of the elementary school years for successful oral language and reading acquisition to occur. Word recognition skills alone will not enable children to use the "intonation, pauses, and emphasis that signal the structure of the sentence and the meaning of the text" required of the standards (p. 100), nor "self-correct through strategies that include syntax and word-meaning clues" (p. 101), nor "make predictions about what will happen next and why" (p. 104). In the terms of these standards, to be a successful reader at the end of Grade 1, students will need to make use of both their word recognition skills and their oral language skills, particularly their academic language skills.

Throughout this book we will stress that *all* students need to acquire academic language. However, we will also stress the particular importance of instruction in academic language for ELL students. There are two reasons for this. One is that the language of texts is different from spoken language, and while children may be competent in social conversation, they may well not have the more complex, academic language structures often found in books. The other reason is that as children begin to acquire content knowledge through reading, they need to be familiar with the specific vocabulary and syntactic structures of the domain studied. For example, math uses specific structures such as "if . . . then . . ." as well as precise vocabulary like *addend* and *quotient*; science requires students to have the necessary language to describe, compare, question, classify, analyze, and hypothesize; and in social studies students will need the language structures to express cause and effect and how to introduce primary source material in direct and indirect speech to support a point of view.

A Model of Teacher Knowledge for Effective Reading Instruction

We began this chapter with a description of the skills and knowledge that we need to have to be effective teachers of reading. In addition to these knowledge and skills, we included knowledge of academic language. Now we consider how we integrate all the knowledge and skills in reading and academic language and apply them to teach reading.

To fully capture the complexity of what is involved in teaching reading, we have developed a model for effective teaching of reading that is shown in Figure 2.2. Language plays a key role in this model and, while a

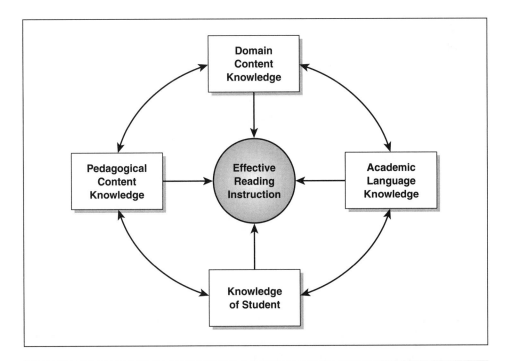

Figure 2.2 Model of Teacher Knowledge for Teaching and Assessment

Adapted from Heritage, Silva, and Pierce (2007).

pertinent component for the effective teaching of any student, it is particularly critical when assuming the effective teaching of ELL students (Téllez & Waxman, 2005). In our model, we have assumed Lee Shulman's (1986) distinctions of teacher knowledge and organized all the facets of teacher knowledge for teaching reading into four categories:

1. Domain content knowledge of reading

2. Academic language knowledge

3. Pedagogical content knowledge

4. Knowledge of students

We'll now discuss each category of knowledge in detail.

DOMAIN CONTENT KNOWLEDGE

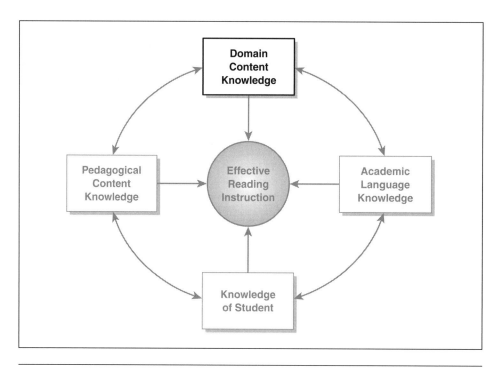

Figure 2.3 Model of Teacher Knowledge for Teaching and Assessment

Domain content knowledge in reading includes knowing in detail the five core areas of reading identified by the National Reading Panel and all the subcomponents of each area. Teachers will need to know all the subcomponents of phonological awareness (e.g., blending and segmenting compound words, syllables, *onset and rime*, and phonemic awareness).

For the area of phonics, teacher knowledge will necessarily include the alphabetic principle and sound symbol relationships including knowledge of consonants, vowels, diagraphs, syllables and *morphemes,* and a developmental sequence of phonics.

Teacher knowledge of vocabulary and specialized lexicons will extend to understanding the contribution of vocabulary to reading comprehension, especially the fact that much vocabulary acquisition is based on an understanding of how words can be derived from other words.

Comprehension knowledge involves knowing about different *text structures, metacognition,* and the kind of comprehension strategies that good readers use. Among the knowledge elements that teachers need about *fluency* are accuracy, rate, and prosody. Content knowledge also includes knowing about the developmental sequence of reading acquisition.

> ## KEY TERMINOLOGY
>
> **Onset and Rime:** An onset is the initial consonant(s) sound of a syllable (the onset of pig is p-; of sheep, sh-). A rime is the part of a syllable that contains the vowel and all that follows it (the rime of pig is -ig; of sheep, -eep).
>
> **Text Structure:** Refers to the features of text and how they are organized to guide readers to identify information and make connections among ideas.
>
> **Metacognition:** Involves monitoring one's own learning. In reading, metacognition includes monitoring understanding while reading, and knowing when and how to use reading skills or strategies to remediate the causes of noncomprehension.
>
> **Fluency:** Refers to high-speed word recognition and the ability to group words into meaningful grammatical units for interpretation while reading.

Developmental Sequence of Reading

Chief among theories that integrate knowledge of these discrete skills is that of a developmental sequence of reading. A renowned reading scholar, the late Jeanne Chall (1983), advanced a developmental model of reading, through which children proceed in predictable stages. The six stages of reading development generally occur at particular ages, but it is important to remember that not all children will spend the same amount of time at each stage.

During the early stage of Chall's model (preschool to kindergarten), children learn the language to express themselves, they develop phonological and print awareness, knowledge of the alphabet, and a rudimentary knowledge of plot structure.

In Stages 1 and 2 (typically acquired in Grades 1, 2, and 3), children "learn to read." That is, they learn the alphabetic principle, word recognition skills, including decoding words they do not immediately recognize, strategies to make meaning from text, and how to develop fluency skills.

Stages 3 to 5 are regarded as the "reading to learn" stages. In Stage 3 (usually Grades 4 to 8), reading is used as a tool and students encounter a wide variety of texts and contexts with increased complexity, along with linguistic and cognitive challenges.

In Stages 4 and 5 (Grade 9 through college), language and cognitive demands continue to increase and readers are able to analyze texts critically and understand issues and concepts from multiple points of view. By Stage 5, readers are able to synthesize background knowledge to create new, complex knowledge. They also now have the ability to synthesize critically the works of others, and are able to form their own perspective on a subject. In Chapter 5, we will see how teacher knowledge of these stages of reading is operationalized into student *learning progressions* to create a continuum of development that provides the basis for reading instruction and assessment. Learning progressions are also introduced in Chapter 4 to describe the continuum of oral language development that provides the basis for instruction and assessment of speaking and listening skills.

ACADEMIC LANGUAGE KNOWLEDGE

Academic language content knowledge is a complementary component to reading content knowledge. Recall our earlier discussion of the importance of simultaneously developing reading skills and academic language skills. If teachers are going to assist their students to acquire academic language in support of reading development, they will certainly

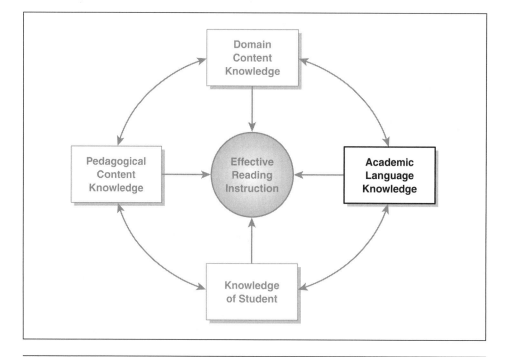

Figure 2.4   Model of Teacher Knowledge for Teaching and Assessment

need to know about the linguistic levels that were described earlier in this chapter: word level, sentence level, and discourse level. They will need to know the specific vocabulary that children should learn to make meaning of the text and the importance of learning not just the definition of a word but acquiring the appropriate background knowledge that will convey the meaning of the word.

Teachers will also need to know about syntactic structures. For example, to assess the earliest stages of grammatical development, teachers will need to recognize the structure of simple sentences such as statement, question, and command forms. As students progress, teachers will need to be prepared to make more sophisticated distinctions between verb tenses and distinguish between parts of speech such as nouns, adjectives, verbs, and adverbs. By the later elementary grades, teachers must be familiar with complex sentences that contain embedded clauses and can be made more cognitively and linguistically demanding through the addition of prepositional and adverbial phrases.

When we look at some of the factors that Reid Lyon (1998) highlights as contributors to noncomprehension of text– insufficient background knowledge, inadequate knowledge of the words used, and a lack of familiarity with the syntactic structures, we can see very clearly that teachers' academic language knowledge is equally as important to effective teaching as reading content knowledge. Finally, because of the interactive nature of academic language and children's linguistic experiences that we have described earlier, teachers will need to know what aspects of academic language will need explicit instruction for which children in their classrooms.

PEDAGOGICAL CONTENT KNOWLEDGE

We have examined the range of content knowledge that teachers need to ensure their students success in reading—and there is a lot. However, there is something else to consider. No matter how much content knowledge teachers have, if they do not have knowledge of which teaching approaches best fit what they want to teach, the students may not learn. So

KEY TERMINOLOGY

Reciprocal Teaching: A comprehension strategy used in a group setting. The teacher models a specific way of approaching text: summarizing, questioning, clarifying, and predicting. Students then use the process to discuss a text they have read (Brown, Palinscar, & Armbruster, 1984).

Word Sorts: Children sort word cards according to the letter patterns. For more on these types of word study activities, see *Words Their Way* (Bear, Invernizzi, Templeton, & Johnston, 2003).

Scaffolding: Establishing what a student can do by him/herself allows the teacher to work within the student's Zone of Proximal Development (ZPD) or the level at which learning occurs through their social interaction. In the ZPD, students need assistance to solve a problem from an "expert other," after which knowledge is internalized and the task can be achieved independently (Vygotsky, 1978).

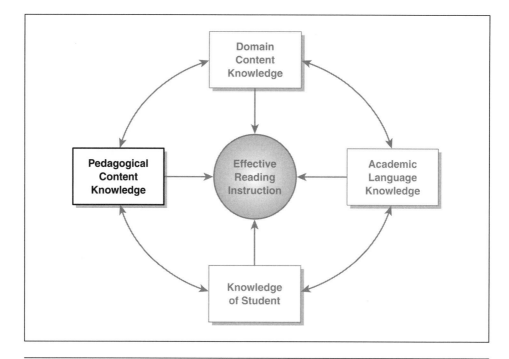

Figure 2.5   Model of Teacher Knowledge for Teaching and Assessment

teachers need to have pedagogical content knowledge; that is, they need to have a tool kit of teaching strategies that they can draw from to select an appropriate approach for whatever they are teaching. For example, when teaching letter-sound correspondences to emergent and beginning readers, a teacher might decide to do *word sorting* with a small group of children and draw their attention to the sound elements and letter patterns in words; when developing comprehension skills, a teacher might use a *reciprocal teaching* strategy with the whole class. And if the students are not learning from the selected approach, the teacher will choose another one. Modeling the steps necessary to successfully complete a task along with the language needed to accomplish the task, and bridging or using prior knowledge to build new knowledge, are just two *scaffolding* techniques that teachers can use and are particularly valuable with ELL students who are learning academic content at the same time they are learning English (Walqui, 2006).

The pedagogical content knowledge tool kit needs to be full of different kinds of tools, and teachers need to know which one to select to do the job in hand. Effective reading instruction, then, involves integrating reading content knowledge with academic language knowledge, and the interaction of these knowledge areas with pedagogical content knowledge.

KNOWLEDGE OF STUDENT

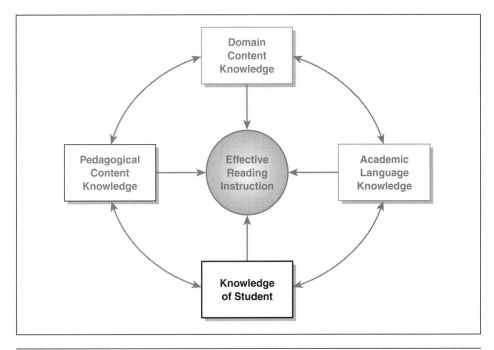

Figure 2.6   Model of Teacher Knowledge for Teaching and Assessment

To be able to bring into play the three types of teacher knowledge we have described so far, teachers need information about their students. So, the fourth category in our model is knowledge of student. In this category, there are three areas of knowledge: content, academic language, and background knowledge. Content refers to the children's skill level in reading and where these skills lie on a continuum of reading development. Academic language concerns knowledge about the vocabulary, grammatical structures, and discourse features that the child can understand and produce. Background refers to knowledge of students' prior experiences, their motivation and interest in learning to read, their primary language and their culture—all of which represent important resources that teachers can use when they are planning for reading instruction. Indeed, a child's knowledge of

KEY TERMINOLOGY

Funds of Knowledge: Refers to a learners' knowledge and experiences with reading both inside and outside the classroom; their identities of themselves as learners (in this case as readers or writers); as well as their attitudes, values, beliefs, and their relationships with learning, and their teachers (Gonzalez, Moll, & Amanti, 2005).

Culturally Relevant Teaching: An approach to teaching that acknowledges that all students are capable of academic success. Teachers see themselves as members of a community and establish and maintain connectedness with all students in order to develop a community of learners through collaboration and the scaffolding of learning. Teaching is built on the premise that knowledge is constantly being evaluated and can be judged critically. Assessment incorporates multiple forms to give students broad opportunities to demonstrate excellence (Ladsen-Billings, 1995).

the topic may be as important for comprehending what is read as vocabulary knowledge and reading skills (Garcia, 1991).

Teacher knowledge of a student's beliefs, values, and cultural practices is also critical for a student's learning outcomes. Knowing the *funds of knowledge* that each student brings to the classroom can be used by teachers to help make learning contexts familiar and thus effective to more students who may have experienced learning very differently outside the classroom.

Culturally relevant teaching is the practice of responding to the needs of English language learners who come from linguistically and culturally diverse backgrounds. It involves teachers' conceptions of self and others, social relations with students, and conceptions of knowledge that place the student and his or her home community at the center of pedagogical approaches. For example, teachers can create what is known as a "third space" whereby they negotiate classroom discourse practices with students in order to incorporate student values, beliefs, and language practices into a "hybrid" of school and student-valued discourses (Gutierrez, Rymes, & Lason, 1995).

In our model of effective teaching in the area of reading, content knowledge (which involves the two interrelated areas of reading content knowledge and academic language knowledge), pedagogical content knowledge, and knowledge of students are invoked in a mutually dependent and dynamic interaction. The pedagogical approach will be determined by the reading and academic language content, that is, what the teachers need to teach, and by the knowledge of students, including their levels of development, their cultural backgrounds, and their specific learning needs. To acquire a broad range of knowledge about their students so that they can match content and pedagogy to the students' needs, teachers must employ effective assessment practices.

EFFECTIVE ASSESSMENT PRACTICES

Earlier we noted that to know what to teach, when to teach it, and what teaching approach to take, teachers need information about student learning. Information about student learning will come from four main types of assessments:

- Summative assessment
- Interim or benchmark assessment
- Formative assessment
- Diagnostic assessment

What Is Summative Assessment?

Summative assessments have been described as assessments *of* learning, as opposed to assessment *for* learning, because results from these kinds of assessments (often *standardized tests*) give information on the *status* of student learning relative to other students rather than information that can be used on a day-to-day basis to *support* learning (Black & Wiliam, 2004).

The annual statewide *standards-based tests* required by the No Child Left Behind (2001) legislation are examples of summative assessments. All students (with the possible exceptions of kindergartners and first graders) take the tests. The results provide information that summarizes student learning at a particular time and answer the question "How many students are meeting the state standards?" As such, these tests provide comparative data for the public and policy makers about the status of student achievement in schools on an annual basis. As Lucy Calkins and her colleagues (1998) point out:

> **KEY TERMINOLOGY**
>
> **Standardized Tests:** Measure student performance in the same way—all students take the same test under the exactly the same conditions so that students' performance can be evaluated in comparison to a sample of their peers (referred to as a normative sample).
>
> **Standards-Based Tests:** Student's performance is evaluated against a set of standards or criteria as opposed to a sample of their peers.
>
> **Aggregated Data**: Student data are combined so that individual performance or performance of particular groups cannot be identified (e.g., data that show a summary of the performance of *all* the fifth grade students on the statewide test are aggregated data).
>
> **Disaggregated Data:** Data presented in a way that individual or group performance can be recognized (e.g., data that show how a subgroup of fifth grade students performed—fifth grade girls, or fifth grade girls in after-school programs—or show how individual fifth grade students performed).

Keeping track of all children's progress on the same standardized tests can be a way to challenge everyone to treat all children in similar ways so that all children have the opportunity to achieve similar standards. (p. 21)

From the perspective of teachers, results from annual tests using *aggregated data* at grade levels to show weaknesses in certain areas can prompt teachers to examine their teaching and assessment practices to see what they could do better in future years. With advancements in technology, there are various online tools available to help districts, schools, and individual teachers store, report, and analyze both aggregated and *disaggregated data* for student assessment performance.

Student scores on tests can provide disaggregated data for individual students or target groups to lead teachers to conduct further assessments so that they get more diagnostic information. Examining test scores over time can also help schools make evaluations about the effectiveness of curricula, teaching, and other practices in the school. These also give direction on changes to be made for improvement.

Yet as guides for teachers about what to teach and when and how to teach it, these kinds of assessments are limited because:

- They tell teachers how well the students did on the test, but they do not give enough information about *what* the students did well on or *why* the students did well, or why they didn't. For example, an annual summative test can indicate that a student, a class, or an entire grade level has not reached proficiency on a test, but the reasons for their achievement level are not apparent. Could it be the students do not have the requisite vocabulary or comprehension strategies? Could it be the reading program? Could it be that not enough time is spent on reading? Or could it be a combination of all of the above?
- The tests are administered toward the end of the school year, and while they may provide information that will help teachers make improvements in their teaching for the next year's students, they will not give information to guide their instruction for the current year's students.
- The tests cover a whole year's worth of instructional goals and therefore are not the most sensitive measures of progress, particularly the progress of struggling readers. Much more fine-grained frequent information is needed to ensure that teachers are responding appropriately to children's needs so that they will make progress in their reading development.

What Are Interim or Benchmark Assessments?

Recognizing that annual state tests provide too little information, too late for teachers to use for planning instruction, increasingly, districts and schools are moving to a practice of using interim or benchmark assessments, typically administered to all students at regular intervals throughout the year. These kinds of assessments are checks on progress and can answer the question, "Who is and who isn't on the way to meeting standards?" (Stiggins , 2006) The results of these tests can help administrators and teachers "catch" those students who are at-risk of being left behind and make plans to accelerate their learning.

One problem with these tests is that although they predict in general how students will do in a subject area, they mostly fail to reliably identify the specific standards or skills on which students need help; they lack reliable diagnostic information on the specifics of where students may need help, much less the underlying source(s) of learning difficulty on which subsequent action would optimally be based. Instead, most commonly, they simply identify students who need remediation without providing specific information about what kinds of additional support will be beneficial for the individual student. The follow-up action to these assessments (or in Dylan Wiliam's terms, what is "formed" by the assessment) is typically additional remediation instruction, which may well include formative assessments to discover the specifics of students' learning needs.

Often, curricula that are used by districts can provide useful interim assessments. The Open Court Reading Program (Bereiter et al., 2005) is one such example, and involves student assessment at six weekly intervals. Although these assessments cover six weeks of instruction, they can be valuable progress monitoring tools and can be used formatively if the information is subsequently used to guide instruction. They could be even more valuable if used in conjunction with more frequent formative assessments. Together they can help to determine strengths and weaknesses of individual students and provide guidance to teachers about where to focus instruction.

What Is Formative Assessment?

Formative assessment is assessment *for* learning. It is assessment that takes place *during* the course of learning and is a source of feedback to both teachers and students to improve teaching and learning (National Research Council [NRC], 2000). In contrast to summative and benchmark assessments that provide a snapshot of learning at periodic intervals, formative assessment provides a video stream of information to guide day-to-day instruction.

Central to formative assessment is feedback to students. Increasingly, more emphasis is being placed on the role that students play in the assessment process. No matter what their age, helping students understand where they are in the learning and what their learning goals will be, and being involved in monitoring their own learning, is a hallmark of good teaching (NRC, 2000).

Formative assessment is the focus of Chapter 3 so we will not dwell on it too long here other than to stress that there is no single way to conduct formative assessment. Formative assessment is a process that uses many different methods to collect evidence of student learning. For example:

- Performance tasks (e.g., teacher listens to child reading aloud)
- Written tasks (e.g., child writes literature response)

- Personal communication (e.g., reading conferences—child and teacher discuss text, teacher questions and student responds)
- Tests (e.g., oral or written test of discrete phonics skills)
- Curriculum-embedded assessments (reading program assessments)

What Is Diagnostic Assessment?

According to Webster's *Ninth New Collegiate Dictionary*, to diagnose is "to analyze the cause or nature of a problem" and diagnostic is defined as "the art or practice of diagnosis" (p. 349). Diagnostic assessment, then, is a means to identify the nature or cause of an educational problem. The term diagnostic is often used synonymously with formative assessment. Formative assessments *can* be diagnostic if they reveal *what* the source of a problem is, and diagnostic assessments that are specifically designed to probe the likely source of a problem *can* be formative if they lead to appropriate instructional action.

In the course of formative assessment, teachers might find that students have a reading problem but cannot pinpoint the specific nature of the problem. At this juncture, they could use a diagnostic probe, either one that they design themselves as another kind of formative assessment, or a published diagnostic assessment for specific subskill areas in reading, such as the *Comprehensive Tests of Phonological Processing* (Wagner, Torgesen, & Rashotte, 1999) and the *Gray Oral Reading Tests* (Wiederholt & Bryant, 2001)

Published assessments ideally need to have met accepted *standards of technical quality.* The teacher's goal is to figure out the source of the problem and find an instructional solution so that the child's reading can progress. This solution might also include a referral for special services in addition to instructional modifications and classroom adjustments.

> **KEY TERMINOLOGY**
>
> **Standards of Technical Quality:** In 1999, the American Educational Research Association, the American Psychological Association, and the National Council on Measurement in Education established standards to provide criteria for the evaluation of tests, testing practices, and the effects of tests use. For example, issues are raised when results of academic achievement tests are interpreted as valid measures with ELL populations who may differ from the general student population on whom these tests are typically piloted and normed (American Educational Research Association, American Psychological Association, & National Council on Measurement in Education, 1999).

Assessments in Action

Now, taking the example of Antonio, a third grade ELL student, and his teacher, we will consider now how these different types of assessments can work together and give a range of constituents the information they need.

At the beginning of the school year, Antonio is not meeting grade level expectations. His teacher knows this because she has information from summative assessments; his statewide test scores from the end of the previous school year show that he is well below proficient on state standards. Antonio's teacher can see from her review of the state test results that he is below basic in reading comprehension and is weak in both word analysis and comprehension strategies. She also has his end of the year school report card, which summarizes his attainment for second grade and indicates that he is well below expectations in reading comprehension. Yet, even with this information, she is not sure why he is performing so poorly. So, she decides that she wants to have more detailed information that will help her figure out what instruction she needs to provide.

During reading instruction time, she decides to ask Antonio to read aloud. Antonio has chosen a book from his independent reading book box and he begins to read. Although he has a number of sight words and attempts to read other words using the visual cue of initial consonants, he often reads aloud a word that does not make sense, but never stops to self-correct. His teacher thinks that one problem could be that he does not use meaning cues. This information is truly formative because, on the basis of it, she decides to intervene there and then and "teach to" a specific strategy.

Ms. Harris: Let's think about a reading strategy here. If you are not sure of a word, you can look at the picture and the beginning sound to make a guess about the word. If I wanted to know what this word was, for example (teacher points to the word "frog"), I can look at the picture that goes with the word and I can see a frog. Yes, this word starts with "fr-." And "frog" makes sense in the sentence. The word must be "frog." Why don't you try it?

Antonio reads several sight words accurately, but when he comes to the word *toad* on the page he looks up at the picture. He looks back at the word and says "t-t-t" and then looks back at the picture. He says "Tod?" and looks up at Ms. Harris.

Ms. Harris: Let's look at the two letters in the middle of the word. When those two letters are together in a word do you know what sound they say?

Antonio: /o/?

Ms. Harris explains that "oa" makes the sound /ō/. She then writes the words *boat*, *load*, and *toad* and asks Antonio to read the words. This time he reads the words correctly.

Antonio: Toad is the same word that it is in my book. What is a toad? Is it like a frog?

Ms. Harris realizes that not only did Antonio not have the letter-sound correspondence knowledge, but he did not have sufficient topic knowledge about frogs to combine with his initial and final sound knowledge to recognize the word.

Ms. Harris and Antonio go over what has happened in the story so far and Antonio continues to read. When he reaches the sentence "Today, you look very green, even for a frog," he reads every word accurately, but looking puzzled by the sentence, he reads it again and then looks up at Ms. Harris.

Antonio: That's a funny sentence.

Ms. Harris: Why do you think that is a funny sentence? Does it make you want to laugh?

Antonio: No, not that—the way the words are is funny—I don't get it.

Ms. Harris interprets this as meaning he could be confused by the sentence structure, which includes a subordinate clause. She and Antonio talk about what the sentence means, and she asks him to explain the meaning in his own words.

Antonio: Frogs are green. Today Frog looks very green.

Antonio continues to read to the end of the chapter and then he and Ms. Harris discuss what the chapter is about.

Based on her observations and interactions with Antonio during the reading session, Ms. Harris decides that she will take a number of actions. She will pay close attention to the syntactic structures he uses in oral and written language to get a better gauge of his syntactic knowledge and build on this to develop his understanding of sentence structures. She also plans to focus her sentence level work (see Chapter 5) for Antonio and others at his language level on subordinate clauses. She will also work with him on vowel digraphs and on integrating visual cues with meaning cues. Ms. Harris also decides that she will do a published diagnostic phonic assessment in the near future to check to see if Antonio is having problems with other sound symbol correspondences that might be impeding his reading progress.

Furthermore, based on today's reading, Ms. Harris is not sure that all the books in Antonio's independent reading box are at the right level for Antonio to practice his reading skills, so she will take a look at those, too.

Ms. Harris plans to give Antonio some feedback about his reading, but before she does she wants to give him the opportunity to reflect on how he read today.

Ms. Harris: Thank you for reading to me today. How did you think you read today?

Antonio: Okay.

Ms. Harris: Can you remember the reading strategy we talked about?

Antonio: Look at the letter and the picture to get the word?

Ms. Harris: Yes, that's the one. And you tried it when we came to the word *toad*.

Antonio: And I couldn't get it.

Ms. Harris now decides to give Antonio feedback about his reading.

Ms. Harris: I think you were not able to read the word "toad" correctly because you did not know the sound that "oa" makes and you were not sure what a toad is. Does that sound right to you? (Antonio agrees).

Ms. Harris: Do you remember when you said that sentence was funny? (Antonio nods). Well, some sentences are like that—so when we do our sentence level work we'll be looking at more sentences that are like the one you read. When you come across other sentences that are like that in the future, they won't sound funny to you and they will make more sense. We'll work together on these goals so that you will become a stronger reader—does that sound good? (Antonio smiles and nods).

When Ms. Harris is next focusing on these skills during her instruction, she will remind Antonio of his goals. She adopts this practice for all students so they are able to monitor their own learning better and can be mutually supportive of each other's goals. Next time she meets to read with Antonio she will ask him what his goals have been and then discuss with him at the end of the session how well he thinks he has met his goals.

In a short space of time, the teacher was able to make a judgment about Antonio's reading performance and decide a course of action that would support his progress. She will continue to gather formative evidence from the classroom that will either corroborate her initial interpretation of his needs or will give her additional information on which to base her instruction. Antonio will also be a part of the assessment process and will keep focused on his goals and with his teacher monitor his progress.

Antonio's teacher continues to use formative assessment strategies linked to her instructional goals for meeting the required reading standards through the first quarter of school. Toward the end of the quarter, all her students take a benchmark test. When Antonio's teacher looks at the results of the benchmark tests, she can see that Antonio, although showing progress, is not yet on target to meet the state standards. However, his result is not a surprise to her. Because of her formative assessment practices she knows where Antonio is on her learning progression toward standards. She will use the results of the benchmark tests to help her define instructional goals for the next quarter and, of course, she will continue assessing Antonio's learning formatively so that she can be sure her instruction responds to his needs.

In this example, summative, benchmark, and formative assessment are working together and satisfying the needs of different stakeholders. The aggregated results of the summative assessments can show the public, policy makers, and administrators how many students are meeting standards. At an individual level, they also show Antonio's teacher and his parents that he is not meeting expected standards. The formative assessment helps the teacher pinpoint the source of Antonio's problems so that she, Antonio, and his parents can focus on his learning priorities. The benchmark assessment results can tell the teacher if Antonio is on track to meet standards or not. Additionally, benchmark test results across the grade level can also inform administrators and teachers in the school who is on track to meet standards and who is not, providing the basis for curricula or program modifications before the end of the year summative tests.

Teacher Knowledge

Earlier in this chapter we discussed the importance of four different kinds of teacher knowledge for teaching reading. However, these types of teacher knowledge are equally important to assessment. If we go back to Antonio for a moment, we can see how his teacher used her reservoir of knowledge to assess and teach reading skills. Her knowledge of formative assessment enabled her to use the opportunity of Antonio's read-aloud to assess his skills. Against the backdrop of her knowledge of reading, she was able to determine the skills he was lacking, and the developmental sequence of reading she had in mind informed her that she needed to help Antonio integrate visual and meaning cues. Because of her academic language content knowledge, she knew that his reading was being impacted by syntactic and vocabulary knowledge. And, because of her pedagogical content knowledge, she was able to draw from her tool kit an appropriate tool to make an instructional intervention while Antonio was reading. All four categories of knowledge were interacting in a process of assessment and instruction.

In this chapter, we have laid the critical foundation upon which the rest of this book is built. We began by defining reading and academic language and how they are intimately related to school success. We covered, in some depth, the different types of teacher knowledge involved in teaching reading. A range of assessment practices and purposes were briefly reviewed as part of the broader suite of types of teacher knowledge. Throughout the chapter, we introduced key terminology to help ensure a solid understanding of the domain of reading, the features of academic language, teacher knowledge, and assessment.

Next, in Chapter 3, we will expand further on formative assessment and describe how teacher knowledge and formative assessment practices can be integrated in a single model of effective assessment for learning. Chapter 3 examines formative assessment for reading instruction in far greater depth, giving examples of its purpose, scope, and the kinds of instruction that get formed as a result of its implementation.

REFERENCES

American Educational Research Association, American Psychological Association, & National Council on Measurement in Education. (1999). *Standards for educational and psychological testing.* Washington, DC: American Educational Research Association.

Bailey, A. L. (2007). *The language demands of school: Putting academic English to the test.* New Haven, CT: Yale University Press.

Bailey, A. L., Butler, F. A., Stevens, R., & Lord, C. (2007). Further specifying the language demands of school. In A. L. Bailey (Ed.), *The language demands of school: Putting academic English to the test* (pp. 103–156). New Haven, CT: Yale University Press.

Bear, D. R., Invernizzi, M., Templeton, S. R., & Johnston, F. (2003). *Words Their Way, Third Edition.* Upper Saddle River, NJ: Prentice Hall.

Bereiter, C., et al. (2005). *Open court reading 2005* (2005 ed.). New York, NY: SRA/McGraw-Hill.

Black, P., & Wiliam, D. (2004). The formative purpose: Assessment must first promote learning. In M. Wilson (Ed.), Towards coherence between classroom assessment and accountability: Part II. 103rd yearbook of the National Society for the Study of Education (1st ed., pp. 20–50). Chicago: University of Chicago Press.

Brown, A. L., Palinscar, A. S., & Armbruster, B. B. (1984). Instructing comprehension-fostering activities in interactive learning situations. In H. Madl, N. L. Stein, & T. Trabasso (Eds.), *Learning and comprehension of text.* Hillsdale, NJ: Lawrence Erlbaum Associates.

Calkins, L., Montgomery, K., & Santman, D. (1998). *A teachers guide to standardized reading tests: Knowledge is power.* Portsmouth, NH: Heinemann.

Chall. J. S. (1983). *Stages of reading development*. New York: McGraw-Hill.

Chamot, A. U., & O'Malley, J. M. (1994). *The CALLA handbook: Implementing the cognitive academic language learning approach*. Reading, MA: Addison-Wesley Publishing Company.

Chiappe, P., & Siegel, L. S. (1999). Phonological awareness and reading acquisition in English and Punjabi-Speaking Canadian children. *Journal of Educational Psychology*, 91, 20–28.

Chiappe, P., Siegel, L. S., & Wade-Woolley, L. (2002). Linguistic diversity and the development of reading skills: A longitudinal study. *Scientific Studies of Reading*, 6, 369–400.

Cummins, J. (1981). The role of primary language development in promoting educational success for language minority students. In California State Department of Education (Ed.), *Schooling and language minority students: A theoretical framework* (pp. 3–49). Los Angeles: National Dissemination and Assessment Center.

Cummins, J. (2000). *Language, power and pedagogy: Bilingual children in the crossfire*. Clevedon, England: Multilingual Matters, Ltd.

Delpit, L. (1995). *Other people's children: Cultural conflict in the classroom*. New York: The New Press.

Dutro, S. (2003). *An introduction to a focused approach to English language instruction. California Reading Association Conference*. San Diego, CA: California Reading & Literature Project.

Garcia, G. E. (1991). Factors influencing the English reading test performance of Spanish-speaking Hispanic students. *Reading Research Quarterly*, 26, 371–392.

Goldenberg, C. (1993). The home-school connection in bilingual education. In B. Arias & U. Cassanova (Eds.), *Bilingual education: Politics, practice, and research* (pp. 225–250). Chicago: National Society for the Study of Education.

Goldenberg, C., Rueda, R. S., & August, D. (2006). Synthesis: Sociocultural contexts and literacy development. In D. August & T. Shanahan (Eds.), *Developing literacy in second-language learners: Report of the National Literacy Panel on language minority children and youth* (pp. 249–267). Mahwah, NJ: Lawrence Erlbaum Associates.

Gonzalez, N., Moll, L. C., & Amanti, C. (2005). *Funds of knowledge: Theorizing practices in households, communities, and classrooms*. Mahwah, NJ: Lawrence Erlbaum Associates.

Gutierrez, K., Rymes, B., & Lason, J. (1995). Script, counterscript, and underlife in the classroom, James Brown versus *Brown v. Board of Education. Harvard Educational Review*, 65(3), 445–471.

Heath, S. B. (1982). What no bedtime story means: Narrative skills at home and school. *Language in Society*, 11, 49–76.

Heath, S. B. (1983). *Ways with words: Language, life and work in communities and classrooms*. New York: Cambridge University Press.

Heritage, M., Silva, N., & Pierce, M. (2007). Academic English: A view from the classroom. In A. L. Bailey (Ed.), *The language demands of school: Putting academic English to the test.* (pp. 171–211). New Haven, CT: Yale University Press.

Hicks, D. (1994). Individual and social meanings in the classroom: Narrative discourse as a boundary phenomenon. *Journal of Narrative and Life History*, 4(3), 215–240.

Ladson-Billings, G. (1995). Toward a theory of culturally relevant pedagogy. *American Educational Research Journal, 12*, (3), 465–491.

Lyon, G. R. (1998). Overview of reading and literacy research. *Education News.* Retrieved on October 5, 2006, from http://www.educationnews.org/ Curriculum/Reading/Overview_of_Reading_and_Literacy_Initiatives.htm

McVeigh, L. *Miss hen's feast* (2004). Boston: Houghton Mifflin.

National Reading Panel (NRP 2000). *Teaching children to read: An evidence-based assessment of the scientific research literature on reading and its implications for reading instruction* (NIH Pub. No. 00–4769). Washington, DC: National Institute for Child Health and Development.

National Research Council. (2000). *How people learn: Brain, mind, experience, and School: Expanded edition.* Committee on Developments in the Science of Learning and Committee on Learning Research and Educational Practice, Commission on Behavioral and Social Sciences and Education. In J. D. Bransford, A. L. Brown, & R. R. Cocking (Eds.). Washington, DC: National Academy Press.

New Standards Primary Literacy Standards Committee. (1999/2004). *Reading and writing grade by grade.* Washington, DC: National Center on Education and the Economy and the University of Pittsburgh.

No Child Left Behind Act (2001). Pub. L. No. 107–110, 115 Stat. 1425.

Philips, S. U. (1972). Participant structures and communicative competence: Warm Springs children in community and classroom. In C. B. Cazden, V. P. John, & D. Hymes, (Eds.), *Functions of language in the classroom* (pp. 370–394). New York: Teachers College Press.

Reppen, R. (2001). Register variation in student and adult speech and writing. In S. Conrad and D. Biber (Eds.), *Variation in English: Multi-dimensional studies* (pp. 187–199). Harlow, Essex, England: Pearson Education.

Scarborough, H. (2001). Connecting early language and literacy to later reading (dis)abilities: Evidence, theory and practice. In S. B. Neuman & D. K. Dickinson (Eds.), *Handbook of early literacy research* (pp. 97–110). New York: The Guilford Press.

Schleppegrell, M. J. (2001). Linguistic features of the language of schooling. *Linguistics and Education, 12*(4), 431–459.

Schleppegrell, M. J. (2004). *The language of schooling: A functional linguistics perspective.* Mahwah, NJ: Lawrence Erlbaum Associates.

Shulman, L. S. (1986). Those who understand: Knowledge growth in teaching. *Educational Researcher, 4*, 14.

Snow, C. E. (1977). The development of conversation between mothers and babies. *Journal of Child Language, 4*(1), 1–22.

Stevens, R. J., Slavin, R. E., & Farnish, A. M. (1991). The effects of cooperative learning and direct instruction in reading comprehension strategies on main idea identification. *Journal of Educational Psychology, 83*(1), 8–16.

Stiggins, R. (2006). *Balanced assessment systems: Redefining excellence in assessment.* Princeton, NJ: Educational Testing Service.

Téllez, K., & Waxman, H. C. (2005). *Quality Teachers for English Language Learners.* A report prepared for The Laboratory for Student Success, The Mid-Atlantic Regional Educational Laboratory, Temple University Center for Research in Human Development and Education. Retrieved March 8, 2007, from http://www.temple.edu/lss/pdf/ReviewOfTheResearchTellezWaxman.pdf

Vygotsky, L. (1978). *Mind in society.* Cambridge, MA: Harvard University Press.

Wagner, R., Torgesen, J., & Rashotte, C. (1999). *Comprehensive Test of Phonological Processing (CTOPP)*. Bloomington, MN: Pearson Education.

Walqui, A. (2006). Scaffolding instruction for English language learners: A conceptual framework. *Bilingual Education and Bilingualism*, *9*(2), 159–180.

Webster's ninth new collegiate dictionary. (1989). Springfield, MA: Merriam-Webster Inc.

Wells, G. (1985). Preschool literacy-related activities and success in school. In D. R. Olson, N. Torrance, & A. Hildyard (Eds.), *Literacy, language, and learning: The nature and consequences of reading and writing* (pp. 229–255). Cambridge, UK: Cambridge University Press.

Wiederholt, J. L., & Bryant, B.R. (2001). *Gray Oral Reading Tests (GORT),* (4th ed.). Austen, TX: PRO_ED Inc.

3 Formative Assessment

*"Where Are My Students
on Their Journey?"*

Used with permission.

In Ms. Lozano's second grade classroom of English language learners at Para Los Niños Charter Elementary School in downtown Los Angeles, the students have been studying rocks and minerals in science. So far in their study, they have explored different types of rocks, investigating and describing properties of the rocks and minerals and classifying them according to their properties. Throughout their study, the children are introduced to curriculum content language (CCL) terms like *minerals, rocks, sedimentary, igneous, metamorphic,* and *conglomerate* as labels for their rock classifications.

In all her science lessons, Ms. Lozano encourages the children to ask questions that arise from their observations. To support their English language development, she has taught them about who, what, when, where, and how questions, as well as how to structure questions in English. They have also compared the structure of questions in Spanish and in English.

Today, Ms. Lozano is building on the knowledge that the children developed from their observations and classifications and is reading a text to them about the formation of rocks. In her prior instruction, she has focused on the characteristics of information text, including, for example,

> ## KEY TERMINOLOGY
>
> **Instructional Conversation**: Instructional conversations are lessons that involve oral discussion that engage students in simultaneously developing concepts and language (e.g., Cazden, 1988; Goldenberg, 1991; Tharp & Gallimore, 1991). They have been described as "instructional in intent . . . conversational in quality" (Goldenberg, 1991, p. 9).

how the language of narrative and information text differs, and how information text makes use of subheading, diagrams, and pictures within text with captions. She reads aloud, highlighting the headings and showing the diagrams as she reads the explanatory text.

After Ms. Lozano has read the text to the class, she begins an *instructional conversation* in which she explores ideas from the text about rock and mineral formation. She and the children have a long and animated discussion about how different types of rocks are formed. Ms. Lozano makes sure she asks questions she had planned beforehand to help structure the conversation and build the children's understanding of the concepts.

After the class discussion, Ms. Lozano asks the children to "turn and talk" to one another and discuss what they have learned from the read-aloud. As they talk, she moves around the classroom listening in to what they say and using a graphic organizer to jot down notes to herself about students' misconceptions and points of confusion. One pair of students seems confused about the difference between how sedimentary and igneous rocks are formed so she briefly notes it to herself. She also tries to determine if the pair's confusion stems from linguistic or conceptual misunderstanding. How she intervenes instructionally is based on her interpretation of the information she gathers and notes to herself.

After the paired conversations, she asks the students to individually write a question on a Post-it note that they think the text answers. She also asks them to write their name on the reverse side of the Post-it. Before they begin, she reminds them briefly about how questions in English are structured. She also tells them that their questions need to relate to the content of the text they have read together and that she or their classmates should be able to answer the questions by rereading the text.

When the students have written their questions, they stick their post-its onto large pieces of paper that she has taped to the whiteboard in the classroom. At the end of the lesson, the board is covered in a flurry of Post-it notes. She concludes the lesson by telling the students that the next day they will review the questions and see if there is agreement among them that these are questions that the text answers.

The children leave for the day, and Ms. Lozano starts to examine the questions the students have written. In Figure 3.1, you can see some of the questions the children wrote on their post-its.

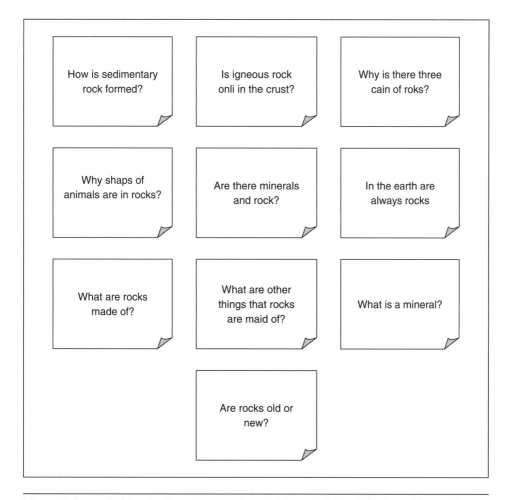

Figure 3.1   Children's Questions on Post-it Notes (with original spelling and sentence structure)

Ms. Lozano notes that the questions show varying levels of understanding and language skills. Some students reveal a literal comprehension of the text by asking questions that can be answered directly from what is stated in the text, for example, "What is a mineral?" Other students are more sophisticated in their questions, and despite the fact that they have not constructed the question accurately, they show they are aware that the text has described fossil formation, "Why [are] shap[e]s of animals in rocks?" She also notes that students are using CCL vocabulary such as *minerals, igneous, sedimentary, surface,* and *erupt* and "mortar" words, which include the general academic language vocabulary that cuts across content areas such as *formed, shapes,* and *kinds of.*

Finally, she notices that while most are structuring their questions according to the conventions of English, at least one has possibly translated the question structure of Spanish into English, which reads as a statement, not a question: "In the earth are always rocks"—a likely translation from the Spanish question, "¿En la tierra, siempre hay piedras?" Ms. Lozano reflects on the structure of the question this student produced. While the structure of the question in English seems more like a statement than a question, if the words were reordered and the word "there" was inserted it would read, "Are there always rocks in the earth?" Ms. Lozano is aware that this student had verbalized questions to her in English that he thought the text could answer and had used the appropriate structure before putting his questions in writing. She notes the student's unusual sentence structure in her graphic organizer. She also decides to observe more systematically the way this student in particular structures other writing to see if any similar patterns emerge so that she can respond to his language needs.

Based on her interpretation of the children's questions Ms. Lozano also decides how she will structure the review of the questions with the students tomorrow. In her lesson, she plans to discuss with them the structure of questions in English in contrast to Spanish, to reinforce the CCL vocabulary associated with rock and mineral formation, and to examine evidence in the text that can provide answers to questions. In examining evidence, she wants to stretch the children to think beyond the literal level so that they can ask deeper questions with answers that require inferences to be made from the text.

In our example, we see Ms. Lozano merging instruction and assessment. Instructionally, she builds on prior knowledge to extend her students' understanding of rocks and minerals in the context of reading and discussing informational text, and provides practice in using language structures that have been the focus of prior instruction. In terms of assessment, she is able to use the students' questions to give her evidence of how well she has met her instructional goals. The evidence that is evoked from this activity informs what she will do next in her instruction. Before the activity, she also provided students with *success criteria* for this activity and

she will be able to provide them with feedback based on these criteria, about the
degree to which the criteria were met, and
how their questions can be improved. This
process of using evidence to provide feedback so that teaching and learning can be
adapted to meet learning needs is the
essence of formative assessment (Black &
Wiliam, 2004). Many more examples of formative assessment in action in
Ms. Lozano's and other teachers' classrooms are given in Chapters 4, 5, and 6.

> **KEY TERMINOLOGY**
>
> **Success Criteria:** The specific criteria for
> what a successful performance in learning
> looks like; what a teacher would want her
> students to say and do.

BACKGROUND ON FORMATIVE ASSESSMENT

In 1967, Michael Scriven used the terms "formative" and "summative" to
describe the two distinct roles that evaluation of curriculum might play.
Shortly after that, Benjamin Bloom (1969) applied Scriven's formative and
summative distinction to learning. While acknowledging the traditional
role of assessment in judging and classifying students (i.e., summative
assessment), he suggested an alternative view:

> Quite in contrast is the use of "formative evaluation" to provide
> feedback and correctives at each stage in the teaching-learning
> process. By formative evaluation we mean evaluation by brief tests
> used by teachers and students as aids in the learning process. While
> such tests may be graded and used as part of the judging and clas-
> sificatory function of evaluation, we see much more effective use of
> formative evaluation if it is separated from the grading process and
> used primarily as an aid to teaching. (Bloom, 1969, p. 48)

Subsequently, "formative" and "summative" have become generally
accepted terms to define the fundamental functions of assessment.
Summative assessment is a means to document and *judge* a phase of learning
(National Research Council [NRC], 2001; Shavelson, 2006; Shepard et al.;
2005). In contrast, formative assessments provide evidence during the course
of learning that is used to *assist* learning (Black, Harrison, Lee, Marshall, &
Wiliam 2003). A landmark in formative assessment of practice was a meta-
analysis conducted by Paul Black and Dylan Wiliam in 1998. They reviewed
over 250 studies from around the world on the impact of effective formative
assessment practices on student learning. They reported that effective formative assessment could yield improvements in student achievement by 0.4–0.7
standard deviations with the largest gains being realized by low achievers.
Subsequent studies have found appreciable effects of formative assessment

on student achievement on externally mandated standardized tests (Black et al., 2003; Clymer & Wiliam, 2006/2007).

The general consensus from the academic literature is that formative assessment is the process of using information about students' learning in the course of instruction to make day-to-day teaching decisions to improve learning (Atkin, Black, & Coffey, 2000; Bell & Cowie, 2001; Harlen, Gipps, Broadfoot, & Nutall, 1992; NRC, 2000). And, because of the potential benefits to student learning of formative assessment practices, teachers and administrators are paying increased attention to how they can incorporate formative assessment into classroom practice.

In the box below, you can read more of what the experts say about formative assessment.

What the Experts Say About Formative Assessment

- Richard Stiggins (2002)
  Assessing *for learning* involves teachers using "the classroom assessment process and the continuous flow of information about student achievement that it provides in order to advance, not merely check on, student learning" (p. 759).

- Paul Black & colleagues (2003)
  "An assessment activity can help learning if it provides information to be used as feedback by teachers, and by their pupils in assessing themselves and each other, to modify the teaching and learning activities in which they are engaged. Such assessment becomes *formative assessment* when the evidence is used to adapt teaching work to meet learning needs" (p. 2).

- Harry Torrance and John Pryor (1998)
  These scholars have argued that formative assessment refers to a social interaction between teacher and student that is intended to have a positive impact on student learning.

- D. Royce Sadler (1989)
  Sadler described a model of formative assessment that emphasizes feedback to students though the idea of feedback loops:
  Few physical, intellectual, and social skills can be acquired satisfactorily simply through being told about them. Most require practice in a supportive environment which incorporates feedback loops. Feedback loops include a teacher who knows which skills are to be learned, who can recognize and describe fine performance, demonstrate a fine performance, and indicate how a poor performance can be improved. (p. 120)

SEVEN DIMENSIONS OF FORMATIVE ASSESSMENT

There are seven essential dimensions of formative assessment that, taken together, distinguish them from other kinds of assessments:

1. **Purpose of the Assessment:** Teachers must be able to identify the "gap" between the learner's current status of understanding with respect to the desired learning goals and apply informed instructional actions to close the gap. Purpose also includes being clear about what you want from the assessments and having confidence that the assessment is valid (i.e., it actually assesses what you think it will assess).

2. **Degree of Spontaneity**: Formative assessment emerges spontaneously in the midst of instructional activity, or is planned in advance to elicit evidence through questioning, discussion, writing, or analysis of student artifacts.

3. **Interpretive Framework:** Learning progressions provide an interpretive framework that enable formative assessments to locate students' current learning status on a continuum along which students are expected to progress.

4. **Feedback:** Formative assessment is a process that provides feedback to the teacher about current levels of student understanding. It also feeds back into the teaching and learning to guide what the next steps in learning should be and provides feedback to students about their learning and how they can improve.

5. **Student Involvement:** Students have an explicit role in formative assessment and through peer- and self-assessment they reflect on their learning and actively take steps to move their learning forward. Effective feedback supports student self-assessment.

6. **Time Interval:** The period between when the teacher collects the information and when she uses it for planning instruction is short. Action is taken in the course of learning.

7. **Locus of Control**: The teacher decides when to use formative assessment strategies, what strategies will be used, who will be assessed, and when the assessment will take place.

We will now look at each one of these dimensions in more detail to better understand the ways in which they characterize formative assessment.

1. Purpose

The purpose of formative assessment is to a help us identify the gap between children's current status in relation to desired learning goals so that we can adapt our instruction to their learning needs. We need to know the current status of student learning so that we can match what and how we teach to where the learners are on their journey to meeting the goal, and move learning forward in ways that make the goal achievable. For instance, if we identify the gap and then pitch our instruction at a level that is too much of a stretch for the student from their current status, their learning may be compromised. Similarly, if we pitch it at a level that is too low and too close to their current status of learning, it will not be moved forward to the degree that it could. So, in the Goldilocks metaphor, we need to find the "just right gap" and match our instruction accordingly.

The "just right gap" in instructional terms has been conceived by educational psychologists as the Zone of Proximal Development (ZPD). This zone is the area where Vygotsky (1978; 1986) hypothesizes learning and development take place. It is defined as the distance between what the child can accomplish during independent problem solving and the level of problem solving that can be accomplished under the guidance of an adult or in collaboration with a more expert peer. Through this guidance, growth occurs and ultimately the child can achieve a higher level of problem solving than he or she could previously. In other words, the adult or more expert peer provides support to move learners from what they already know to what they can do next.

This process of giving support to learning has been characterized by the term "scaffolding" (Wood, Bruner, & Ross, 1976). This is a process of "setting up" the situation to make the child's entry successful and then gradually pulling back and handing the role over to the child as he becomes skilled enough to manage it.

The essence of effective teaching is to identify where the student is in relation to a learning goal and to scaffold learning within the student's ZDP to move the student forward toward the goal. Our job as teachers is to ensure that the student receives appropriate support in the acquisition of new learning so that the learning is incrementally internalized and ultimately becomes part of the student's independent achievement. In reading, for example, children are initially given support to learn decoding skills and eventually internalize this knowledge in order to decode rapidly and efficiently on their own.

To identify the gap in children's learning, we need to be very clear about the purpose of our assessment—why we are doing it and what we hope to learn. For example, is the purpose of the assessment to find out what comprehension strategies a student is using, or is it to discover a student's level of interest in reading about a particular topic? Knowing the purpose of the assessment will enable us to choose the appropriate strategy to evoke the evidence and adapt our instruction accordingly.

Validity

Another way of thinking about the purpose of the assessment is in terms of the validity of our interpretation of the evidence. Validity is the key issue in educational measurement and centers on whether an assessment is measuring what it is intended to measure and whether it can can serve well the intended purpose of the assessment. It is important to remember that validity always relates to a specific use of the assessment or the interpretation of evidence yielded by the assessment.

> **KEY TERMINOLOGY**
>
> **Construct**: A construct is the specific characteristic (e.g., the ability, skill, understanding, psychological trait, or personal quality) that the test is intended to measure. For example, reading comprehension, number sense, scientific inquiry, anxiety, and creativity are all constructs.

For example, if you are selecting a test to find out how well your students understand a specific level of expository text, then the test would need to measure the construct of reading comprehension of expository text. This means that the test must measure the range of abilities, skills, and understandings comprising the construct of reading comprehension of expository text.

Bear in mind that if the test does not accurately measure the construct then your interpretation of how well students can comprehend expository text will be flawed and the consequential instruction may be inappropriate or even detrimental. If we cannot draw valid inferences from our assessments, then we will not be able to scaffold students' learning effectively.

Validity is an important issue for *all* assessments, but particularly for those tests where the consequences of student performance are very high—for example, the annual state tests that can have significant consequences such as student retention. These kind of tests, as well as many of the reading diagnostic tests from test publishers, will have (or should have) undergone a rigorous process to establish their *technical quality*.

What happens as a result of an assessment is also a validity issue and referred to as consequential validity. Consequential validity means an evaluation of the consequences of the inferences and actions resulting from the use of tests and the interpretation of test results. Formative assessment is about consequences. Gordon

> **KEY TERMINOLOGY**
>
> **Technical Quality**: The test is measuring what it purports to measure (validity). It consistently measures what it is intended to measure irrespective of changes (e.g., in who scores it, or when it is administered in the assessment situation) (reliability).

Stobart (2006) helps us understand formative assessment and consequential validity. Citing Wiliam & Black (1996) and Wiliam (2000), Stobart states, "By definition, the purpose of formative assessment is to lead to further learning. If it fails in this then, while the intention was formative, the process was not" (p. 136). So, if what you do instructionally in light of your interpretation of the assessment evidence is inappropriate for students' learning (e.g., your interpretation of reading comprehension test is inaccurate and you focus on the wrong aspect of comprehension in your teaching), then the consequences of your assessment are invalid.

Because formative assessment opportunities can arise spontaneously during a lesson, or are instructional activities that can yield information about children's learning, they will not be able to meet all the technical quality standards that summative or interim assessments need to meet. Nonetheless, assessment quality and validity evidence are still important concerns in formative assessment.

Formative assessments should be aligned with instructional goals, be appropriate to purpose (for instance, be at an appropriate level of detail to provide information for action), and there should be some evidence that they lead to further learning (i.e., that teachers have taken the right course of action to move learning forward so that the consequence of the assessment is of benefit to students).

2. Methods of Assessment and Degrees of Spontaneity

Formative assessment involves collecting evidence using a variety of assessment methods—there is no one single method. Methods of formative assessment are often characterized as informal or formal. We find it more helpful to think about assessments in terms of their degree of spontaneity, rather than in a binary characterization. Some assessment opportunities will be entirely spontaneous and unfold during the course of regular classroom activities. Others will be planned in advance and designed to occur within a specific lesson or after a series of lessons. Others, still, could be a combination of both planned and spontaneous.

Formative assessment methods can be broadly defined as:

- On the run/In the moment
- Planned for interaction
- Embedded in curriculum

On the Run/In the Moment

On-the-run assessment, or in-the-moment assessment, occurs during the course of teaching a lesson and arises spontaneously. In other words, the teacher has not planned for the formative assessment, but during instructional activity, evidence of student learning is evoked and she seizes the moment to take instructional action there and then, sometimes referred to as a "teachable moment." For example, in a small group discussion she realizes that the students are having difficulty expressing the main idea of the text and she decides to do a minilesson on getting the main idea rather than continue with the lesson she had planned. This type of interaction has been described as a pop-up lesson (Heritage, Silva, & Pierce, 2007) because it is not part of the original planning but literally pops up during a sequence of instruction in response to evidence of learning.

Planned-for-Interaction

In planned-for-interaction, teachers decide beforehand how they will evoke evidence of learning during the course of instruction. Teachers' questions comprise a significant part of their teaching and, if carefully planned in advance of instruction, can be a valuable tool to elicit student levels of knowledge, skills, and understanding in reading. For example, in an upcoming reading conference, a teacher plans to focus on inferential skills. She carefully plans her questions beforehand to make sure that the questions will evoke the evidence that she wants about her students' inference-building skills. So, for instance, she plans to frame her questions as "why do you think (something happened in the text)," rather than "what happened?" Thus, this form of assessment does not have the degree of spontaneity that the on-the-run assessments hold.

Curriculum-Embedded Assessments

Curriculum-embedded assessments are those that teachers and curriculum developers embed in the ongoing curriculum to create opportunities for evoking evidence of learning. For example, the Open Court Reading Program includes regular assessments that can be used formatively to provide information about how students' reading is developing and instructional action can be taken in response; a test of specific skills such as the Basic Phonic Skills Test will give teachers information about how children's decoding skills are developing to guide subsequent instruction. Teachers could then create an assessment of their own to find out if their students are able to use prediction skills in reading comprehension, and decide at which points to embed these types of assessments into the curriculum to evoke evidence about this aspect of reading comprehension.

3. Interpretive Framework

While meeting standards is the primary purpose of our instruction, most state standards, in and of themselves, do not provide a clear interpretive framework for understanding where students are relative to desired goals. In fact, many state standards do not necessarily even provide a clear picture of what learning is expected. If formative assessment is to provide guidance for us on where students are in their learning, and what the best next steps are for them, it needs to be linked to an interpretive framework or learning progression. The learning progression should clearly articulate the subgoals that constitute progression toward the ultimate goal (i.e., the specified standards). Learning progressions provide the big picture of what is to be learned, which is important for both teachers and students to know and to keep in mind during the course of learning, and they help teachers locate students' current learning status on the continuum along which students are expected to progress.

Students also need to have short-term goals, broken down from the learning progression and described in terms of success criteria. Success criteria, the key ingredients that the student needs in order to fulfill the learning goal, are the guide to learning *while* the student is engaged in the learning task. The success criteria, derived from the learning progression, provide the framework within which formative assessment takes place and interpretation of evidence is made possible. To better understand this, let's return to our opening example of Ms. Lozano's class.

The teachers and administrators at Ms. Lozano's school have spent a long time developing learning progressions in science knowledge, concepts, and skills that are linked to content standards. To accompany the learning progression, they have also developed a continuum of curriculum content language that outlines key vocabulary and structures for each stage of the progression. When Ms. Lozano is observing her students, having discussions with them, or reviewing their written work, the learning progression acts as an internal guide for her. She knows what she wants to assess at points along the learning progression and is able to interpret her students' responses in light of the progression in learning. She also knows what she needs to teach next to move the children's learning forward. Recall also that Ms. Lozano is able to provide her students with success criteria as a guide to think about their learning—their questions need to relate to the content of the text they have read together and that she or their classmates should be able to find answers to the questions by rereading the text.

With a learning progression, we can systematically collect evidence of where our students are on their journey and build formative assessment into our practice as a matter of course. The benefits of formative assessment to children's learning will not be realized to their fullest potential if formative assessment is treated as a series of ad hoc activities rather than a systematic process of evidence gathering. The learning progression can help anchor our formative assessments, and, even when they arise spontaneously, our interpretations of how children are learning will be made based on the trajectory of learning represented in the progression.

You will see more clearly how formative assessment is anchored by learning progressions in Chapters 4, 5, and 6. Chapter 5 explicitly presents a continuum of learning in reading comprehension that serves the dual purpose of helping the teacher to determine what subgoals need to be assessed and what next steps should to be taken in instruction.

4. Feedback

A core idea in the formative assessment academic literature is feedback. Formative assessment is a process that provides feedback to the teacher about current levels of learning that can help teachers to close the gap. It also feeds back into the teaching and learning to guide what the next steps in learning should be. Moreover, formative assessment can also supply teachers with feedback about the effectiveness of their instructional plans, strategies, methods, and curriculum.

Of equal importance as feedback to teachers is feedback to students. By feedback we do not mean telling students if their answers are right or wrong. As Paul Black (2003) observes "such practice is merely frequent summative assessment" (p. 2). Effective feedback involves teachers sharing criteria for success with students at the outset of the learning activity. The criteria help students to know what is expected of them and enable teachers and students to assess progress and obtain feedback. Research shows that the quality feedback that teachers give to their students makes a difference to learning. Quality feedback is clear, descriptive, criterion-based feedback and indicates to students where they are in a learning progression, how their response differed from that reflected in the desired learning goal, and how they can move forward (Black & Wiliam, 1998; Butler & Neuman, 1995; Kluger & DeNisi, 1996). In Chapter 2, we saw how Ms. Harris gave Antonio specific feedback about his reading performance and what he needed to do to improve. Because of this feedback, he and his teacher could work together to move his learning forward.

5. Student Involvement

The kind of feedback we have just described is taken one step further in Sadler's (1989) model of formative assessment. Rather than being passive recipients of teachers' behavior students become active participants in the process of teaching and learning. Students know what the criteria for success are for their learning, and they are able to engage in self-assessment, essentially becoming partners with their teachers.

The idea of self-assessment is in accord with cognitive theories that note a central role for metacognition (i.e., thinking about thinking) in students' learning. We will discuss metacognition further in Chapter 5 in terms of reading comprehension skills, but for now, in the context of assessment, metacognition involves students in understanding how they are learning and what they are learning and when they need more information (National Research Council, 2001). To be involved in self-assessment, students need to learn the strategies of self-assessment (e.g., understanding of goals and criteria for success, reflection, and identifying next steps in their learning). Teaching and supporting self-assessment, therefore, is an integral part of the teachers' explicit role in formative assessment.

As a process that provides feedback for both students and teachers, to be effective, formative assessment must be cyclical. It is not a one-shot deal. Instead, formative assessment involves teachers and their students in identifying the current status of learning in relation to success criteria, taking steps to close the gap by modifying instruction and learning, assessing again to give further information, modifying instruction and learning, and so on. Thus, effective formative assessment constitutes an inquiry cycle that repeats itself numerous times throughout the course of instruction as opposed to summative assessment, which occurs at the end of a period of learning to show what has been learned.

6. Time Interval

In Chapter 2, we discussed the limitations of summative assessments (e.g., the annual statewide assessments) to provide the kind of information that teachers need for ongoing instruction. One of the limitations is that the interval between when the test is administered and when teachers receive its results is usually too long for it to be immediately relevant or specific enough for either the teacher's or the students' needs. By contrast, the information from formative assessment is much more timely and therefore can be used to make day-to-day instructional decisions.

Formative assessment can be located within different time intervals or cycles: long, medium, and short cycle (Wiliam & Thompson, 2006). A long cycle could be a year or more between the time the assessment information is collected and when that information is applied to instructional needs. For example, a teacher might collect information about students' understanding of a particular genre and decide that the following year when she teaches that genre again she will do it slightly differently to avoid some of the misunderstandings that have been evident among her current students.

Medium cycles happen between lessons within a one-day to two-week period. Our example at the beginning of the chapter illustrates a medium cycle. Ms. Lozano reviews information from one day's lesson to make decisions about the next day's lesson.

Short cycles of formative assessment occur within the lesson and can extend from five seconds to the full period of the lesson. In Chapter 2, we saw a short assessment cycle when Ms. Harris used information about Antonio's reading to make immediate adjustments to her teaching, and Ms. Lozano intervened in a pairs discussion when she heard the children expressing confusion.

Formative assessments that are in a long cycle may not necessarily support a teacher's current students' learning but may assist with long-term curricular goals, teaching, and program improvements that will benefit next year's students. Medium- and short-term cycles are those that inform ongoing instruction, and these are the focus of this book.

7. Locus of Control

In large-scale assessment (i.e. statewide and district-wide tests), teachers are told what tests to administer and when to administer them, and typically they have to administer them to all students. These measures gather information about the performance of students in the entire state, district, and school. In contrast, teachers have control over formative assessment. They can decide which students they want to assess, how often they want to assess them, what strategies they will use to gauge learning; whether they will assess individual students, groups, or the whole class; and what they will do with the information they obtain from the assessments. In formative assessment, teachers are using their judgment about the evidence they need to promote learning *during* the course of instruction.

PUTTING IT ALL TOGETHER

Having read about the seven dimensions of formative assessment, you might now be thinking how on earth do you do all this in your classroom? And you might even be thinking *why* should you do it? In answer to the second question, remember that research clearly shows the benefits to student learning of formative assessment. If you do adopt formative assessment practices, there is a very good chance that your students' achievement will improve considerably. In answer to the first question, the adage "Rome wasn't built in a day" applies. Fully implementing formative assessment in your classroom will take time and effort, and you will need the support of your colleagues. However, the payoff to your students must surely be worth the effort. In Chapter 7, we will focus on ways that you can develop formative assessment skills in the context of your own school. But for now, we turn to putting formative assessment practices together with the aspects of teacher knowledge described in Chapter 2.

In Chapter 2, we stressed the importance of teacher knowledge for effective reading instruction: domain content knowledge of reading, academic language knowledge, pedagogical knowledge, as well as knowledge of students. We also showed a model of how these different types of knowledge operate interdependently in teaching reading.

Now we will look at how these aspects of teacher knowledge, which have been argued as necessary for formative assessment, play out in the model (Heritage, 2007). Figure 3.2 shows where the different components of teacher knowledge contribute to the process of formative assessment and also how this knowledge interacts with teachers' skills in interpreting information for instructional action.

To help us understand how teachers' knowledge and skills work together, we return to the example of Ms. Lozano and her second grade students. Let's first consider what knowledge Ms. Lozano brought to the implementation of her formative assessment strategy:

- **Domain Knowledge:** Including knowledge of the language and structure of informational text (in this case science texts), science content (basic geology), and academic language knowledge (vocabulary and syntactic structures, particularly the structure of questions). Ms. Lozano draws from all of this knowledge in her interpretive framework and instructional activity before and after formative assessment.
- **Student Prior Knowledge:** What kinds of texts' structures and features the students are already familiar with, the kinds of language structures students have encountered in instruction and also ones that they might be bringing with them from a first language, and the science domain knowledge that the students already have.
- **Formative Assessment Knowledge:** Which formative assessment strategy/tool to use to obtain information about where students are with respect to a learning goal, how to structure a formative assessment, determining alternate sources of formative assessment information, and knowing when to formatively assess.

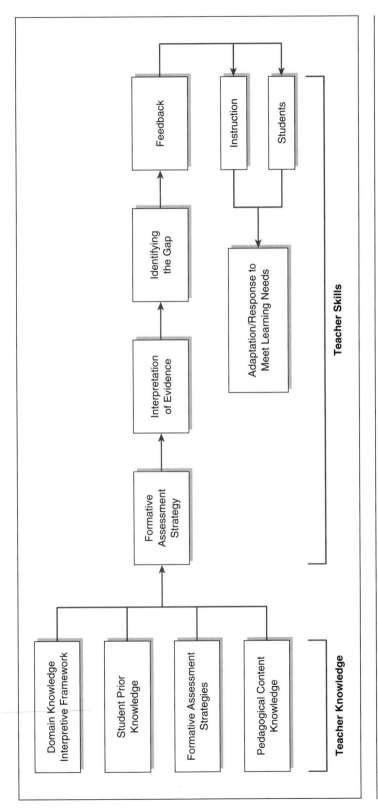

Figure 3.2   Teacher Knowledge and Teacher Skills in Formative Assessment

- **Pedagogical Content Knowledge:** How to structure the lesson to build on students' prior learning to develop new understandings and provide for practice in emerging language skills; what instructional decisions and adjustments/adaptations to make after interpreting the information obtained from formative assessment; when to incorporate formative assessment information into instruction (immediately, or in later instruction); determining what and how much feedback to give and when and whether or not subsequent formative assessments are needed.

With this knowledge background, Ms. Lozano was able to use her skills of interpreting evidence of learning in relation to desired goals. Evidence alone is insufficient to inform instruction. Only when the evidence is interpreted does it become information that can be used to guide instruction. Her domain knowledge and academic language knowledge provided her with the interpretive framework to determine the students' current learning status in relation to the learning goals and to identify the gap.

Knowing the gap between the students' current status and learning goals will enable her to draw once again from all her knowledge sources to adapt her instruction to the students' needs. As we saw, this might be an immediate adaptation or a later one (the next day's lesson). In addition to feeding back information to her instruction, she uses her skills of providing clear and descriptive feedback to students in the next lesson about their questions. This feedback is informed by her knowledge of students and by her domain and pedagogical content knowledge. Finally, she will draw from her knowledge of formative assessment to decide if and when she will make subsequent formative assessments.

SUMMING UP

In this chapter, we have discussed the essential elements of formative assessment. To sum up:

- Formative assessment information is used to make changes. "Assessments are formative, if and only if something is contingent on their outcome, and the information is actually used to alter what would have happened in the absence of the information" (Wiliam, 2006, p. 284).
- Formative assessment is a continuous process, integrated into instruction that gathers evidence about *how* student learning is progressing toward instructional goals. To provide such evidence, formative assessment must be clearly and directly linked to instructional goals.

- Formative assessment involves a variety of assessment methods and strategies—there is no one way to conduct formative assessment.
- Formative assessment gives students feedback and involves them in self-assessment about how their learning is progressing toward desired goals so that they can be active agents in learning, working with teachers to close the gap between current levels of understanding and desired learning goals.

In the following chapters, we will discuss literacy-related applications of formative assessment. Specifically, we will closely look at: listening and speaking skills (Chapter 4), reading comprehension (Chapter 5), and extensions to writing and, in particular, Grade 6 where English language arts become more challenging and more embedded within discrete content areas (Chapter 6).

REFLECTION QUESTIONS

1. How does what you now do in your classroom to assess student learning compare with what has been presented in the chapter?

2. What are your strengths in assessing student learning and which areas that you have read about in this chapter would you like to develop further?

3. What new or additional formative assessment strategies can you envision incorporating into your classroom? What support do you think you will need, and who among your colleagues may be able to provide it?

REFERENCES

Atkin, J. M., Black, P., & Coffey, J. (Eds.). (2001). *Classroom assessment and the National Science Education standards.* Washington, DC: National Academy Press.

Bell, B., & Cowie, B. (2001). *Formative assessment and science education.* Dordrecht, Netherlands: Kluwer Academic Publishers.

Black, P. (2003). *Formative and summative assessment: Can they serve learning together?* Paper presented at AERA, SIG Classroom Assessment Meeting. Chicago.

Black, P., Harrison, C., Lee, C., Marshall, B., & Wiliam, D. (2003). *Assessment for learning: Putting it into practice.* New York: Open University Press.

Black, P., & Wiliam, D. (1998). Assessment and classroom learning. *Assessment in Education: Principles, Policy and Practice, 5*(1), 7–73.

Black, P., & Wiliam, D. (2004) The formative purpose: Assessment must first pro-mote learning. In M. Wilson (Ed.), *Towards coherence between classroom assessment and accountability: 103rd Yearbook of the National Society for the Study of Education* (Pt. 2, pp. 20–50). Chicago: University of Chicago Press.

Bloom, B. S. (1969). Some theoretical issues relating to educational evaluation. In R. W. Tyler (Ed.), *Educational evaluation: New roles, new means: The 63rd yearbook of the National Society for the Study of Education* (Pt. 2, pp. 26–50). Chicago: University of Chicago Press.

Butler, R. & Neuman, O. (1995). Effects of task and ego achievement goals on help-seeking behaviors and attitudes. *Journal of Educational Psychology, 87*(2), 261–271.

Cazden, C. (1988). *Classroom discourse: The language of teaching and learning.* Portsmouth, NH: Heinemann.

Clymer, J. B., & Wiliam, D. (2006/2007). Improving the way we grade science. *Educational Leadership, 64*(4), 36–42.

Goldenberg, C. (1991). *Instructional conversations and their classroom application.* (Educational Practice Report 2) Washington, DC: National Center for Research on Cultural Diversity and Second Language Learning.

Harlen, W., Gipps, C., Broadfoot, P., & Nuttall, D. (1992). Assessment and the improvement of education. *The Curriculum Journal, 3*(3), 215–230.

Heritage, M. (2007). Formative assessment: What teachers need to know and do. *Phi Delta Kappan, 89*(2), 140–146.

Heritage, M., Silva, N., & Pierce, M., (2007). Academic English: A view from the classroom. In A. L. Bailey (Ed.), *The language demands of school: Putting academic English to the test* (pp. 171–210). New Haven, CT: Yale University Press.

Kluger, A. N., & DeNisi, A. (1996). The effects of feedback interventions on performance: A historical review, a meta-analysis, and a preliminary feedback intervention theory. *Psychological Bulletin, 119*(2), 254–284.

National Research Council. (2000). *How people learn: Brain, mind, experience, and school* (Expanded ed.). Committee on Developments in the Science of Learning, and Committee on Learning Research and Educational Practice, Commission on Behavioral and Social Sciences and Education. J. D. Bransford, A. L. Brown, and R. R. Cocking (Eds.). Washington, DC: National Academies Press.

National Research Council. (2001). *Knowing what students know: The science and design of educational assessment.* Committee on the Foundations of Assessment. J. Pellegrino, N. Chudowsky, & R. Glaser (Eds.). Washington, DC: National Academies Press.

Sadler, D. R. (1989). Formative assessment and the design of instructional systems. *Instructional Science, 18*, 119–144.

Scriven, M. (1967). The methodology of evaluation. In R. W. Tyler, R. M. Gagné, & M. Scriven (Eds.), *Perspectives of curriculum evaluation* (Vol. 1, pp. 39–83). Chicago: Rand McNally.

Shavelson, R. J. (2006). *On the integration of formative assessment in teaching and learning with implications for teacher education.* Retrieved October 19, 2006, from the Stanford Education Assessment Laboratory Website: http://www.stanford.edu/dept/SUSE/SEAL/

Shepard, L. A., Hammerness, K., Darling-Hammond, L., Rust, F., Snowden, J. B., Gordon, E., et al. (2005). Assessment. In L. Darling-Hammond & J. Bransford (Eds.), *Preparing teachers for a changing world: What teachers should learn and be able to do* (pp. 275–326). San Francisco, CA: Jossey-Bass.

Stiggins, R. J. (2002). Assessment crisis: The absence of assessment FOR learning. *Phi Delta Kappan, 83*(10). Retrieved December 5, 2007, from http://electronicportfolios.org/atl/stiggins-assessmentcrisis.pdf

Stobart, G. (2006). The validity of formative assessment. J. Gardner (Ed.), *Assessment and Learning* (pp. 133–147). London: SAGE.

Tharp R., & Gallimore, R. (1991). *The instructional conversation: Teaching and learning in social activity* (Research report No. 2). Washington, DC: National Center for Research on Cultural Diversity and Second Language Learning.

Torrance, H., & Pryor, J. (1998). *Investigating formative assessment.* Buckingham, UK: Open University Press.

Wiliam, D. (2000). Recent developments in educational assessment in England: The integration of formative and summative functions of assessment. Paper presented at SweMaS, Umea, Sweden, May.

Wiliam, D. (2006). Formative assessment: Getting the focus right. *Educational Assessment, 11*(3&4), 283–289.

Wiliam, D., & Black, P. (1996). Meanings and consequences: A basis for distinguishing formative and summative functions of assessment? *British Educational Research Journal, 23*(5), 537–548.

Wiliam, D., & Thompson, M. (2006). Integrating assessment with instruction: What will it take to make it work? In C. A. Dwyer (Ed.), *The future of assessment: Shaping teaching and learning.* Mahwah, NJ: Lawrence Erlbaum Associates.

Wood, D., Bruner, J., & Ross, G. (1976). The role of tutoring in problem solving. *Journal of Child Psychology and Psychiatry, 17*, 89–100.

Vygotsky, L. (1978). *Mind in society.* Cambridge, MA: Harvard University Press.

Vygotsky, L. (1986). *Thought and language.* Cambridge, MA: MIT Press.

4 Laying the Foundations for Reading Comprehension

Assessing Listening and Speaking Skills

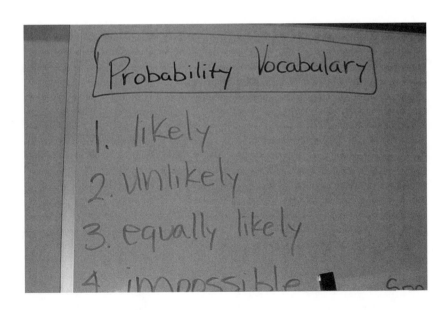

A heading at the top of the page read, "Lining up Animals."

"So what do you think of this one?" asked Mr. Adachi.
"It's crappy!" many of the students called out.

—Kenjiro Hantani (2005, p. 88)

Developing strong oral language skills in English is a critical foundation for understanding what we come to read. Listening and speaking are what Penny McKay (2006) calls "the mainstay of both language learning and academic learning for young learners and a central tool in teaching and assessment in the classroom" (p. 176). Later, in Chapter 5, we will see examples of how the vocabulary, grammatical structures, and discourse skills that children first acquire in the oral domain are linked to reading comprehension.

We begin this chapter on these foundational components of literacy with another story of classroom practice, this time as told by Kenjiro Hantani (2005), a Japanese author, educator, and child advocate. In *A Rabbit's Eyes,* he writes about life in an elementary school in a particularly poor neighborhood in a grimy, industrial part of a Japanese city. A second grade teacher, Mr. Adachi, has been trying to get his students to converse critically about artwork, namely give their evaluations of the crabs drawn in their arts and crafts textbook. Hantani continues:

"Ms. Kotani, who was observing the class from the back of the room, was shocked. What could be the point of getting students to criticize the model picture in the textbook?

"What's crappy about it?" Mr. Adachi continued.

About half the students raised their hands.

"Okay, Haruko," he said, calling on a student.

"It's crappy 'cause they're all the same," she said.

"Could you be a bit more specific?"

They're all the same shape and the same color. It's boring."

"Okay, roger that," said Mr. Adachi, pointing to the next student.

"Crabs are living things right? But these crabs're all lined up straight, kinda like apples or oranges or something. It's weird. They ought to be crawlin' all over the place."

"Roger that," said Mr. Adachi. You couldn't tell whether he agreed with the boy or not. He just continued having one student speak after another. Ms. Kotani was impressed: second graders were actually speaking out critically" (pp. 88–90).

With a series of questions and nonverbal prompts to join in, we see that Mr. Adachi is able to get the children to verbalize their artistic responses to "Lining up Animals." We see that Mr. Adachi's continuing questions also reveal to him at the very beginning of the lesson the different levels of student knowledge, their degrees of interest in the subject, and, critically for the topic of this chapter, how well the students are able to meet the language demands of the task itself. Penny McKay reminds us that such practices are what pedagogue and reformer Paulo Freire (1972) has called the "oral work" of teachers. Through this oral work, a teacher can gauge students' prior knowledge of a topic (in this case, students noticed the false lack of variation in the crab shapes, colors, and behaviors depicted—something many would know firsthand from living close to the coast), determine their motivation to engage in learning (in no uncertain terms Mr. Adachi knows most find the artwork "crappy" and "boring"), and assess their current level of abilities to carry out a task. (Mr. Adachi has impressed at least one of his colleagues with how much he has been able to get his students to verbally express themselves through this activity.)

Oral language is sadly often neglected in U.S. schools. We assume that once children reach the age of compulsory education, the language learning they need for understanding the information they receive from others and for communicating their own ideas, thoughts, and desires will have largely taken place before they arrive in kindergarten. As a college teacher of language development, one of the authors of this chapter has come across this fallacy time and again. Indeed most textbooks at the college level include a single, final chapter dedicated to the entirety of oral language development after age 5. And yet the fair and valid assessment of young school-aged children requires special attention to developmental considerations and cultural variation in acquisition contexts (Bailey, 2008). Only recently have texts appeared that are targeted at oral language development in the K–12 population (e.g., Menyuk & Brisk, 2005), and this is primarily because English is increasingly being acquired by school-age children who have English as a second or additional language. This neglect has expressed itself in two key ways that impact teaching and assessment:

1. Inadequate or omitted listening and speaking standards for the academic oral language skills of students

2. A lack of available assessments for the oral language skills of typically developing children

A notable and encouraging exception to this situation is the recent attention placed on standards for and assessment of the English language development (ELD) of English language learners under the No Child Left Behind legislation (2001). However, general education teachers can be at a loss for information about what oral language skills are and what their development entails, as well as be unfamiliar with how oral language assessment can assist them in teaching reading. Luisa Moats (2000) has put this critical teaching need most succinctly:

> The teacher who understands language and how children are using it can give clear, accurate, and organized information about sounds, words, and sentences. The teacher who knows language will understand why students say and write the puzzling things they do and will be able to judge what a particular student knows and needs to know about the printed word. (p. 1)

In this chapter, we outline the domain content knowledge teachers need to know in order to effectively assess the listening and speaking skills of their students. As much as Hantani's Mr. Adachi makes this look like an effortless conversation with his students, in fact, to do this well demands a lot of knowledge and skill. We present real examples of formative assessment to uncover the depth of domain content knowledge and pedagogical content knowledge involved in assessing oral language. We will be able to see how these examples of oral language assessment fit within the assessment model we outlined in Chapters 2 and 3 and how oral language can generate valuable information for teachers to use in their reading instruction.

WHAT ARE ORAL LANGUAGE SKILLS?

Listening and speaking are the oral language skills upon which literacy is built (Dickinson, McCabe, Anastasopoulos, Peisner-Feinberg, & Poe, 2003). While many oral language skills may be honed over several years prior to kindergarten for native speakers of English, in the case of ELL students, these skills are more often learned simultaneously with learning to read in the English language. Consequently, ELL students will need systematic and explicit instruction in many of these areas. Vocabulary in English, understandably, has been found to be less well developed in ELL students than in native English-speaking students and is likely not to develop as robustly if left to simple incidental exposure alone. Rather, vocabulary will need to be taught in ways that provide repeated opportunities to hear and to use new words in as many oral and print contexts as possible. It will also need to be taught in ways that give all students strategies for their own independent learning of new vocabulary (e.g., August & Shanahan, 2006; Baker, Simmons, Kameenui, 1998; Blachowicz, Fisher, Ogle, & Watts-Taffe, 2006; Geva, Yabhoub-Zadeh, & Schuster, 2000; Menyuk & Brisk, 2005; Wagner, Muse, & Tannenbaum, 2007). We initially divide oral language skills into receptive skills, that is, *listening comprehension,* and expressive or productive skills, that is, speaking skills. While it is useful to consider them as separate modalities of the full communicative repertoire used in school and elsewhere (e.g., listening, speaking, reading, and writing), assessing listening and speaking often requires both modalities to be assessed at the same time. Indeed, much classroom interaction demands the interweaving of all four modalities, with a constant back-and-forth between tasks that requires listening and reading comprehension and responses that require verbal and written displays of understanding (Gibbons, 1998).

Separating what a student comprehends from what a student can express verbally can be difficult and, because of this, we often talk of oral language abilities without making the finer distinction between the skills and developments that go into listening comprehension and those that go into speaking. However, with ingenuity we can and should attempt to tease apart these two skill areas to achieve a better understanding of where students might struggle and where they can succeed. Often comprehension of language precedes a student's ability to express him or herself verbally. New English language learners may even experience a silent period during which their receptive skills grow and they gather "data" about the language they are hearing around them. Only later might they feel comfortable or able to speak. Their listening comprehension abilities may far outweigh their speaking abilities (Tabors, 1997). Making the distinction between comprehending language and producing it is also important for making effective decisions in reading instruction.

In this chapter and Chapters 5 and 6, we have created learning progressions for stages of development in key language and literacy skills. The stages are intended as road maps or guides to assess development and plan instruction accordingly. They are not tied to any particular curriculum. While ideally the creation of learning progressions should be informed by standards' frameworks, in this instance we draw predominantly from research in child language development given the dearth of formal standards for oral language development in native English-speaking children.

Listening Comprehension: What Is it?

Listening comprehension is the ability to make meaning from oral language input. Clearly the ability to listen to and comprehend

directions and instructions is important for a student's classroom participation and engagement with the entire school curriculum, but it is also
critical in the process of learning to read. This is true of all students, not
just those learning to speak English as a second or additional language.
If any student cannot make sense of oral language, then his or her
chances of making sense of even simple sentences, let alone complex
grammatical structures and *extended discourse* in print, will be impacted.
For diagnostic purposes, knowing if a student can or cannot make sense
of oral language will help in devising strategies for reading comprehension. If students cannot make sense of a story or a series of directions as
spoken to them, we will know that their inability to comprehend what
they are decoding may be tied more broadly to their level of proficiency
in oral English.

What the Experts Say About Listening Comprehension and Reading

Listening comprehension is highly related to reading comprehension. Andrew
Biemiller (1999) has shown that in the early elementary grades, children's level of
listening comprehension determines the degree to which they can comprehend
what they read. That is, listening comprehension is in advance of the reading
comprehension of young readers.

The recent National Literacy Panel headed by Diane August and Timothy
Shanahan (2006) reviewed studies that show a positive relationship between listening comprehension and reading comprehension for English language learners. For example, in a study by Royer and Carlo (1991) at the elementary level,
listening comprehension in English was one of the best predictors of the English
reading comprehension of Spanish-speaking students.

What Teachers Must Know About Listening Comprehension

The domain knowledge that a teacher must have to effectively teach
and assess in the area of listening comprehension includes an understanding of *phonological* processing, *receptive vocabulary* development, comprehension of *grammatical structures*, as well as knowledge of *discourse*
and *pragmatic* rules that govern age- and socially-appropriate ways for
students to be attentive listeners in the differing contexts of school.

Vocabulary and Syntax

Teachers must know that in order to remain attentive to others' talk,
their students need to retain the sound information they have processed

long enough to make sense of the speech stream (a student's representation of the English phonological system). Then students must map the individual or combinations of sounds that they have identified and retained in their short-term or working memory to the meaning of a concept or object that they have stored in long-term memory (the *lexicon*).

Estimates of the size of receptive vocabulary vary tremendously, but they put children coming to school with a lexicon of about 2,500–6,000 words (Beck & McKeown, 1991). The range is due to differences in how researchers count words, either by each individual word form (e.g., *work, works, worked, worker,* etc.), or by first clustering words into families, with a word like *work* serving as the base word and *inflectional* and *derivational* forms like *works* and *worker* already accounted for. However we choose to count, a child's lexicon typically grow rapidly from about the time of his/her first birthday through the third year by a process known as "fast-mapping." This means that after just a few exposures, children can attach the meaning of a new word they hear to a specific *referent* in their environment (Carey, 1978). For

> ## LISTENING COMPREHENSION AND DIVERSE LEARNERS
>
> The development we have described in this chapter constitutes the basic mechanics of listening comprehension, and difficulties for students can arise if there is any compromise to these processes (e.g., hearing impairment, phonological processing deficit, specific language impairment [SLI]), or deviation from them (e.g., English as a second language leading to unfamiliarity with the sounds of the English language, or lack of knowledge of English words for objects and concepts). Assessing listening comprehension is important because it will help a teacher address which among these is the source of a student's difficulties. If a compromise to the basic hearing and auditory processing system or SLI is suspected, such occurrences are outside the area of expertise of general educators and a teacher will need to seek further guidance from a speech/language pathologist or clinician. The remediation of these causes of listening comprehension difficulties is also outside the scope of this book with its focus on formative assessment for in-class instruction.

example, after hearing the word *blanket* when a blanket is placed around the child, whenever a blanket comes loose from his or her bed, and when a blanket is lifted down from the closet shelf, a child comes to attach the properties of blanket-like objects to the combination of sounds that make up the word *blanket*.

What teachers need to be aware of, however, is that by age 5, just one or two exposures (Quick Incidental Learning or QUIL) will give a child sufficient information to map a new word he or she hears to a meaning he or she can infer from context (Rice, 1990). Much of this listening comprehension is in receptive vocabulary—the words that children acquire from hearing the words spoken to them. Studies have shown that children from low-income family backgrounds typically hear far fewer words in their preschool years than children from middle-income families. This gap in word exposure unfortunately grows over time and sets children on different trajectories for later academic outcomes (Hart & Risley, 1995). Typically, a student's lexicon increases during the first through third grades to about 20,000 individual words, and then doubles again to about 40,000 words by fifth grade. Teachers need to know that much growth occurs over this period because students are using their increasing knowledge of English *derivational morphology* to comprehend new words from the base words already learned (Anglin, 1993).

KEY TERMINOLOGY

Story Grammar: Organization of the sequence of events in fictional stories (often using a visual schema). The structural components include a problem that requires a response by the character(s) in the story.

Referent: The person, object, or concept being referred to in speech or writing.

When children are decoding and comprehending print independently, they can acquire new vocabulary and grammatical structures from reading unfamiliar texts. At this point, oral language comprehension need no longer constrain reading comprehension—rather written language becomes a major source of a student's new language knowledge (Nagy & Herman, 1987; Sternberg, 1987). Indeed, once students are reading to learn, written language becomes *the* source of most new vocabulary growth as students use the surrounding context they read to make meaning of the new words they decode (Sternberg, 1987). Importantly, a student will still need to attach meanings to about 95% of the words they read in a text to comprehend the overall meaning of the text (Laufer, 1989).

Discourse and Pragmatics

Teachers also need to know about the discourse and pragmatic rules that govern age- and socially-appropriate ways of being a good listener and comprehender across a large range of different settings. Discourse is language organized beyond the level of the single sentence. By age 5, students will need to have knowledge of the plot structure or *story grammar* of the stories they hear read to them. Over time, this knowledge will need to grow to include both familiar and unfamiliar story grammars as students increase their repertoire of story types (Rumelhart, 1980). They will need to listen to and comprehend a teacher's explanations and descriptions of content material and directives for following task sequences and completing activities. These language functions will also increase in complexity and diversity throughout the elementary years. Students will also need to understand their peers' personal narratives, descriptions, and accounts, as well as their directives in small groups and in pairs, and on it goes—the need to listen and comprehend in every conceivable situation and navigate the language demands of the immense range of tasks that students encounter in school (Bailey, 2007).

Metacognition

In school, more than anywhere else perhaps, we must be active listeners, that is, paying close attention to what is being said and using our metacognitive (more specifically in this instance, meta-attention) abilities to deliberately monitor if we are making sense of what is being said, and not just patiently waiting for our turn to speak. By the time they enter school, students must be seen to be actively listening by signaling that they are paying attention. At different grade levels this may take on different characteristics and need different degrees of support and reminders from the teacher. Kindergarteners are still in the process of learning to pay attention and what to pay attention to. Teachers will have their own classroom rules for what makes a good listener—with rules for listening often posted around the room (e.g., "sit quietly while someone else is talking," "wait my turn to speak," etc.). The later grades will also have posted rules often including more sophisticated listening skills that focus on students monitoring their own comprehension. One way this is manifested is by having students engage in their own formative self-assessment through formulating their own questions (e.g., "How many steps were in the directions?" "Can I retell the events of the story?") (Clarke, 2005).

A Learning Progression for Listening Comprehension Skills

Our continuum of development for listening comprehension skills is presented in three stages at each of the linguistic levels we introduced in Chapter 2—the *word, sentence,* and *discourse* levels. Discourse is the oral language equivalent to the *text* level we will use in Chapters 5 and 6. The learning progression includes the development of prior or background knowledge to capture the fact that students need to learn how to integrate new information with what they already know. While each stage is separately introduced below for ease of use, Resource A reproduces these and the equivalent stages for speaking skills in their entirety.

Stage 1 represents the initial starting place of all students. These stages are not linked to specific grades as different students will be at different places along the learning progression at different points in their elementary school years. There may also be unevenness across word, sentence, and discourse level knowledge within individual students. Those students who are learning English as a second or additional language may be distinguished from native English students at any grade by the relatively few common words, grammatical structures, *discourse genres* and idiomatic uses of language they have been exposed to and thus can comprehend.

Stage 1: Listening Comprehension

Word Level

- Comprehend a range of frequently used words (e.g., common vocabulary in the domains of social language [SL] and school navigational language [SNL])
- Identify and intentionally add a small number of new words to broaden **receptive vocabulary** in the areas of mortar words and curriculum content language (CCL) (by adding new words) and deepen the **lexicon** (by adding new meanings and nuances to known words)

Sentence Level

- Use word order conventions to make meaning of syntactically simple sentences (e.g., subject+verb+object = declarative statement; verb+subject+object = question form; verb+object = imperative form)
- Use high frequency *inflectional morphology* (plural+s) to make meaning of syntactically simple sentences

Discourse Level

- Begin to build spoken language genre knowledge (organization of language and ideas) by interpreting the meanings of a range of oral discourse contexts (conversations with a peer, short teacher monologues, simple one-step instructions/directions)
- Begin to build printed language genre knowledge by acquiring story grammar knowledge and interpreting the meanings of a range of short, simple texts read aloud by the teacher (storybooks, simple expository texts, poetry, puns)
- Comprehend frequently used idioms, clichés, and expressions used in the classroom (e.g., Once upon a time, The End, Are you sitting nicely?)

Prior/Content Knowledge

- Begin to connect new information heard to that already learned so that general background and content knowledge grow in both depth and breadth

---

Figure 4.1 Stage 1: Learning Progression for Listening Comprehension

Stage 2 differs from Stage 1 primarily in terms of the breadth of the repertoire of listening skills that students are expected to know.

Stage 2: Listening Comprehension

Word Level

- Comprehend a broader range of frequently used words (e.g., common vocabulary in the domains of SL and SNL)
- Identify and intentionally add an increasingly large number of new words to broaden receptive vocabulary in the areas of mortar words and CCL (by adding new words including the academic synonyms of more commonly used words [e.g., feline for cat]), synonyms to provide more precision or information [e.g., replied and asked for said] and continue to deepen the lexicon (by adding new meanings, shades of meaning [e.g., anger versus furious] and nuances to known words)
- Begin to use word analysis skills to aid in comprehension (e.g., use high frequency derivational morphology (e.g., adjective+ness = noun) to identify parts of speech or understand new meanings (un+adjective and un+verb = opposite in meaning to root word)

Sentence Level

- Expand repertoire of recognizable sentence structures to include frequently used complex syntax (e.g., relative clauses)
- Use less common inflectional morphology to make meaning of syntactically complex sentences (e.g., participial modifiers [verb+ing] such as, *The boys running were late for their class*)

Discourse Level

- Continue to build spoken language genre knowledge (organization of language and ideas) by interpreting the meanings of a broader range of oral discourse contexts (dialogues between two peers, longer teacher monologues, two- and three-step instructions/directions)
- Continue to build printed language genre knowledge by interpreting the meanings of a broader range of simple texts read aloud by the teacher (storybooks with familiar and unfamiliar story grammars, simple expository texts, poetry, puns)
- Comprehend frequently used idioms, clichés, and expressions used in the classroom (e.g., Give it your best, The more the better)

Prior/Content Knowledge

- Continue to connect larger amounts of new information heard to that already learned so that general background and content knowledge grow in both depth and breadth

---

Figure 4.2   Stage 2: Learning Progression for Listening Comprehension

Stage 3 differs from Stage 2 primarily in the degree of complexity of input and the greater sophistication students must have for accurately comprehending what they hear.

Stage 3: Listening Comprehension

Word Level

- Comprehend a wide range of common and uncommon words in the domains of SL and SNL
- Continue to identify and intentionally add unfamiliar words to broaden receptive vocabulary in the areas of mortar words and CCL (by adding new words) and deepen the lexicon (by adding new meanings, shades of meaning, and nuances to known words)
- Make inferences about a speaker's stance towards content from his or her word choices (e.g., retorted for replied)
- Continue to use word analysis skills to aid in comprehension (e.g., use rarer derivational morphology (e.g. verb+ate [fixate] = new verb meaning; adjective+ify [solidify] = verb)

Sentence Level

- Comprehend the full range of simple and complex grammatical structures (e.g., nominalization of verb forms [to form versus formation] to increase amount of information contained within a sentence) and increase sentence length (e.g., multiple prepositions in a single sentence)
- Continue to use common and uncommon inflectional morphology to make meaning of syntactically complex sentences

Discourse Level

- Continue to build spoken language genre knowledge (organization of language and ideas) by interpreting the meanings of a broader range of oral discourse contexts (dialogues between multiple peers, extended teacher monologues, plays/dramas, multistep instructions/directions)
- Continue to build printed language genre knowledge by interpreting the meanings of a broader range of simple and challenging texts read aloud by the teacher (storybooks with familiar and unfamiliar story grammars, works of literature, complex expository texts, primary source texts in content areas such as history, poetry, plays, puns)
- Comprehend frequently used idioms, clichés, and expressions used in the classroom (e.g., Don't beat about the bush, All's well that ends well)

Prior/Content Knowledge

- Continue to connect complex and large amounts of new information heard to that already learned so that general background and content knowledge grow in both depth and breadth

---

Figure 4.3   Stage 3: Learning Progression for Listening Comprehension

Speaking Skills: What Are They?

After children begin to listen and comprehend language, and long before they learn to read, they typically learn to speak. As we mentioned in Chapter 2, Chall's (1983) model of reading development presupposes a stage prior to formal instruction in reading when children are learning the oral language to express themselves.

What Teachers Must Know About Speaking Skills

The domain knowledge that a teacher must have for the formative assessment of speech production is extensive. In a later text box, we refer teachers to further readings that provide more detail about school-age children's oral language development. What we describe next can only be a brief overview of the speaking skills teachers must know for assessment purposes.

Teachers need to know that speaking skills include children's knowledge of the sound system of English, the age-appropriate *expressive vocabulary* and grammatical structures they should be producing, and the diverse discourse aspects of language that children need to acquire.

By the time they enter formal schooling, many students have developed some *phonemic awareness*, learning how to manipulate the sounds of the language. This ability continues to grow and indeed teachers should know that students may become more *metalinguistically* aware of the sound system of the language as they see it represented in print as they learn to read.

As described in the section on listening comprehension, children come to school with a rapidly growing lexicon so that by some counts, the average fifth grader knows the meaning of about 40,000 words. However, teachers must be aware that much of this knowledge remains passive, with far fewer words being part of a child's productive or expressive vocabulary. For example, by some estimates, as adults we may know upwards of 50,000–200,000 individual words. However, we use but a small portion of these in our everyday speech. Approximately, just 2,000–3,000 different words account for most of what we have to say (Baker, Simmons, & Kameenui, 1989; Nagy & Anderson, 1984).

Students have also acquired many of the grammatical structures of the language before entering school, but for teaching purposes it is important to know that students will need to continue to add less commonly used structures (e.g., adverbial clauses) to increase the length and complexity of their sentences during the elementary school years (Schleppegrell, 2004). In particular, students add syntax to their oral language that is more often encountered in written language (e.g., nominalizations) and is associated with the acquisition of an academic language *register.*

Discourse level skills cover a student's knowledge of the organization of stories and expository or informational genres, as well as pragmatic or language use skills, such as using language to achieve a range of *language functions* (e.g., *request, describe, explain*) (e.g., Bailey, Butler, Stevens, & Lord, 2007). During discourse, students must also take into account the perspective of an audience in making linguistic choices, such as using *anaphoric references,* and using the appropriate register to achieve the right amount of formality for a given context. For example, "Grab the end of this" is a phrase to use to informally command a friend, but "Would you take hold of this end please" is a phrase to use to request the help of a classroom teacher.

KEY TERMINOLOGY

Anaphoric References: Words, such as pronouns, are used to stand in for given nouns: "A man was walking down the street. He was wearing a tall hat"). Explicit ties between the same referent appearing multiple times in discourse or text make language cohesive and therefore comprehensible for listeners and readers.

High-Point Narrative: The organization of the structural components in an oral personal narrative. This organization will make a story coherent for a listener exposed to this style of discourse. These components include orientation information, a series of complicating actions or events, the high point of the story (a concentration of evaluative comments), and a resolution to the problem in the story. Peterson & McCabe, 1983

By age 5, many children will have acquired turn-taking skills and learned how to give contingent responses so that their conversational skills will be sufficiently honed for them to ask and answer questions about their comprehension of classroom material. They will also have begun to acquire the necessary skills to organize their own personal stories into coherent and cohesive narration.

Recall from Chapter 2 that socially-appropriate uses of language will influence what discourse skills are learned by different groups of students. For example, students who have been exposed to narrative genre in largely European-American influenced homes will have begun to favor the use of a linear, so-called classic narrative that follows a *high-point narrative* structure. Students continue to show growth in this area of discourse development by adding evaluative comments to their stories to increase their length (Bamberg & Damrad-Frye, 1991; Peterson & McCabe, 1983). Of course, teachers must be aware that both stories and conversations are also made more sophisticated over time by increases in the diversity of expressive vocabulary and in the complexity of grammatical structures children produce.

What the Experts Say About Speaking Skills and Reading

Speaking skills in the areas of sound, meaning, structure, organization, and use of the language are all related to various aspects of reading (e.g., National Reading Panel, 2000; National Research Council, 1998; Scarborough, 2001; Snow, Tabors, & Dickinson, 2001; *Snow, 2003*; Stanovich, 1986; Storch & Whitehurst, 2002).

For example, phonological awareness predicts later decoding skills (Wagner et al., 1997), and a large oral vocabulary or lexicon is related to success in making meaning of text; that is, as a child decodes the sounds represented in a written word, having knowledge of the meaning of the word from already acquiring it in the oral domain increases reading comprehension (e.g., Stanovich, 1986).

Use of complex grammatical structures and organization of discourse during *decontextualized* situations such as telling a personal narrative are also important oral language skills related to literacy (e.g., Bailey & Moughamian, 2007; Griffin, Hemphill, Camp, & Wolf, 2004; Snow, Tabors, & Dickinson, 2001; Reese, 1995). During these situations, oral language more closely mirrors that of written language, whereby audiences rely on a speaker/writer to be fully explanatory or explicit in their meaning making.

The importance of a strong oral language foundation for reading is highlighted by the fact that the oral language skills and topic knowledge of ELL students are found to affect reading comprehension even when decoding skills are taken into account (Garcia, 1991).

A Learning Progression for Speaking Skills

Our continuum of development in the area of speaking skills is presented, again, in three stages, each covering the *word, sentence,* and *discourse* levels of language. At Stage 1, students can express themselves in simple ways, in a limited range of contexts, and, in the case of ELL students, may use unanalyzed strings that are several words learned as a single unit (*Iwannago* [= I+want+to+go] . . . X as in "I want to go outside, I want to go to recess"), or chunks of oral language that are useful phrases that they have committed to memory ("I'm all done"). These strings and chunks often fulfill frequently occurring language functions, such as requests or descriptions.

Stage 1: Speaking Skills

Word Level

- Produce frequently used words (e.g., common vocabulary in the domains of Social Language [SL] and School Navigational Language [SNL])
- Identify and intentionally use a small number of new words to broaden expressive vocabulary in the areas of common mortar words and simple Curriculum Content Language (CCL) (by using new words) and deepen the lexicon (by using the new meanings and nuances of known words)

Sentence Level

- Produce syntactically simple sentences
- Use high frequency inflectional morphology to produce syntactically simple sentences

Discourse Level

- Begin to display spoken language genre knowledge by producing discourse on familiar topics in a small range of frequently occurring contexts (short conversations with a peer, short responses to teacher requests, simple requests for clarification of teacher directions)
- Produce frequently used idioms, clichés, and expressions found in the classroom, often learned in chunks or unanalyzed strings (e.g., Once upon a time, Mayago [= May+I+go] to recess?)
- Use language in service of common social functions (express needs, command) and simple/common academic language functions (describe, label)

Figure 4.4   Stage 1: Learning Progression for Speaking Skills

At Stage 2, students primarily increase the breadth of their repertoire of speaking skills.

Stage 2: Speaking Skills

Word Level

- Produce a broader range of frequently used words (e.g., common vocabulary in the domains of SL and SNL)
- Identify and intentionally use an increasingly larger number of new words to broaden expressive vocabulary in the areas of mortar words and simple CCL (by using new words) and continue to deepen the lexicon (by using the new meanings and nuances of known words)
- Make new words of differing parts of speech from known words using derivational morphology

Sentence Level

- Produce greater variety of grammatical structures (e.g., inclusion of adjectival and prepositional phrases)
- Use less common inflectional morphology to produce syntactically more complex sentences

Discourse Level

- Continue to expand use of spoken language genre knowledge by producing discourse on familiar topics in a broader range of contexts (conversation with a peer, conversation with a group of peers, production of simple monologues such as personal narratives or a short book report, responses to teacher multipart requests, requests for clarification of teacher and peer directions)
- Produce frequently used idioms, clichés, and expressions found in the classroom
- Use language in service of a wider range of social functions (command, request) and increasingly complex academic language functions (explain, summarize)

Figure 4.5   Stage 2: Learning Progression for Speaking Skills

At Stage 3, students can produce a wide range of complex oral language skills and display sophisticated knowledge of language use in social and academic contexts.

Stage 3: Speaking Skills

Word Level

- Produce a wide range of common and uncommon words in the domains of SL and SNL
- Continue to identify and intentionally use a wider range of new words to broaden expressive vocabulary in the areas of uncommon mortar words and low frequency CCL (by using new words) and continue to deepen the lexicon (by using the new meanings and nuances of known words)
- Continue to make new words of differing parts of speech from known words using derivational morphology

Sentence Level

- Produce full range of simple sentences and complex grammatical structures (e.g., relative clauses) and increase sentence length
- Use common and uncommon inflectional morphology to produce syntactically complex sentences

(Continued)

Discourse Level

- Continue to expand use of spoken language genre knowledge by producing discourse on familiar and unfamiliar topics in a broader range of contexts (conversation with multiple peers, production of extended monologues such as personal narratives or book and science reports, responses to teacher multipart requests, requests for clarification of teacher and peer directions)
- Produce frequently used idioms, clichés, and expressions found in the classroom
- Use language in service of a wide range of simple and complex social functions (command, persuade) and simple and complex academic language functions (describe, explain, summarize, hypothesize)

Figure 4.6   Stage 3: Learning Progression for Speaking Skills

Further Reading on Oral Language Skills

Luisa Moats, in *Speech to Print: Language Essentials for Teachers*, provides a comprehensive course on different domains (phonetics, phonology, morphology, semantics, and syntax) of oral language she argues teachers need to know to make sense of their students' reading development.

Moats, L. C. (2000). *Speech to Print: Language essentials for teachers.* Baltimore: Paul Brookes Publishing.

A recent overview of language development with focus on language and the educational experiences of diverse learners including those with English as a second language is provided by Paula Menyuk and Maria Brisk.

Menyuk, P. & Brisk, M. E. (2005). *Language development and education: Children with varying language experiences.* New York: Palgrave-MacMillan.

The new *Encyclopedia of Language and Education* has an entire volume dedicated to assessment of language, which includes chapters on classroom-based language assessment, dynamic assessment, and the language assessment of multilingual students.

Shohamy, E., & Hornberger, N. H. (Eds.) (2008). *Encyclopedia of language and education, Vol. 7: Language testing and assessment.* Berlin: Springer.

Linking Listening Comprehension and Speaking Skills Together

While it is frequently useful to know how well a student is comprehending what he or she hears on a topic separately from how well he or she can converse about the topic and vice versa, in reality, much of what a student experiences during the school day is the intertwined nature of listening and speaking. Teachers will therefore often need to assess listening and speaking as they occur together, as well as assess them as separate skill areas. This can best be illustrated with a series of formative assessments of listening and speaking skills which are embedded in the science teaching at Para Los Niños Charter Elementary School (PLN). While this extended example of implementing formative assessments is focused on ELL students at various stages of ability in listening comprehension and speaking, we should not forget that native English-speaking students also continue to develop oral language skills throughout the elementary school grades. There is much diversity in the language abilities of these students, and you will need to gather information about which stages of listening comprehension and speaking best describe your own students' current language abilities as well. Resource C, at the end of this chapter, presents numerous strategies in the form of a *formative assessment wheel*. The wheel is a convenient schema for thinking about the broader collection of strategies you might use to assess listening comprehension and speaking skills.

Implementing Formative Assessment Strategies for Listening and Speaking: All Stages

The following teaching and assessment sequence took place at PLN in the second grade classroom of Ms. Cardenas. During a series of science lessons about the earth and its composition and geological processes, Ms. Cardenas took the opportunity to infuse formative assessments of both listening comprehension and speaking skills into the various learning activities over several days. Of course, she was also keen to know what geology her students were learning along the way.

As we described in Chapters 1, 2, and 3, the formative assessments are linked to learning progressions, in this case to the listening comprehension skills and speaking skills continua. This extended example of formative assessment practice will show how a framework for science learning is also taken into account. Specifically, the PLN framework for science lays out the course of learning for the entire school year and includes the language (both oral and print) that students will be expected to know already or learn in service of science concept learning and inquiry. This particular unit led to a fun and informative representational task (model building) by which the teacher could gauge the overall learning that had taken place.

The geology unit began with a formative assessment strategy that used *guiding questions*, "What do you think is inside the earth?" along with "What do you think the earth is made of?" This is the first type of questioning Ms. Cardenas uses, but you will see that she uses questions (both her own and those of her students) as formative assessment strategies at different times throughout this example (Clarke, 2005). These questions and other formative assessment strategies that correspond to Resource C are illustrated throughout. First, however, the children respond to her questions by sharing their ideas with the entire class about the earth and what they thought was inside it. She then recorded the student oral responses using a graphic organizer for formative assessment of content, listening, and speaking learning (see the one created by Ms. Cardenas below in Figure 4.7, and see Resource B for a template graphic organizer).

As Ms. Cardenas was writing the student responses to the guiding questions, she was assessing student oral language along with science content knowledge and understanding. We can illustrate how she used her knowledge by examining one aspect of the learning progression for Stage 2 below. (Refer back to Figures 4.4, 4.5, and 4.6 for descriptions of all three stages of Speaking Skills.)

Stage 2: Speaking Skills

Word Level

- Identify and intentionally use an increasingly larger number of new words to broaden expressive vocabulary in the areas of mortar words and simple CCL (by using new words) and continue to deepen the lexicon (by using the new meanings and nuances of *known* words)

Ms. Cardenas's specific *success criterion* for this aspect of the learning progression was evidence of the students' accurate use of different types of academic vocabulary. As she examined her graphic organizer, it became clear to her that by using the guiding questions formative assessment strategy, she had uncovered considerable confusion, with some students making inaccurate distinctions between mortar words such as *inside* versus *outside* and *inner* versus *outer*, and still others confusing academic language—specifically the curriculum content language that carries scientific meaning, in this case words and phrases such as *surface level* and *degrees of depth*. From this formative assessment strategy, Ms. Cardenas was able to learn which words were successfully being used and which still needed review for some students.

Content Learning Assessed	Student Responses/Teacher Observations/ Evaluations/Other Comments
Student responses: Conceptual understanding	*The earth has rocks.* *The earth is like a rock.* *Inside the earth there's fire.* *Inside the earth there is bones [sic]* *Water inside the earth.* *Dirt.* *Seeds and roots are inside.*
Student responses: Misconceptions	*The sun is inside the earth.* *Stars inside.*
Clarifying questions (from students)	None
Inquiry questions (by teacher)	*What do you think is inside the earth?* *What do you think the earth is made of?*
Language Learning Assessed (Listening)	**Student Responses/Teacher Observations/ Evaluations/Other Comments**
Word Level: Vocabulary (high frequency, mortar, and/or CCL words)	Need to check on comprehension of positional words—will need to have students follow directions
Sentence Level: Syntactic structures	Simple directive sentences
Discourse Level: Organization of language, language functions	Listening accurately to various combinations of directions
Language Learning Assessed (Speaking)	**Student Responses/Teacher Observations/ Evaluations/Other Comments**
Word Level: Vocabulary (high frequency, mortar, and/or CCL words)	Difficulties distinguishing between: *Inside versus outside* *Inner versus outer* *Surface level versus degrees of depth*
Sentence Level: Syntactic structures	Directive-imperative forms
Discourse Level: Organization of language, language functions	Students give multiword directions to their classmates

Figure 4.7   Graphic Organizer for Formative Assessment of Listening and Speaking

Next, Ms. Cardenas needed to determine if she had a conceptual problem or a language-learning problem on her hands. This concern can be true with all students, but teasing out the distinction is especially true when teaching ELL students. Knowing the cause of the problem will be important for interpreting comprehension difficulties in the reading domain, as we will see in Chapter 5.

In order to clearly define the difference between *inside* and *outside*, she provided a "pop-up lesson" or in-the-moment instruction to demonstrate with concrete examples what *inside* and *outside* could mean (Heritage, Silva, & Pierce, 2007). Such a lesson stops the forward movement of planned content to focus instead on any lingering misconceptions that students may have. In this instance, these misconceptions were revealed by her formative assessment strategy. For the pop-up lesson, Ms. Cardenas first demonstrated *inside* and *outside* by using a paper bag. Students then had opportunities to follow oral directions given by the teacher using basic classroom objects with which they were already familiar and knew the names. For example:

Ms. Cardenas: Put your pencils *inside* your folders.

Ms. Cardenas: Now place all your pens *outside* your desk.

Ms. Cardenas then introduced the additional positional words that would lead to the development of the students' understanding and practice of the new academic vocabulary:

Ms Cardenas: Are all your papers now on the surface of the desks, on top of your desks? Pablo, your pens are still *inside* your desk. Where are they?

Pablo: Inside.

Ms. Cardenas: Yes, we can also say that they are in the *inner* part of your desk. I want to see them on the *outer* part of your desk, okay?

To further the practice of oral language, Ms. Cardenas gave students still struggling to follow the whole class directions additional opportunities to give directions to their classmates, thereby continuing to practice their oral language.

Next, Ms. Cardenas cut an onion to demonstrate the vocabulary required for understanding a video she intended to use in a future lesson. As she cut the 45-degree angle cross section of an onion, she asked the students:

Ms. Cardenas: What do you notice about the inside of an onion? Sketch your observations in your journal. Then turn and talk to your partner and tell them what you noticed about the inside of the onion.

Using her next formative assessment strategy, *turn and talk,* Ms. Cardenas had all her students share their impression of the onion with their neighbors. During this time, she was able to walk around the classroom listening to the students' language, and pulling out and completing another sheet of her graphic organizer with the following content statements of the students: "The onion inside has lines. The onion inside has curves. You can see the inside gets smaller and smaller. The inside is like a rainbow."

Ms. Cardenas noticed that most of the students were now using the word *inside.* In order to build on prior knowledge, she also proceeded to share with all the students the statement she had heard about the similarity of the onion to the rainbow. The children agreed that the cross section looked like a rainbow they had previously studied. Ms. Cardenas then took this opportunity to capitalize on this prior knowledge and introduced the word *layer* to the students:

Ms. Cardenas: Just as the rainbow has *layers* of color, so deep inside the earth there are *layers.*

Ms. Cardenas followed this with a discussion of *depth* by using an apple. By slowing removing the skin and cutting up the apple in front of the class, Ms. Cardenas told the students about the *surface, skin, layer,* and *the core at the center* of the apple. Ms. Cardenas then gave many opportunities for students to sketch, write labels, and turn and talk to their partners before finally summarizing the vocabulary learned: *inside* versus *outside, outer* versus *inner, core, layers, deep,* and *center.*

The vocabulary prepared the students for the CCL required to view an earth science video, *Journey to the Center of the Earth,* from the Magic School Bus series. The video continued to build the students' exposure to CLL in this area of geology as well as provide a graphic portrayal of the physical processes at work inside the earth. The visual representation of new knowledge is particularly helpful with the ELL students at Stage 1. It allowed these students to anchor new vocabulary to new concepts in the area of geology. As the students viewed the video, they made sketches of interesting sections related to the layers of the inner earth and the core. The vocabulary words were already previously recorded in their journals, and students could refer to their newly acquired science terms. Additionally, the teacher used the language from the video to extend their vocabulary further. The following words were added to the content language: *crust, mantle, outer core,* and *core.* Students had opportunities to ask clarifying questions and pose questions for further investigation by writing them on the board.

Ms. Cardenas used the student *clarification questions* and *questions for further investigation* as part of her collection of formative assessment strategies.

> ## KEY TERMINOLOGY
>
> **Readers' Workshop:** A method of teaching reading that fosters a love for reading by allowing student choice of texts at their current level of reading and provides differentiated instruction to meet individual student needs. This approach is well suited to formative assessment strategies such as individual conferencing and observation of student reading abilities and attitudes in order to plan instruction.

These questions provided information for her own understanding of their vocabulary acquisition and development of topic knowledge. She then supplemented this initial introduction to the science topic with follow-up reading. First, Ms. Cardenas read aloud from *Planet Earth/Inside Out* by Gail Gibbons (1995). She typically uses expository text to further provide instruction to students during *readers' workshop.*

Specifically, Ms. Cardenas had students reread their clarifying questions and questions for further investigation that were on the board. As she read from the book, students were prompted to raise their hand when they thought the passage was addressing a question. The teacher also modeled the use of an *"I wonder . . ." question*:

Ms. Cardenas: As I read this passage, I wondered, "How deep are the layers? Could anyone really travel to the earth's core?"

This is an approach that she has learned in the writings and workshops of reading expert Lucy Calkins (2001) who has created a "talk-curriculum" to support the development of reading. Ms. Cardenas then wrote her question on a sticky note and modeled her thinking by posting the sticky to the page she was reading.

The students then continued reading independently from the chapter and used sticky notes to jot down questions that they thought were answered by the text. They also had opportunities to jot down any "I wonder" questions of their own. Ms. Cardenas then collated the information that these and other student questions can yield about student learning to review later and use as another formative assessment strategy. With this information, she can monitor their question formation abilities and intercede with more practices for those students having problems.

Next, Ms. Cardenas supplemented the student reading time with a time set aside for *journal writing* in their science notebooks (Figure 4.8). These notes were not formal pieces of writing to be evaluated, but were meant to mirror the practices used by scientists in conducting science.

As such, the students were directed to make notes for themselves on what they had learned so far.

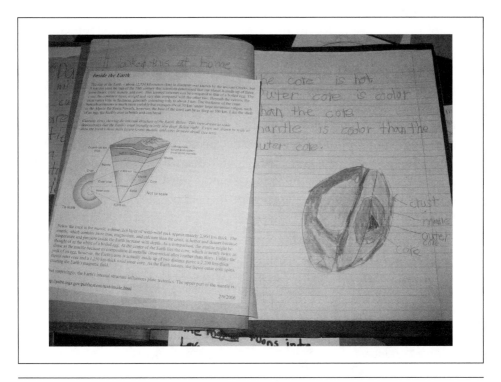

Figure 4.8   Example of Journal Writing to Link Oral Language Discussions to Literacy in Science.

Used with permission.

The students also used sticky notes to jot down additional questions that they had as they arose while they were reading the passage. As the children continued reading over several days, they had additional opportunities for sharing aloud their "I wonder" questions with a partner and for Ms. Cardenas to monitor their growth in science and language learning through these questions and the turn-and-talk formative assessment strategy.

The viewing, reading, and journaling activities were subsequently followed up with open-ended conversations in groups of four to five students. Ms. Cardenas continued her formative assessment of speaking skills used in this unit during small group *discussion*. The groups talked about what they had heard and read. Ms. Cardenas circulated among them, listening and making written notes of what the children were saying to one another in terms of their understanding. Obviously, in exactly the same set-up, she could have chosen to focus on how well they listened to one another. However, in this instance her purpose was to focus on speaking skills, particularly on the students' inclusion of CCL vocabulary and on their abilities to pose grammatically correct, topic-focused questions to one another. Having one clear purpose for the formative assessment is a good strategy; Ms. Cardenas can always choose to make a second sweep of the classroom to observe discussion and note how well students listen and comprehend one another's comments by whether they give contingent responses to one another and/or make clarification requests.

Over the next few days, the small groups created *representational models* of their learning that can be a formative assessment strategy to gather information about students' comprehension of the main concepts being taught. In this instance, clay and paint models represented what they had learned about the core and mantel of the earth, as well as volcanic processes (Figure 4.9). The models were not replications of existing models but stemmed entirely from the students as visual representations of their conceptual understanding of what they had seen, heard, and read over the entire series of geology lessons.

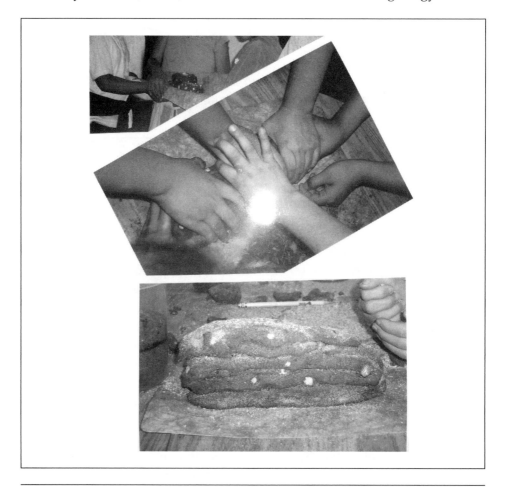

Figure 4.9   Examples of Creating Representational Models of Learning.

Used with permission.

Some students chose to show the layers of the earth and the formation of volcanoes with the magma rising to the surface from the inner core under pressure (Figure 4.10).

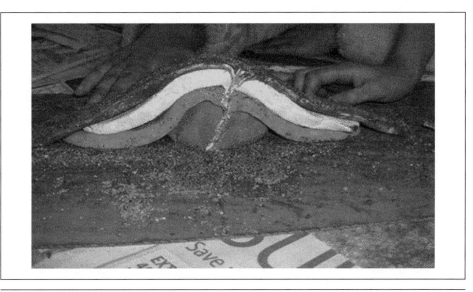

Figure 4.10 Example of a Representational Model of an Erupting Volcano.

Used with permission.

Yet other students made cross sections of the earth to show what was inside the hemispheres (Figure 4.11).

Figure 4.11 Example of a Cross-Sectional Model of the Earth

Used with permission.

The detail and accuracy of these models were then evaluated by Ms. Cardenas as indicators of how well the students had listened to her, and to their peers, over the course of all the lessons. While suitable for gauging the learning of all students, representational modeling is a formative assessment strategy particularly useful with ELL students because it can capture listening abilities and understanding of content without confounding these with ability to produce oral English.

In Chapter 3, we presented a model for how teachers integrate a range of knowledge and skills during formative assessment. We will now refer to the model (Figure 4.12) to more closely examine the final formative assessment strategy utilized by Ms. Cardenas and summarize what evidence of student learning she has gathered overall.

As final step, Ms. Cardenas conducted individual *conferencing* with each student to check on his or her learning of geologic concepts, along with her or his ability to comprehend her questions and talk about the material. This task clearly draws on all four of the teacher knowledge domains defined in Figure 4.12. Specifically, this choice of formative assessment strategy gave the students opportunities to tell their teacher about the models they had created and why they had chosen various materials. While summative in its overall purpose, Ms. Cardenas could use this strategy to detect if there were any gaps in the content and/or language learning of individual students. In this way, she could still use the information in a formative way to address these gaps instructionally in the future.

She generally began her conferencing sessions with an open-ended question or simple directive to the student:

Ms. Cardenas: Tell me about your model and what it shows.

In response, students had opportunities to use CCL vocabulary and display their topic knowledge gained during the extensive oral discussions and reading. Many students referred back to the initial lessons describing the earth as like an onion or an apple. This situation forced students to use the comparative words such as *like, just like, same as,* and *it reminds me of . . . a rainbow* or *the time when we cut the onion,* or *the time when we cut the apple.* Because Ms. Cardenas was fully aware of the science learning progression used throughout her school, she was able to draw on her knowledge of students' prior learning experiences not only with her but also from previous grades when she heard students use words from earlier units of study, such as *solids, liquids, gases,* and *temperature.* She recorded the student responses on her graphic organizer, paying close attention to all their vocabulary choices, the variety and accuracy in their grammatical structures, and the different discourse features, specifically

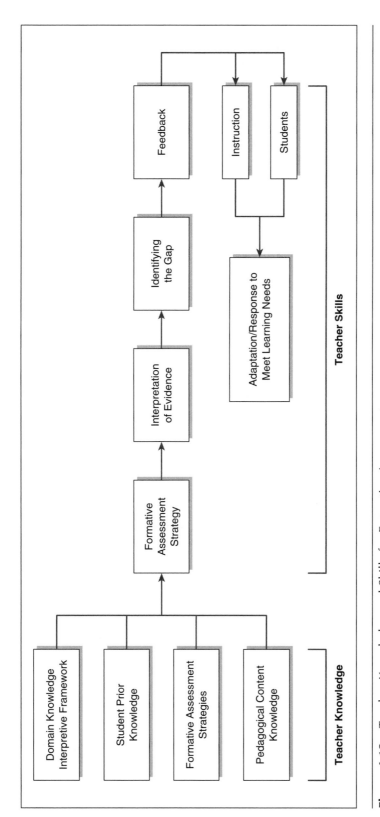

Figure 4.12 Teacher Knowledge and Skills for Formative Assessment

the language functions the students used in conferencing, such as *descriptions and explanations* for what they had made.

The information she got for her efforts not only provided her with feedback for her own future instructional decisions but also allowed her to give feedback to students about their science misconceptions and their oral language challenges. Students could then select activities to meet their own learning needs, such as practicing question and answer skills with more expert peers. From all this, Ms. Cardenas was able to form a comprehensive view of what her individual students had learned *and* what they would still need to learn in the future, as they take their language skills to new levels—and where we turn to in the next chapter—reading comprehension.

REFLECTION QUESTIONS

1. How much do you focus on the formative assessment of listening comprehension skills in systematic ways in your classroom?

2. How much do you focus on the formative assessment of speaking skills in systematic ways in your classroom?

3. Which features of spoken academic English do you expect students in your classroom to know and how do you monitor development of these features in students?

4. Where do your own students fall on the learning progressions for listening comprehension and speaking skills?

5. What additional skills should be added to the learning progressions to best capture your expectations for the oral language skills of native-English-speaking students?

6. What additional skills should be added to the learning progressions to best capture the ELD standards of your state?

RESOURCE A

Stages of Listening Comprehension and Speaking Skills

STAGE 1

Listening Comprehension

Word Level

- Comprehend a range of frequently used words (e.g., common vocabulary in the domains of social language [SL] and school navigational language [SNL])
- Identify and intentionally add a small number of new words to broaden *receptive vocabulary* in the areas of mortar words and curriculum content language (CCL) (by adding new words) and deepen the *lexicon* (by adding new meanings and nuances to *known* words)

Sentence Level

- Use word order conventions to make meaning of syntactically simple sentences (e.g., subject+verb+object = declarative statement; verb+subject+object = question form; verb+object = imperative form)
- Use high frequency *inflectional morphology* (plural+s) to make meaning of syntactically simple sentences

Discourse Level

- Begin to build spoken language *genre* knowledge (organization of language and ideas) by interpreting the meanings of a range of oral *discourse* contexts (conversations with a peer, short teacher monologues, simple one-step instructions/directions)
- Begin to build printed language *genre* knowledge by acquiring story grammar knowledge and interpreting the meanings of a range of short, simple texts read aloud by the teacher (storybooks, simple expository texts, poetry, puns)
- Comprehend frequently used idioms, clichés and expressions used in the classroom (e.g., Once upon a time, The End, Are you sitting nicely?)

Prior/Content Knowledge

- Begin to connect new information heard to that already learned so that general background and content knowledge grow in both depth and breadth

Speaking Skills

Word Level

- Produce frequently used words (e.g., common vocabulary in the domains of SL and SNL)
- Identify and intentionally use a small number of new words to broaden expressive vocabulary in the areas of common mortar words and simple CCL (by using new words) and deepen the *lexicon* (by using the new meanings and nuances of *known* words)

Sentence Level

- Produce syntactically simple sentences
- Use high frequency *inflectional morphology* to produce syntactically simple sentences

Discourse Level

- Begin to display spoken language *genre* knowledge by producing *discourse* on familiar topics in a small range of frequently occurring contexts (short conversations with a peer, short responses to teacher requests, simple requests for clarification of teacher directions)
- Produce frequently used idioms, clichés, and expressions found in the classroom, often learned in chunks or unanalyzed strings (e.g., *Once upon a time, Mayago [= May+I+go] to recess?*)
- Use language in service of common social functions (*express needs, command*) and simple/common academic language functions (*describe, label*)

STAGE 2

Listening Comprehension

Word Level

- Comprehend a broader range of frequently used words (e.g., common vocabulary in the domains of SL and SNL)

- Identify and intentionally add an increasingly large number of new words to broaden *receptive vocabulary* in the areas of mortar words and CCL (by adding new words including the academic synonyms of more commonly used words [e.g., *feline* for *cat*]), synonyms to provide more precision or information [e.g., *replied* and *asked* for *said*] and continue to deepen the *lexicon* (by adding new meanings, shades of meaning [e.g., *anger* versus *furious*], and nuances to *known* words)
- Begin to use word analysis skills to aid in comprehension (e.g., use high frequency *derivational morphology* (e.g., adjective+*ness* = noun) to identify parts of speech or understand new meanings (*un*+ adjective and *un*+verb = opposite in meaning to root word)

Sentence Level

- Expand repertoire of recognizable sentence structures to include frequently used complex syntax (e.g., relative clauses)
- Use less common *inflectional morphology* to make meaning of syntactically complex sentences (e.g., participial modifiers [verb+*ing*] such as *The boys running were late for their class*)

Discourse Level

- Continue to build spoken language *genre* knowledge (organization of language and ideas) by interpreting the meanings of a broader range of oral *discourse* contexts (dialogues between two peers, longer teacher monologues, two- and three-step instructions/directions)
- Continue to build printed language *genre* knowledge by interpreting the meanings of a broader range of simple texts read aloud by the teacher (storybooks, simple expository texts, poetry, puns)
- Comprehend frequently used idioms, clichés, and expressions used in the classroom (e.g., *Give it your best, The more the better*)

Prior/Content Knowledge

- Continue to connect larger amounts of new information heard to that already learned so that general background and content knowledge grow in both depth and breadth

Speaking Skills

Word Level

- Produce a broader range of frequently used words (e.g., common vocabulary in the domains of SL and SNL)

- Identify and intentionally use an increasingly larger number of new words to broaden expressive vocabulary in the areas of mortar words and simple CCL (by using new words) and continue to deepen the *lexicon* (by using the new meanings and nuances of *known* words)
- Make new words of differing parts of speech from known words using *derivational morphology*

Sentence Level

- Produce greater variety of *grammatical structures* (e.g., inclusion of adjectival and prepositional phrases)
- Use less common *inflectional morphology* to produce syntactically more complex sentences

Discourse Level

- Continue expanded use of spoken language *genre* knowledge by producing *discourse* on familiar topics in a broader range of contexts (conversation with a peer, conversation with a group of peers, production of simple monologues such as personal narratives or a short book report, responses to teacher multipart requests, requests for clarification of teacher and peer directions)
- Produce frequently used idioms, clichés, and expressions found in the classroom
- Use language in service of a wider range of social functions (*command, request*) and increasingly complex academic language functions (*explain, summarize*)

STAGE 3

Listening Comprehension

Word Level

- Comprehend a wide range of common and uncommon words in the domains of SL and SNL
- Continue to identify and intentionally add unfamiliar words to broaden *receptive vocabulary* in the areas of mortar words and CCL (by adding new words) and deepen the *lexicon* (by adding new meanings, shades of meaning, and nuances to *known* words)
- Make inferences about a speaker's stance towards content from their word choices (e.g., *retorted* for *replied*)

- Continue to use word analysis skills to aid in comprehension (e.g., use rarer *derivational morphology* (e.g. verb+*ate* [*fixate*] = new verb meaning; adjective+*ify* [*solidify*] = verb)

Sentence Level

- Comprehend the full range of simple and complex *grammatical structures* (e.g., nominalization of verb forms [*to form* versus *formation*] to increase amount of information contained within a sentence) and increase sentence length (e.g., multiple prepositions in a single sentence)
- Continue to use common and uncommon *inflectional morphology* to make meaning of syntactically complex sentences

Discourse Level

- Continue to build spoken language *genre* knowledge (organization of language and ideas) by interpreting the meanings of a broader range of oral *discourse* contexts (dialogues between multiple peers, extended teacher monologues, plays/dramas, multistep instructions/ directions)
- Continue to build printed language *genre* knowledge by interpreting the meanings of a broader range of simple and challenging texts read aloud by the teacher (storybooks with familiar and unfamiliar story grammars, works of literature, complex expository texts, primary source texts in content areas such as history, poetry, plays, puns)
- Comprehend frequently used idioms, clichés, and expressions used in the classroom (e.g., "Don't beat about the bush," "All's well that ends well")

Prior/Content Knowledge

- Continue to connect complex and large amounts of new information heard to that already learned so that general background and content knowledge grow in both depth and breadth

Speaking Skills

Word Level

- Produce a wide range of common and uncommon words in the domains of SL and SNL

- Continue to identify and intentionally use a wider range of new words to broaden expressive vocabulary in the areas of uncommon mortar words and low frequency CCL (by using new words) and continue to deepen the *lexicon* (by using the new meanings and nuances of *known* words)
- Continue to make new words of differing parts of speech from known words using *derivational morphology*

Sentence Level

- Produce full range of simple sentences and complex *grammatical structures* (e.g., relative clauses) and increase sentence length
- Use common and uncommon *inflectional morphology* to produce syntactically complex sentences

Discourse Level

- Continue to expand use of spoken language *genre* knowledge by producing *discourse* on familiar and unfamiliar topics in a broader range of contexts (conversation with multiple peers, production of extended monologues, such as personal narratives or book and science reports, responses to teacher multipart requests, requests for clarification of teacher and peer directions)
- Produce frequently used idioms, clichés, and expressions found in the classroom
- Use language in service of a wide range of simple and complex social functions (*command, persuade*) and simple and complex academic language functions (*describe, explain, summarize, hypothesize*)

RESOURCE B

Graphic Organizer

Formative Assessment of Listening and
Speaking During Content Classes

Content Learning Assessed	Student Responses/Teacher Observations/ Evaluations/Other Comments
Student responses: Conceptual understanding	
Student responses: Misconceptions	
Clarifying questions (from students)	
Inquiry questions (by teacher)	
Language Learning Assessed (Listening)	**Student Responses/Teacher Observations/ Evaluations/Other Comments**
Word Level: Vocabulary (high frequency, mortar, and/or CCL words)	
Sentence Level: Syntactic structures	
Discourse Level: Organization of language, language functions	
Language Learning Assessed (Speaking)	**Student Responses/Teacher Observations/ Evaluations/Other Comments**
Word Level: Vocabulary (high frequency, mortar, and/or CCL words)	
Sentence Level: Syntactic structures	
Discourse Level: Organization of language, language functions	

Figure 4.13   Formative Assessment of Listening and Speaking During Content Classes

RESOURCE C

Additional Formative Assessment Strategies
for Listening and Speaking Skills

Below is a Formative Assessment Wheel. It contains the strategies already introduced in this chapter, along with several additional strategies. Below, we provide examples of many of these strategies. This is not an exhaustive list of strategies but the wheel is meant to remind you that it is the *collection* of many different strategies that will give you reliable evidence and a more complete picture of student progress (While not focused on formative assessment exclusively, see also Penny McKay's (2006) *Assessing Young Language Learners,* Cambridge University Press, for excellent suggestions for assessing the oral language skills of children learning a second language.) Both the type and size of the "slices" of the wheel will differ for each student. Keeping this is mind will help ensure that you do not rely too much or too little on just one strategy.

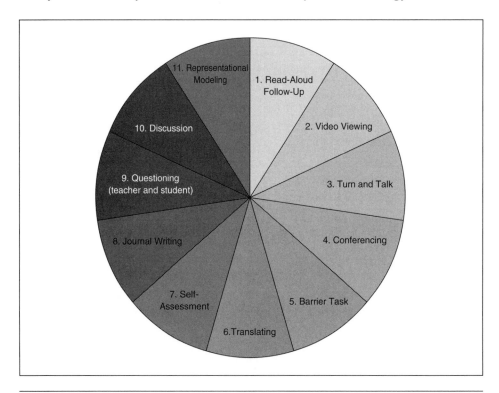

Figure 4.14 Formative Assessment Wheel: Strategies for Listening and Speaking

1. Read-Aloud Follow-Up

For gathering formative information from a read-aloud task, texts should be age/grade appropriate and if assessing English language learners, chosen based on the level of English language development. After the read-aloud, listening comprehension and/or speaking abilities can be assessed in a variety of verbal and nonverbal (e.g., total physical response) ways:

- *Verbal Retell (sequencing events)*: for listening comprehension (accuracy and amount of text retold) and for speaking abilities in the area of lexical diversity, sophistication of sentence structure, and coherent and cohesive discourse
- *Picture Drawing (sequencing events)*: for listening comprehension (accuracy and amount of text represented graphically)
- *Yes/No Questions*: for listening comprehension (accuracy and amount of text recalled)
- *Visual Arts*: for listening comprehension (accuracy and amount of text represented in model creations)
- *Performance Art (play, dance):* for listening comprehension (accuracy and amount of text represented dramatically)

Figure 4.15　Example of Reenacting Science Facts and Processes Through Dance.

Used with permission.

2. Video Viewing

   Programming should be age/grade appropriate and if assessing English language learners, chosen based on the level of English language development. This stimulus for assessment is particularly effective for use with English language learners because the visual input will not be as language-dependent as reading aloud from story and expository texts. After viewing, listening comprehension and/or speaking abilities can be assessed in the same manner as read-aloud assessments (see #1 above).

3. Turn and Talk

   The teacher instructs students to turn to their neighbors and discuss the material that was just presented. Turn and talk activities can be supported by posters of conversation starters/prompts placed around the room for students to spontaneously use or for the teacher to remind students of their potential help. The teacher then circulates around the room to listen in on the dialogues, using her graphic organizer to take notes on student listening comprehension (accuracy and amount of text retold) and their speaking abilities in the area of lexical diversity, sophistication of sentence structure, and coherent and cohesive discourse abilities.

4. Conferencing

   One-on-one conferencing with students allows them to tell first-hand about their learning. The teacher can use prompts to provide students with opportunities to display listening comprehension (accuracy and amount of text retold) and their speaking abilities including their use of CCL and other key vocabulary, sentence structures, and conversational skills.

5. Barrier Task

   In this classic communication task, a student gives another student the verbal input needed to draw a picture behind a barrier to determine if the second student can accurately reproduce what the first student is describing. This captures the listening comprehension skills of the second student and the abilities to give fully elaborated description and directions in the first student.

6. Translating

   In the case of English language learners, a teacher can ask a more advanced student to translate what is being said in English to a less proficient student, as well as ask the student to translate back

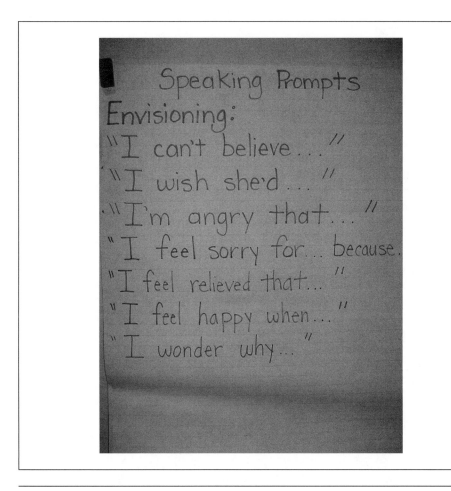

Figure 4.16   Example of Second Grade Speaking Prompts for Expressing Opinion
and Inquiry

into English what the less proficient student has expressed in the
first language. A bilingual teacher can listen to these dialogues
and use her graphic organizer to take notes on student listening
comprehension in both languages and their translation abilities
to and from English.

7. Self-Assessment
For many activities involving listening comprehension, students
can assess their own learning with a simple *finger walk* procedure.
Using their own fingers they can recount the events in a story or
the sequence of steps in a process they have just heard during a
read-aloud or in viewing a video. This will enable them to start
to judge for themselves if they have paid attention to a certain
amount of information, say three of four pieces, each represented
by a finger.

REFERENCES

Anglin, J. M. (1993). Vocabulary development: A morphological analysis. *Monographs of the Society for Research in Child Development, 58*(10).

August, D., & Shanahan, T. (2006). *Developing literacy in second-language learners: Report of the National Literacy Panel on language minority children and youth.* Mahwah, NJ: Lawrence Erlbaum Associates.

Bailey, A. L. (Ed.) (2007). *The language demands of school: Putting academic English to the test.* New Haven, CT: Yale University Press.

Bailey, A. L. (2008). Assessing the language of young learners. In E. Shohamy & N. H. Hornberger (Eds.), *Encyclopedia of language and education, Vol. 7: Language testing and assessment.* Berlin: Springer.

Bailey, A. L., Butler, F. A., Stevens, R., & Lord, C. (2007). Further specifying the language demands of school. In A. L. Bailey (Ed.), *The language demands of school: Putting academic English to the test* (pp. 103–156). New Haven, CT: Yale University Press.

Bailey, A. L., & Moughamian, A. C. (2007). Telling stories their way: Narrative scaffolding with emergent readers and readers. *Narrative Inquiry, 17*(2), 203–229.

Baker, S. K., Simmons, D. C., & Kameenui, E. J. (1998). Vocabulary acquisition: Research bases. In S. C. Simmons & E. J. Kaneenui (Eds.), *What reading research tells us about children with diverse learning needs: Bases and basics* (pp. 183–218). Mahwah, NJ: Lawrence Erlbaum Associates.

Bamberg, M., & Damrad-Frye, R. (1991). On the ability to provide evaluative comments: Further exploration of children's narrative competencies. *Journal of Child Language, 18*(3), 689–710.

Beck, I. L., & McKeown, M. G. (1991). Social studies texts are hard to understand: Mediating some of the difficulties. *Language Arts, 68*, 482–490.

Biemiller, A. (1999). *Language and reading success.* Brookline, MA: Brookline Books.

Blachowicz, C. Z., Fisher, P. J. L., Ogle, D., & Watts-Taffe, S. (2006). Vocabulary: Questions from the classroom. *Reading Research Quarterly, 41*(4), 524–539.

Calkins, L. M. (2001). *The art of teaching reading.* New York: Longman.

Carey, S. (1978). The child as word learner. In M. Halle, J. Bresnan, & G. A. Miller (Eds.), *Linguistic theory and psychological reality.* Cambridge, MA: MIT Press.

Chall, J. S. (1983). *Stages of reading development.* New York: McGraw-Hill.

Clarke, S. (2005). *Formative assessment in the secondary classroom.* London: Hodder Murray.

Dickinson, D. K., McCabe, A., Anastasopoulos, L., Peisner-Feinberg, E. S., & Poe, M. D. (2003). The comprehensive language approach to early literacy: The interrelationships among vocabulary, phonological sensitivity, and print knowledge among preschool-aged children. *Journal of Educational Psychology, 95*(3), 465–481.

Freire, P. (1972). *Pedagogy of the oppressed.* Harmondsworth: Penguin.

Garcia, G. E. (1991). Factors influencing the English reading test performance of Spanish-speaking Hispanic students. *Reading Research Quarterly, 26*, 371–392.

Geva, E., Yabhoub-Zadeh, Z. & Schuster, B. (2000). Understanding individual differences in word recognition skills of ESL children. *Annals of Dyslexia, 50*, 123–154.

Gibbons, G. (1995). *Planet Earth/Inside out.* New York: Morrow Junior Books.

Gibbons, P. (1998). Classroom talk and the learning of new registers in a second language. *Language and Education, 12(2),* 99–118.

Griffin, T., Hemphill, L., Camp, L., & Wolf, D. P. (2004). Oral discourse in the preschool years and later literacy skills. *First Language, 24,* 123–147.

Hart, B., & Risley, T. R. (1995). *Meaningful differences in the everyday experiences of young American children.* Baltimore: Paul Brookes Publishing.

Hantani, K. (2005). *A rabbit's eyes.* New York: Vertical.

Heritage M., Silva, N., & Pierce, M. (2007). Academic English: A view from the classroom. In A. L. Bailey (Ed.), *The language demands of school: Putting academic English to the test* (pp. 171–210). New Haven, CT: Yale University Press.

Laufer, B. (1989). What percentage of text-lexis is essential for comprehension? In C. Lauren and M. Nordman (Eds.), *Special language: From humans thinking to thinking machines.* Clevedon, UK: Multilingual Matters.

McCabe, A., & Rollins, P. R. (1994). Assessment of preschool narrative skills. *American Journal of Speech-Language Pathology, 3*(1) 45–55.

McKay, P., (2006). *Assessing young language learners.* Cambridge, UK: Cambridge University Press.

Menyuk, P., & Brisk, M. (2005). *Language development and education: Children with varying language experience.* New York: Palgrave-McMillan.

Moats, L. C. (2000). *Speech to print: Language essentials for teachers.* Baltimore: Paul Brookes Publishing.

Nagy, W. E., & Anderson, R. C. (1984). How many words are there in printed school English? *Reading Research Quarterly, 19,* 304–330.

Nagy, W. E., & Herman, P. A. (1987). Breadth and depth of vocabulary knowledge: Implications for acquisition and instruction. In M. G. McKeown and M. E. Curtis (Eds.), *The nature of vocabulary acquisition* (pp. 19–36). Hillsdale, NJ: Lawrence Erlbaum Associates.

National Reading Panel. (2000). *Teaching children to read: An evidence-based assessment of the scientific research literature on reading and its implications for reading instruction.* Bethesda, MD: National Institutes of Health.

National Research Council. (1998). *Preventing reading difficulties in young children.* Committee for the Prevention of Reading Difficulties in Young Children. C. E. Snow, M. S. Burns, & P. Griffin (Eds.). Washington, DC: National Academy Press.

No Child Left Behind Act. (2001). Pub. L. No. 107–110, 115 Stat. 1425.

Peterson, C., & McCabe, A. (1983). *Developmental psycholinguistics: Three ways of looking at a child's narrative.* New York: Plenum.

Reese, E. (1995). Predicting children's literacy from mother-child conversations. *Cognitive Development, 10,* 381–405.

Rice, M. L. (1990). Preschooler's QUIL: Quick incidental learning of words. In G. Conti-Ramsden & C. E. Snow (Eds.), *Children's language* (Vol. 7, pp. 172–169). Hillsdale, NJ: Lawrence Erlbaum Associates.

Royer, J. M. & Carlo, M. S. (1991). Transfer of comprehension skills from native to second language. *Journal of Reading, 34*(6), 450–455.

Rumelhart, D. E. (1980). On evaluating story grammars. *Cognitive Science, 4*(3), 313–316.

Scarborough, H. (2001). Connecting early language and literacy to later reading (dis)abilities: Evidence, theory, and practice. In S. B. Neuman &

D. I. Dickinson (Eds.), *Handbook of early literacy research* (pp. 97–110). New York: The Guilford Press.

Schleppegrell, M. J. (2004). *The language of schooling: A functional linguistics perspective.* Mahwah, NJ: Lawrence Erlbaum Associates.

Snow, C. E., Tabors, P. O., & Dickinson, D. K. (2001). Language development in the preschool years. In D. K. Dickinson & P. O. Tabors (Eds.), *Beginning literacy with language: Young children learning at home and school.* Baltimore: Paul Brookes Publishing.

Stanovich, K. E. (1986). Matthew effects in reading: Some consequences of individual differences in the acquisition of literacy. *Reading Research Quarterly, 21,* 360–406.

Sternberg, R. J. (1987). Most vocabulary is learned from context. In M. G. McKeown and M. E. Curtis (Eds.), *The nature of vocabulary acquisition* (pp. 89–106) Hillsdale, NJ: Lawrence Erlbaum Associates.

Storch, S. A., & Whitehurst, G. J. (2002). Oral language and code-related precursors to reading: Evidence from a longitudinal structural model. *Developmental Psychology, 38*(6), 934–947.

Tabors, P. (1997). *One child, two languages: A guide to preschool educators of children learning English as a second language.* Baltimore: Paul Brookes Publishing.

Wagner, R. K., Muse, A. E., & Tannenbaum, K. R. (2007). *Vocabulary acquisition: Implications for reading comprehension.* New York: The Guilford Press.

Wagner, R. K., Torgesen, J. K., Rashotte, C. A., Hecht, S. A., Barker, T. A., Burgess, S. R., et al. (1997). Changing relations between phonological processing abilities and word-level reading as children develop from beginning to skilled readers: A 5-year longitudinal study. *Developmental Psychology, 33,* 468–479.

5 The Essence of Reading

Assessing Reading Comprehension

Used with permission.

D rew, a first grader at Western Elementary School in Los Angeles, is reading aloud to her teacher, Ms. Quon. Drew has good letter-sound knowledge and knows quite a few sight words, but her reading is still quite labored. Ms. Quon has been focusing on helping Drew think about the meaning of what she is reading and has been specifically teaching Drew a set of cues to help her make meaning from the text. While Drew reads, Ms. Quon checks to see how well she uses the meaning-making strategies. We'll focus in on one page of the book and what happens when Drew reads.

Text:	Fish swim in the sea.
Drew (reading very slowly):	Fish . . . . . . swim . . . . . . in . . . . . the . . . . . . water. No. That's not water. It doesn't begin with 'w.' S (says letter name) ssss (letter sound). Sea. Fish swim in the sea.

Although Drew reads slowly, Ms. Quon sees that she is using her cueing strategies effectively. First she uses meaning cues, substituting *water* for *sea*. From her background knowledge about fish, she knows they can swim in water so the text is making sense. However, when Drew reads *water*, she sees a visual mismatch between what she has read aloud and the initial letter of the word. Drew's strategy then is to initiate a search, first by letter name and then by letter sound, to find the right word. She preserves the meaning when she self-corrects and selects the word *sea* (she could have selected other words that begin with "s" instead, but which would not have made sense in this particular text). Then she rereads the whole text.

Ms. Quon then asks Drew to think about what she did when she self-corrected:

Drew:	When I said it, I thought the word doesn't begin with "w" so it couldn't be water. Then I thought, well what could it be and I saw the "s." Then I figured out that it had to be sea because fish can swim in the sea.
Ms. Quon:	You did a very good job of using your strategies to read the text accurately. Let's keep on reading and while you are reading think about two questions: is what you are reading making sense and does what you are seeing match with what you are reading?—just like you did when you noticed that water could not be the right word because it began with the letter "s."

Even though Drew is in the early stages of learning to read, she clearly understands the two simultaneous processes involved in comprehending text: extracting and constructing meaning (RAND Reading Study Group, 2002). She knows that there is a story or message to be constructed from text, and she understands quite a bit about the technical features of written language. We'll now examine in more detail these two processes, which are central to reading comprehension.

EXTRACTING MEANING

Extracting meaning from text depends on the reader's ability to recognize symbols on a page or screen. As we noted in Chapter 2, this requires the fluent decoding of combinations of symbols as words and combinations of words as sentences. Fluent decoding entails a mix of quick, accurate, and efficient word recognition, an understanding of how words function together at the sentence level (i.e., grammar) and knowledge of the uses of punctuation. With this knowledge, a reader can quickly access the surface level of text (i.e., what the symbols stand for)—the first step in reading comprehension.

The ability to extract meaning is one that grows incrementally. When children first start to read, their reading is often slow and labored. This is due, in part, to the fact that they do not have automatic word recognition skills. In the absence of immediate word recognition, children have to segment and blend the individual phonemes of regular words and, in the case of irregular words that are not known on sight, they will have to resort to other means. For example, children could use context as a clue to an unknown word, but this strategy may not always lead to successful, accurate word recognition. Children's ability to recognize words quickly and accurately grows over time; later in the chapter we outline how this growth occurs in our developmental continuum of reading comprehension skills.

As children's knowledge of syntax and grammar increases so does their ability to chunk words into units of grammar as they read. For example, if they know that words that qualify a noun come before the noun, then when they read a phrase like "the big, yellow bus" they will be able to read all the words together in a grammatical chunk. An expanding knowledge of punctuation and how it is used to determine pause and emphasis will also help the child make sense of the text.

Explicit teaching of word recognition skills, syntax and grammar, and the role of punctuation will be necessary to ensure that children acquire the skills and successfully extract meaning. And of course, practice in reading will make a big contribution to the development of these abilities, too.

CONSTRUCTING MEANING

At the same time that readers are extracting meaning from text, they must also be constructing meaning. Constructing meaning involves a wide range of knowledge, including vocabulary knowledge, topic knowledge, and genre and text structure knowledge. Successful comprehension also finds students engaged in a self-monitoring and other metacognitive strategies while they are reading so that they are continuously aware if the text is making sense to them or not. And when the text is not making sense, they also have a wide range of comprehension strategies to draw on and know when to employ them appropriately. Let us take a more detailed look at how all this knowledge contributes to reading comprehension.

Vocabulary Knowledge

We have already noted in Chapters 2 and 4 that vocabulary knowledge is strongly related to reading comprehension. In the beginning stages of reading, children's oral vocabulary plays an important role in helping them make the connection between the spoken word and print.

When they are applying their letter-sound knowledge to decode words in print, they more readily understand the text if they can map the words they are reading to the oral vocabulary they bring to the task (National Reading Panel, 2000). However, as children develop as readers, their reading vocabulary becomes a critical factor in comprehending the text. By reading vocabulary, we mean the number of words they can recognize and know the meaning of in text.

Topic Knowledge

What the Experts Say About Topic Knowledge

In a nice example, E.D. Hirsch, Jr. (2003), shows how topic knowledge of baseball is important for understanding the simple sentence "Jones sacrificed and knocked in a run." For someone who knew nothing about baseball, this would be a very puzzling sentence, even if this person were able to read all the words and had general knowledge of the word "sacrificed." While this sentence makes use of everyday vocabulary, it is used in the specific context of baseball. Unless the reader has knowledge of baseball, the meaning of the words will remain opaque.

Constructing meaning also depends on a reader's prior knowledge of the topic introduced in the text. Successful readers are able to activate their prior knowledge of the topic in the process of reading, compare it to new knowledge presented in the text, and connect the new knowledge to existing knowledge.

Thus, knowledge of the topic enables the reader to make rapid connections between new and previously learned content—a process that supports comprehension. We have all experienced the difficulty of trying to read and make sense of a text with content of which we know absolutely nothing about.

Genre Knowledge

What the Experts Say About Genre Knowledge

Pauline Gibbons (1998) suggests that genre knowledge is a type of schematic or "in-the-head" knowledge similar to content knowledge. She argues that with knowledge, for example, of only a story title such as "The Sly Cat and the Clever Mouse," one could predict many major elements of a story. Readers with genre knowledge then tend to have more strategic resources to draw on for comprehension, reading more easily with an anticipatory set for reading, developing a purpose for their reading, and anticipating and verifying predictions.

To construct meaning of text, a reader needs to also have understanding of genre. Genre refers to the norms of different text types including their social purpose, overall structure, and specific language features. For example, a narrative is informal in tone, is structured around a climactic moment, and includes precise, vivid word choice intended to create imagery in the reader's mind. Conversely, an explanation is generally read for information, more formal in tone, structured around a sequence of ideas or concepts, and it includes general nouns, present tense action verbs, and connectors to join the verbs together in a logical order.

Text Structure Knowledge

An important aspect of genre knowledge is knowledge of how a text is structured. Text structure refers to the features of narrative and expository text and how they are organized to guide readers to identify information and make connections among topics and ideas (Englert & Thomas, 1987). Students who have reading comprehension difficulties often lack skills in identifying main topics and in identifying significant supporting information and relations between the text's main topics. Proficient readers are able to recognize logical relationships such as chronology, cause and effect, comparison, and contrast in text patterns and use them to make decisions about the overall meaning of what they are reading. They are also able to use discourse connectors (e.g., *given that, despite, however*) to form a stance toward information, for example, what is known, unknown, contrasted, minimized, or preferred.

Academic Language Knowledge

Central to how well students are able to construct meaning within different text structures is their academic language knowledge. Take, for example, clauses and how they link together in speech to signal logical relationships and how such links are made in text. In spoken interaction, children will string one clause after the other with conjunctions to signal logical relationships, whereas in text, meanings are condensed in denser clause structures that incorporate logical relationships (Schleppegrell, 2004). Different text structures link clauses in different ways.

What the Experts Say About Oral and Print Language

Mary J. Schleppegrell (2004) helps us understand the difference between clauses in speech and text in the following example:

The invention of the telephone has made it more convenient for people to talk with those that they cannot usually see and spend time with, but the telephone has also become a substitute for spending time with loved ones. Instead of getting everyone together and having a picnic or day together at someone's house, the telephone has seemed to replace this.

The primary logical relationship in the text is contrast, and this is signaled in two different ways. In the first sentence, the clauses are linked by the conjunction *but* similar to how they would be signaled in speech. However, rather than a conjunction, the second sentence uses the prepositional phrase *instead of* to show the relationship of contrast. In spoken interaction, this sentence might have been constructed as, "We used to get together and have picnics *but* the telephone has replaced this." In this sentence, a conjunction links the clauses and signals the logical relationship. (p. 65)

To assist in comprehending a text, students will need to be familiar with the various ways in which clauses are combined.

Comprehension Strategies

Readers need a repertoire of available strategies from which they can select to assist with comprehension. Successful comprehension will actively draw from their knowledge of reading strategies while they are reading, especially when they are aware that the text is not making sense. Below you will find twenty strategies that can assist comprehension.

Comprehension Strategies

1. Establishing an anticipatory set for reading (e.g., looking at the title, author, and type of text to get a sense of what the book is going to be about before starting to read)
2. Developing a purpose for reading—for recreation, for information about a particular subject, for following instructions
3. Activating prior knowledge and combining it with information in the text
4. Organizing and integrating new information with existing knowledge
5. Anticipating and verifying predictions
6. Identifying main topics
7. Reading ahead and cross checking
8. Summarizing during reading
9. Using context for meaning making
10. Integrating cues while reading: visual information, background knowledge, word and sentence meanings, and language structure of the text
11. Questioning the author
12. Drawing conclusions from the text and connecting them to other knowledge
13. Making mental pictures of what is being read
14. Making personal connections with reading
15. Focusing on large chunks of text
16. Self-monitoring while reading
17. Expecting that text will make sense
18. Using punctuation for pause and emphasis to make sense of the text
19. Using background knowledge to make inferences
20. Choosing the appropriate strategy to make meaning

Figure 5.1   Comprehension Strategies

METACOGNITION

Knowing that a text is not making sense while reading involves metacognition, which involves both metacognitive knowledge and self-regulation (Dickson, Collins, Simmons, & Kameenui, 1998). Metacognitive knowledge includes knowledge of oneself as a learner, knowledge of the purpose of the reading and what the task of reading requires, knowledge of the relationship between text, prior knowledge and reading comprehension, and knowledge of when and how to use reading skills or strategies.

The other aspect of metacognition, self-regulation, encompasses planning for reading, monitoring understanding while reading, and if not understanding what is being read, knowing what to do about it *while* reading.

Knowing what the task of reading requires means that readers must be able to determine when and how to use reading strategies. To successfully accomplish this, readers will draw from their repertoire of available strategies, some of which we described above.

Motivation

Motivation is often added to knowledge and self-regulation as a component of metacognition (Borkowski, 1992; Chan, 1994; Pintrich, Anderman, & Klobucar, 1994). Readers' motivational beliefs may influence their use of metacognitive knowledge and self-regulation strategies while they are reading. By motivational beliefs, we mean readers' beliefs about their general level of competency or self-efficacy (Borkowski, 1992; Rottman & Cross, 1990), their feelings of competency to perform specific reading tasks (Johnston & Winograd, 1985; Schunk & Rice, 1992), and their beliefs about the benefits of using a particular strategy (Billmeyer, 2001). In other words, if a child does not feel competent as a reader and does not believe that he or she has the right reading strategies to make sense of what is being read, the child will be less likely to be a successful reader.

Clearly, to move from the beginning stages of learning to read to becoming a sophisticated reader who can use a wide array of knowledge and skills to get to the essence of reading, requires focused and sustained teaching and learning—teachers will need to progressively develop all the competencies we have described to ensure that their students read for meaning.

What the Experts Say About Reading Comprehension

Snow and Sweet(2003) identify three elements in comprehension:

- the reader who is doing the comprehending
- the text that is to be comprehended
- the activity of which comprehension is a part

In Durkin's view (1993), reading comprehension is the essence of reading.

Anderson and Pearson (1984) contend that reading comprehension is influenced by the reader's prior knowledge.

Comprehension is a complex process involving knowledge, experience, thinking, and teaching (Fielding & Pearson, 1994).

A reader constructs memory representations of what is understood and puts this understanding to use (Pressley & Afflerbach, 1995).

The ability to obtain meaning from print depends very strongly on the development of word recognition accuracy and reading fluency (National Research Council, 1998).

Formative Assessment and Reading Comprehension

Now that we have laid out what is involved in reading comprehension, we will focus our attention on how to formatively assess the development of children's reading.

Remember from Chapter 3 that formative assessment involves gathering evidence during the course of instruction that can be used by teachers and students to improve teaching and learning. And formative assessments that are linked to a learning progression help teachers determine students' current status and what needs to happen next to move them forward in their learning.

In this chapter, we present a developmental continuum for developing reading comprehension that is organized in three stages and can be used as a learning progression for instruction and assessment.

After we have described each stage, we will give stories about how several teachers we know, all from different schools with different populations, use formative assessment strategies to gauge where children are along the continuum. Recalling the model of teacher knowledge and the model for formative assessment from Chapters 2 and 3, we will also think about how the teachers in our stories bring their knowledge to bear in the process of implementing and interpreting formative assessment.

Learning Progression

Our progression for developing reading comprehension skills draws from the U.K. National Literacy Strategy (1998) and the Queensland Syllabus for English (2006) for reading as well as the Language Arts Standards from National Council of Teachers of English (2007). Overall, the progression represents the key building blocks for reading comprehension. It is divided into three stages and organized around the categories of word, sentence and text level knowledge and skills, vocabulary, and comprehension skills.

The stages of reading are not intended to be grade level specific. Many children, for example, will come to school with the skills in Stage 1 already in place, while others may take kindergarten and most of first grade to acquire them, and still others may be struggling to acquire the skills after first grade. Rather, the stages are intended as a guide to plan instruction and assess the development of the important building blocks for reading.

Before looking at the stages in detail, let us look at one section (Stage 1, word level) to better understand how the continuum works and how it can be used to plan instruction and assess learning. Stage 1 word level has three components: phoneme awareness, and the alphabetic principle, and vocabulary. Phoneme awareness begins with the isolating and blending phonemes of compound words and progresses to isolating and blending individual phonemes in words. A first step in the alphabetic principle is to understand that letters are visual symbols that represent sound and that letters have names as well as sounds.

Stage 1: Word Level

Phoneme Awareness

- Compound word isolation and blending
- Syllable isolation and blending
- Onset and rime isolation and
- Phoneme isolation: recognizing individual phonemes
- Phoneme blending: combining a sequence of separately spoken sounds (e.g., what word is /s/ /k/ /u/ /l/?—school)

Alphabetic Principle

- Understand that letters are visual symbols that represent sounds
- Understand that letters have names as well as sounds
- Understand that reading a word requires the letters to be read in order

---

By definition, a continuum, or learning progression, implies a linear sequence, and indeed our stages are organized in progressively more difficult understandings and skills. However, in some instances, some of the skills may be developed simultaneously. For example, you might be teaching children about compound word and syllable isolation and blending and introducing them to letter-sound symbol correspondences at the same time, even though they are represented sequentially in the progression. This is something to bear in mind when you use the progression to plan instruction. Some skills have definite precursors (for example, children need to know some letter-sound correspondences before they can start decoding words) but others might be developed together, as in the example above.

Breaking down the progression into manageable increments for instruction not only helps you know what to teach and when to teach it, but also what to assess. Remember in Chapter 3 we discussed the importance of success criteria derived from learning goals for interpreting the children's response to your formative assessment strategy and for providing feedback. Knowing what to teach and assess also enables you to develop success criteria (i.e., what a good learning performance looks like). Take, for example, isolating and blending phonemes. Success criteria would be: recognizing individual phonemes from a sequence of separately spoken sounds and combining the sequence smoothly to say the word correctly (e.g., what word is /s/ /k/ /u/ /l/?—school).

Now we'll look more closely at the categories of the three stages: word, sentence and text level knowledge and skills, and their contribution to reading development.

Word Level

Extracting meaning involves accurate and automatic word recognition. However, there are a number of precursor skills that children must have to be able to recognize words automatically, namely, phoneme awareness, knowledge of the alphabetic principle, and decoding ability. Children must first understand that speech can be broken into small sounds, phonemes, and they must be able to hear the component sounds of words, phoneme awareness. Beginning readers need to able to make the connection between the sounds that they hear (the phonemes) and the printed symbols that represent the sounds (the alphabetic principle). Automatic word recognition develops from this stage to a stage of sight vocabulary and decoding skills acquisition. A sight vocabulary starts with the recognition of high frequency words and extends to the ability to recognize irregular and infrequent words. Decoding skills range from blending simple consonant-vowel-consonant (CVC) words (e.g., *c-a-t*) to higher levels of word analysis, for example using root words to derive the meaning of an unknown word (e.g., *hyd(ro)(ra)*—*hydroplane, hydroelectric, hydrate, hydrant*).

Because knowing the meaning of words is so important for reading comprehension, we include vocabulary knowledge as a component at the word level. Vocabulary knowledge will range from words that introduce and conclude dialogue (e.g., *said, stated, replied, asked*), to specialized academic words (e.g., *rocks, minerals, mass*), to understanding the nuances among synonyms (e.g., angry, annoyed, upset, furious).

Sentence Level

At the sentence level, children learn about the grammar of English in oral and written forms. Grammar can be divided into simple and complex syntactic structures. Examples of simple sentences are, "Sam has a friendly dog. Jeff's dog isn't friendly." An example of a more complex sentence is, "Whereas Sam's dog is friendly to all visitors, Jeff's dog is quite aggressive, routinely baring his teeth to anyone who comes near the house." Facility with complex structures is a critical component of academic language, and research shows that children's knowledge and use of complex syntactic structures are strongly related to reading comprehension (e.g., Chaney, 1992; Turner, Nesdale, & Wright 1987). In addition to a focus on grammar and syntax, sentence level work includes an awareness of punctuation and its functions in print. For example, beginning readers need to be aware of the concept of a sentence and that, in written form, it will be demarcated by a capital letter and a period. Later in elementary school, children should be able to identify possessive apostrophes and recognize to whom or to what they refer.

Text Level

Before children can learn to read, they need to have some basic concepts about print (e.g., print carries a message and moves from left to right). So, our text level component of the continuum begins with an understanding of the concepts of print, knowing that print moves from the top to the bottom of the page and from left to right, for example. Later on, when students are able to read, knowing about text structure is important for comprehension. Identifying organizational features of nonfiction text (e.g., headings, lists, captions), and understanding cause and effect and compare and contrast structures in text, are but a few aspects of structural knowledge of text that are necessary for comprehension.

Being able to distinguish among different genres of text is also important for comprehension. This begins in the early stages of reading when children begin to understand that some texts tell stories, while others give information. Subsequently, students can investigate the range of genres of text from plays and poetry to distinguishing between fact and opinion, to comparing forms or types of humor in text.

Next, we are going to see how the various components we have described are developed progressively across three stages of our continuum.

Stage 1

We begin with Stage 1, the earliest stage of reading. At the word level, children are developing an awareness of the component sounds of words and learning the alphabetic principle—that letters are the symbols that represent the sounds. Children also increase their vocabulary through being read to, through new experiences, and through increasing knowledge in the content areas. Developing vocabulary about the children's immediate surroundings and things that are in their environment is also important at this stage. As children are introduced to new experiences and phenomena, they learn related words. Additionally, they learn precise words related to the task of reading, for example, *word, letter, alphabet,* and *sentence.*

In Stage 1 at the sentence level, early grammar work includes knowing what a sentence is and being able to produce and understand simple sentence structures such as, "Today, I am going to play with my friend" and "The leaves on the tree are green."

Stage 1: Word Level

Phoneme Awareness

- Compound word isolation and blending
- Syllable isolation and blending
- Onset and rime isolation and blending
- Phoneme isolation and blending

Alphabetic Principle

- Understand that letters are visual symbols that represent sounds
- Understand that letters have names as well as sounds
- Sound out and name each letter of the alphabet in lowercase and uppercase
- Understand alphabetical order
- Understand reading a word requires the letters to be read in order

Vocabulary

- Develop vocabulary related to own environment
- Through new experiences, read alouds, and interactions, increase social and content vocabulary
- Develop vocabulary associated with grammar, print, and reading content (e.g., sentence, capital letter, period, alphabet)

Figure 5.2   Stage 1: Learning Progression for Word Level Knowledge

In terms of punctuation, most children learn to write their name with a capital letter in the early years of school and begin to be aware of upper-case and lowercase letters.

The text level at each stage of the continuum comprises understanding of both text and comprehension skills. At Stage 1, understanding of text ranges from recognizing printed words in a variety of settings, to making

---

Stage 1: Sentence Level

Grammatical Awareness

- Understand that a sentence is a group of words that make sense and conveys meaning
- Know that statements provide information and questions ask about something or request information
- Understand and use simple sentence structure

(Continued)

(Continued)

Punctuation

- Know that a capital letter is used for the start of own name
- Recognize capitals and periods in print and know that they are demarcations of sentences

---

Figure 5.3   Stage 1: Learning Progression for Sentence Level Knowledge

one-to-one correspondences between print and written and spoken words, to understanding that print can be written down and read again for different purposes.

Knowing the difference between spoken and written forms of language is an early skill in reading comprehension, while being aware of one's own experience and how to relate it to what is read in the text is also something children become aware of in Stage 1.

Stage 1: Text Level

Understanding of Text

- Understand that print communicates a message
- Recognize environmental print
- Understand that words can be written down to be read again for a range of purposes
- Understand and use correct terms about books and print: book, cover, beginning, end, page, line, word, letter, title
- Know that words need to be read from left to right to make sense
- Know that a line of words with spaces between can make a sentence
- Track the text in the right order, page by page, left to right, top to bottom; pointing while reading/telling a story, and making one-to-one correspondences between written and spoken words

Comprehension Skills

- Aware of the difference between spoken and written forms
- Retell a narrative in sequence
- Aware that some books tell stories while others give information
- Use informational language when recounting the content of expository text
- Respond to simple questions about the content of books read aloud
- Make predictions based on portions of story
- Use knowledge from own experience to make sense of and talk about text

---

Figure 5.4   Stage 1: Learning Progression for Text Level Knowledge

A Story About Formative Assessment: Stage 1

Our story about Stage 1 formative assessment takes place in Ms. Thompson's kindergarten classroom. Here we will take a look at how she used the learning progression for Stage 1 for formative assessment and for subsequent instructional planning.

Ms. Thompson is a very experienced teacher who teaches a kindergarten class at Southfields Elementary School in Los Angeles. The student population is approximately half English language learners and half English only students. Ms. Thompson's students come from a wide range of backgrounds, including students who have had at least one year of preschool to those whose first experience in school is her kindergarten class. A number of her students entered the kindergarten class with well-developed emergent reading skills such as concepts of print, knowledge of letter-sound correspondences, and the ability to retell stories they have heard. Others, who have had less opportunity to develop these skills before arriving in kindergarten, are at the very beginning stages of acquiring important emergent skills.

Today, Ms. Thompson is working with a small group of children whose early skills are just beginning to develop. She is reading a story about a dog whose name is Duke. The text consists of simple declarative sentences (e.g., "Duke was a big dog") and is written in large print under illustrations on each page. As she reads, she shows the children the pictures and she points carefully at each word as she says it. After the story, she discusses with the children what they liked about the story and then she asks them to draw a picture about the part they liked the best. While the children draw their pictures she goes to check on other groups in the class.

After a time, Ms. Thompson returns to her original group and sits down beside Ronnie. Ronnie's language is not well-developed, and he has had very few literacy experiences prior to kindergarten. Ms. Thompson has been focusing on language development with him, providing him (and the rest of the children) with lots of new experiences and encouraging him to talk about them. She has also focused on helping him understand how print works and that there are one-to-one correspondences between print and the spoken word. She plans to use this opportunity (i.e., a planned interaction) to find out how well Ronnie is acquiring both language and print awareness skills.

First, she asks Ronnie to tell her what his picture is about. You can see the picture that Ronnie drew in Figure 5.5.

Ms. Thompson: Ronnie, let's talk about the picture you have drawn. I see that you have drawn a picture of Duke. Can you tell me what he is doing?

Figure 5.5 Ronnie's Picture.

Used with permission.

Ronnie:	That's the dog. That's the house, the ball, and the boy. (Each time Ronnie mentions an object he points to it in his picture.)
Ms. Thompson:	Yes, I see you have the dog, the house, the boy, and the ball in your picture—just like in the story. Can you tell me what is happening in the picture? What part of the story did you draw?
Ronnie:	The boy. The dog and the ball. (Ronnie points to the boy, the dog, and the ball as he says the words.) Playing.
Ms. Thompson:	Do you remember we talked about when we are telling a story we need to put our words into sentences? You have given me some good words about your picture, and I am going to put them into a sentence. The boy and the dog are playing with the ball.
Ronnie:	Yes, in the yard.
Ms. Thompson:	Okay—I can add that to the sentence. The boy and the dog are playing with the ball in the yard. Is that a good sentence about your picture?

Ronnie agrees that it is a good sentence, and Ms. Thompson asks him to repeat the sentence, which he does, correctly.

Ms. Thompson: So let's write that sentence under your picture and then we'll read it.

Ms. Thompson writes the sentence, "The boy and the dog are playing with the ball in the yard" under the picture. Then she tells Ronnie that they are both going to read the sentence together. As they read, Ms. Thompson points carefully to each word. Ronnie reads along with her.

Ms. Thompson: You did a great job reading along with me. Now go ahead and read the sentence on your own. Remember to point to each word as you read it.

Ronnie has learned that print moves from left to right and points at the first word in the sentence, which he reads correctly. He moves from left to right as he reads, but while he repeats the sentence he heard, his finger moves randomly across the print. He either says two words while he is pointing at one word or points at two or three words while he is saying one word only. He repeats the sentence almost word for word except for "are playing" for which he substitutes "play."

Ms. Thompson: I saw that when you started to read that you started on this side of the page—that is great—because when words are written down they always go from left to right. I noticed when you were reading the words that sometimes you were pointing at two words when you were saying only one word and then sometimes you pointed at one word and said two words! A line of words with spaces between the words can make a sentence, like the sentence we wrote under your picture. The letters in the words are close together and the words have spaces in between them like this. (She points out the letters close together in two words and the space in between.) Next time we read your sentence, let's see if you can point to each word as you read it.

Ms. Thompson thanks Ronnie for reading and suggests that he put his picture and sentence in his reading folder. She will ask him to talk about his picture and read his sentence again later in the week.

From this interaction, Ms. Thompson learns that Ronnie is beginning to develop some important Stage 1 understandings, for example, understanding that a sentence is a group of words that make sense and convey meaning and that print moves from left to right. However, she also notes that he is not yet able to point to words while "reading" to signal correspondences between words and what is read, he cannot retell part of a narrative, and that rather than using simple sentences he uses words or phrases. She decides that she will need to work more with Ronnie on helping him express ideas in full sentences, which she will do in class and group discussions, and she will try as much as possible to work one-on-one with him, too. She will also continue to help him understand the correspondence between spoken words and print, modeling this when she is reading to the students from books and environmental print and also using the strategy of writing sentences for him and having him reread them.

Recall from Chapter 3 the model we presented for how teachers integrate a range of knowledge and skills in formative assessment practices. We are going to take another look at the model (shown in Figure 5.6) and think about it in relation to the formative assessment scenario above.

What knowledge and skills does Ms. Thompson use to take advantage of her interaction with Ronnie as a source of evidence for his learning? First, she uses all the categories of teacher knowledge: her domain knowledge, specifically, Stage 1 of the progression; her prior knowledge of Ronnie's previous experiences with his language and his understanding of print; her knowledge of formative assessment strategies (in this case, planned for interaction); and pedagogical content knowledge to know how to teach Stage 1 skills and how assessment could be integrated into instruction. She uses planned interaction around Ronnie's picture as her formative assessment strategy, she interprets Ronnie's responses in light of her domain knowledge, and she is able to identify the gap between Ronnie's performance and her instructional goals. This gives Ms. Thompson the feedback for her instructional plans and also for Ronnie so that he can understand what he needs to do to improve. She was able to use the feedback from the interaction to make an instructional response there and then, thus blending instruction and assessment, and will also use this information later in the week when she reads with Ronnie again and also in her group and class discussion when she will focus on retelling in simple sentences.

Stage 2

Now we'll take look at Stage 2 of our continuum and see how children's skills progress. You will notice at this stage that skills and language knowledge are becoming quite a bit more sophisticated.

At the word level, children begin using their knowledge of letter-sound correspondences for decoding, and progressively increase their knowledge so that they can decode words with increasingly complex spelling patterns. They also develop their reading sight word vocabulary and are more and more able to recognize words on sight.

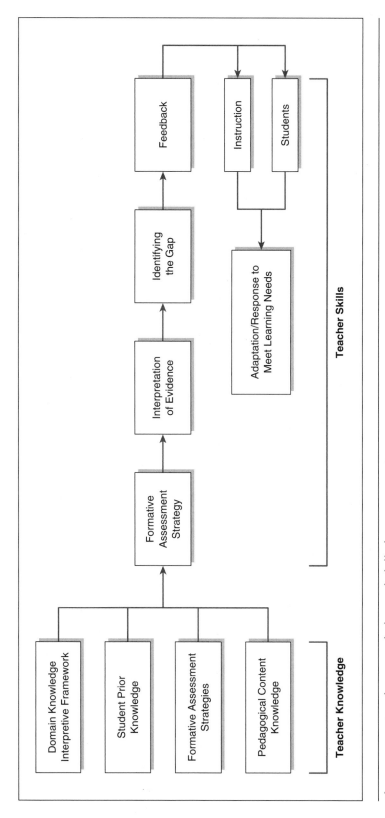

Figure 5.6 Teacher Knowledge and Skills for Formative Assessment

Oral and reading vocabulary continue to increase and at this stage, in addition to acquiring new vocabulary through content areas, students also increase their vocabulary by reading—the more they read, the more their vocabulary grows.

Stage 2: Word Level

Phonics

- Use knowledge of regular letter-sound correspondences to read words
- Read regularly spelled one- and two-syllable words automatically
- Use knowledge of irregular spelling patterns, diphthongs, and digraphs to read words
- Use knowledge of irregular spelling patterns, diphthongs, and digraphs to read words automatically
- Use knowledge of prefixes, affixes, suffixes, and inflections to read words automatically
- Identify syllabic patterns in multi-syllabic words

Sight Words

- Read on sight a range of familiar words (e.g., children's names, captions, labels, and words from favorite books)
- Read on sight an increasing range of high frequency words
- Read on sight the words from texts of appropriate difficulty

Vocabulary

- Increase vocabulary associated with subject matter content
- Increase vocabulary through reading and being read to
- Increase vocabulary associated with grammar, print, reading content, and figurative language (e.g., consonant, syllable, prefix, verb, apostrophe, antonym, simile)
- Use knowledge of prefixes, suffixes, to generate new words

Figure 5.7   Stage 2: Learning Progression for Word Level Knowledge

At the Stage 2 sentence level, students' awareness of the functions of grammar and their ability to understand and produce more complex sentences increases. They also start to recognize and understand the use of figurative language and are able to produce this kind of language in their speech. Punctuation skills increase considerably during Stage 2, and students progressively understand the functions of punctuation and are able to read aloud using pause and emphasis indicated by the punctuation.

Stage 2: Sentence Level

Grammatical Awareness

- Understand subject-verb agreements, plurals, and word order
- Understand and use simple and compound sentences
- Understand verb tense signals when an action takes place
- Use verb tenses and agreements with increasing accuracy
- Use past tense consistently for narration
- Use present tense consistently for explanation
- Know the difference between statements and questions and commands and the predictable structure of each
- Know the functions of pronouns (first, second, and third person) and conjunctions moving from simple to complex (e.g., and, then, to, though, since)
- Know the functions of nouns, verbs, adjectives, adverbs
- Know the functions of adjectival and adverbial phrases
- Understand that clauses can represent what is happening, who is taking part, and the circumstances surrounding the activity
- Know that vocabulary choice is influenced by text type, topic, and the function of the word
- Know that the beginning part of a sentence carries the key information (theme position)
- Understand the role of simple figurative language (e.g., simile)

Punctuation

- Know common uses of capitalization—people, places
- Progressively know the functions of and recognize in print commas, question marks, exclamation points, apostrophes, and speech marks

---

Figure 5.8 Stage 2: Learning Progression for Sentence Level Knowledge

At the text level, students develop an awareness of audience, increase their knowledge of different types of text and genre, understand how to use the features associated with information text to support comprehension, and develop their ability to identify the main idea, supporting details, and connection among the ideas.

Stage 2: Text Level

Understanding of Text

- Understand that texts can be produced for different audiences
- Know that texts are constructed differently for different audiences (e.g., letters, recipes, stories, instructions)

(Continued)

(Continued)

- Know that a topic can be maintained through related pages or sections
- Understand that in narrative the sequencing of events builds up to a high point and ends with a resolution
- Understand that main ideas in narrative are developed through connections among plot, setting, characters, and events
- Recognize the range of text types within genres (e.g., narratives, expository, procedures, reports, poetry)
- Understand how paragraphs and chapters are used to order text
- Understand that chapters are subdivisions of whole text
- Recognize that in expository text main ideas are developed by elaborating on ideas and information with supporting details
- Know that chapters, paragraphs, headings, subheadings, and hyperlinks can be used to link ideas and information in text
- Understand that text can convey meanings that are not directly stated

Comprehension Skills

- Determine the purpose of reading
- Self-monitor while reading
- Use grammar and grapho-phonic knowledge to predict and check the meanings of unfamiliar words and to make sense of what is being read
- Use definition/explanation context cues
- Identify main topic, key events, and supporting details of a text and recall key events in sequence
- Summarize a paragraph by identifying the most important elements
- Summarize a chapter by identifying the most important elements
- Activate prior knowledge and combine it with information in the text to make sense of the text
- Make inferences from information that is closely related to the text
- Make inferences from information that is not directly stated
- Understand how punctuation shapes meaning and use the cues of punctuation to gain meaning
- Use intonation, pauses, and emphasis when reading aloud to signal understanding of meaningful grammatical units
- Focus on large chunks of text

Figure 5.9   Stage 2: Learning Progression for Text Level Knowledge

A Story About Formative Assessment: Stage 2

Our first story about formative assessment strategies linked to Stage 2 takes place in Ms. Clark's first grade classroom at Twenty-third Street Elementary School, located just southeast of downtown Los Angeles's garment district and home to a large population of recent immigrant families from Mexico and Central America. Most of the students attending Twenty-third Street are at English language development (ELD) levels of I and II (beginner and early intermediate). This means that they have limited proficiency in listening, speaking, reading, and/or writing in English. Also, as a Title I school, the majority of students qualify for free breakfast and lunch every day.

The instructional language approach in this classroom is English immersion with only minimal primary language support. The reading curriculum—highly prescriptive, whole group focused, and phonics oriented—is consistent throughout the school and is taught according to a schoolwide pacing plan. Within the confines of the reading program, Ms. Clark, who has just three years' experience, tries to meet individual needs by differentiating instruction during the time when the program calls for independent work time. This is a time when students are working individually or in groups.

Marco is six years old and a native Spanish speaker of immigrant parents from Mexico. His language has been assessed to be at an overall level of ELD II due primarily to his reading and writing abilities that are still at the early intermediate levels. Ms. Clark is concerned about Marco's progress. During the semester, he has consistently scored at "below basic" level on the reading program's six-week assessments. From her observations and interactions with Marco during instruction, she is aware that Marco is not keeping up with his peers in the development of reading skills. She observes that he is at the "glued to print" stage—reading extremely slowly while working out all the sounds of the words. One problem that she has identified from her observations is that he has difficulty with tracking, that is, moving successfully in sequence from one word to the next. She knows that reading by decoding individual words carries a high cognitive demand and makes other aspects of reading, such as tracking, more challenging. To help him with his tracking problem (i.e., scaffolding his reading), each time they read together she moves her finger under each target word.

During today's independent work time, Ms. Clark wants to assess Marco's reading. Recently, her instruction has focused on decoding skills and she wants to find out how well Marco is using these skills in reading. Ms. Clark's assessment strategy involves listening to Marco while he reads the text aloud. In particular, she plans to pay close attention to whether he correctly sounds out the letters and blends them into words, and also how quickly he is able to do this.

The book she asks Marco to read is a decodable book that includes a few high frequency words (*a, is, was*) and mostly regular CVC words (*fun, pop, hat*) with a constrained range of letters that Marco had previously been taught during individualized instruction.

Ms. Clark: Today, Marco, I would like you to read aloud from this book called *Fun in the Sun*. (Ms. Clark shows him the book.) When you are reading and you find a word you don't know, remember to use the decoding strategy that we have been working on.

Marco: Okay. There's a funny picture on the front. The guy in the middle has curly hair and a mustache.

Ms. Clark: That's right. What do you think the book might be about?

Marco: Maybe these three guys on the front are going to the beach?

Ms. Clark: Let's see if you are right. (Ms. Clark opens the book to the first page with text. She points her finger under the first word for him to read.)

Marco: The sun was hot. (He reads slowly but accurately.)

Marco: Pop had a t-o-p . . . pot hat. (Marco has read the word *top* as *pot*.)

Marco: Mom had a red w-i-g . . . giw.

Marco: P-e-g . . . Peg had a b-i-g . . . gib c-a-p . . . pac.

Ms. Clark: Thank you, Marco. Let's stop here and talk about your reading today.

While listening to Marco read aloud, Ms. Clark identified that he is able to read the familiar words quickly and accurately (e.g., *mom, red, sun*), and he is able to track the words in the sentence without difficulty. However, when he attempts to decode words he is less familiar with, or that contain the less familiar letters, Marco laboriously sounds out the letters first one at a time, and then blends them together in reverse order.

Ms. Clark speculates this is because he articulates the sounds of the word so slowly that by the time it comes to blending the individual sounds together to read the word, he starts with the one he has heard the most recently. For example, *m-a-t* becomes *tam*.

A further explanation could be that Marco has not yet developed strong left to right scanning processes. Ms. Clark knows that consistent use of these processes can take children some time to develop because they have to overcome their previously learned logic that all objects remain constant regardless of their orientation (Piaget, 2000). While this logic is true for most things (e.g., a house is a house irrespective of the direction it is facing or the direction from which you may approach it), the exceptions to this principal of object permanence, demanding that our minds pay attention to orientation, are letters, numbers, and words (Tolchinsky, 2004). For example, *b* is not the same as *d*, *p* is not *q*, nor is 21 the same as 12, and certainly *sag* does not mean the same as *gas*. Even after children master left to right scanning for reading purposes, into third grade many children commonly reverse a portion of letters and numbers in their writing.

Based on her interpretation of the evidence from her formative assessment strategy, Ms. Clark provides Marco with feedback about his reading.

Ms. Clark: I noticed that when you were reading you knew the sight words we have worked on and you were able to read those quickly. When you came to other words you didn't know so well, you sounded out the letters and blended them just as we had been practicing in class, but I wonder if you realized what you did when you blended them together?

Marco looks confused and shrugs.

Ms. Clark: Okay, Marco, let's take a look at that last sentence ("Peg had a big cap.") I was a little confused about what it meant when you read it. Can you read it again?

Marco rereads the sentence in exactly the same way as the first time.

Ms. Clark: Did you understand what that sentence was about?

Marco: Not so much. (They look at the sentence and picture above it together.)

Ms. Clark: Well, I think the reason we didn't know what the sentence meant may have to do with how you read these two words at the end of the sentence. (Ms. Clark points to them.) I understand that Peg had *something* but I wasn't sure what. (Marco looks at the sentence and nods his head in agreement.) I noticed that sometimes after you sounded out all the letters in a word, you blended them backwards. Let me show you how to sound out the sounds and then blend them starting at the front of the word.

Ms. Clark writes a few CVC words on a piece of paper. With a marker, she models tracing a line under each letter as she sounds out each letter, and then deliberately brings the marker all the way to the first letter to then underline the letters again as she blends them together in the correct order.

With a second CVC word, she and Marco do this together, each holding the marker. They repeat the process a few more times. Then she asks Marco to read some CVC words by himself, including some that had challenged him earlier in his decodable reading book. Marco independently and successfully blends all the CVC words.

Ms. Clark: You did a great job. Now when you are reading you will have to check that you are blending the letters in the

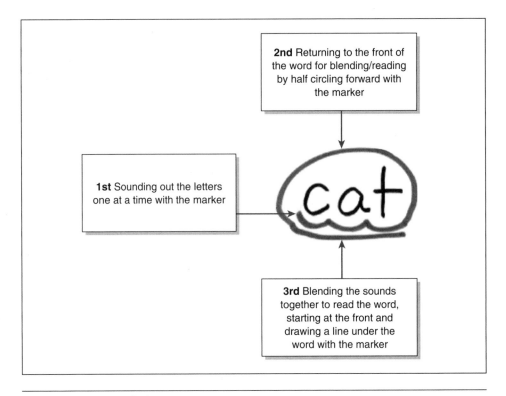

Figure 5.10   Ms. Clark's CVC Strategy

correct order. I also want to tell you about something else you can do when you are reading if the words don't make sense to you.

She discusses the idea that words often refer to things we know about in our everyday lives such as pencils, paper, tables, and chairs. She explains that thinking about words in that way can help us check for understanding in our reading. She then models checking for understanding when she reads a word incorrectly, asking herself, "Does this sound like a word I know? No, it doesn't, so I'm going to check that I have blended the letters together correctly." She blends the letters together correctly. "Yes, now it sounds like a word I know. I am going to check the picture, too, so that I can be sure I have read the correct word." She goes over with Marco the strategies she has modeled and how using these will help him become a stronger reader. He now has new strategies to be aware of when he reads, and he can use these to move forward as a reader. Next time Marco reads aloud to Ms. Clark, she will monitor how well he is incorporating the strategies when he reads. In the meantime, she will also give Marco gentle reminders of the strategies when he is working independently.

In this story, we see how Marco's teacher was able to use the read-aloud as a source of evidence for his reading development to create a "teachable moment" and blend assessment and instruction into one activity.

Another Stage 2 Story About Formative Assessment

Our next formative assessment story linked to Stage 2 takes place at a university affiliated lab school in southern California, University Elementary School. The school is relatively small in size with just over 400 students who are diverse in ethnicity and socioeconomic status. The school adopts a balanced approach to literacy, providing children with many opportunities for listening to books read aloud, independent reading, and talking about books, while systematically developing their reading, skills. Teachers team teach and plan their instruction together.

One of the primary level teachers is Ms. Ramirez, who teaches a mixed kindergarten and first grade classroom for English only and ELL students. Based on information from previous formative assessment, she has decided that some of her more advanced students need to develop the ability to make inferences from information that is closely related to the text. She also wants to expand their genre knowledge. To achieve these objectives, she organizes them into groups of three or four for independent reading, during which time they will all read the same book independently, and then come together to participate in a guided discussion with Ms. Ramirez.

Ms. Ramirez has chosen the mystery, *Nate the Great,* for one of the groups. She gives them a reading journal to complete during independent reading time and also at home when they continue to read the book. In the journal, she provides questions for the students to answer after they have read particular sections; their responses then become the basis for their group discussion. Ms. Ramirez reviews the student journals before she meets with the group so that she can decide how she wants to structure the discussion to best support their skill development.

In Figure 5.11, the first page of the journal, we can see what Ms. Ramirez has written to the children.

Ms. Ramirez has set up the assignment as a fun clue-gathering activity—a "who done it?"—and structured it to attain the goals of active, goal-oriented reading using inferential problem solving.

Ms. Ramirez has posed two questions to the students, and in Figure 5.12 we can see Artemio's response to the questions.

Ms. Ramirez interprets Artemio's response to the first question to indicate that, while he can comprehend the text well enough to deduce a correct fact about the picture, he still has difficulty elaborating his answers in writing, (e.g., his response to the question about the picture is only that, "it's yellow"); Artemio also does not yet express his ideas in writing with appropriate academic language. In the above example, Artemio's use of the word *it's* in subject (or topic) position is more aligned with the structure of dialogue. In fact, it seems that Artemio is responding as if the question, "What facts do we have about the picture?" was spoken out loud to him. He is not aware that the protocol for academic writing does not assume the same level of shared knowledge, and he is expected to include the subject reference (the painting) within his response, (i.e., *The painting* is yellow). Ms. Ramirez finds this same trend in the written responses of her other students in the reading group and decides that, on a day following their upcoming discussion, she will hold a mini lesson on academic language expectations for written responses, within the larger framework of teaching her students how to make appropriate language choices related to their awareness of context (e.g., if speakers or writers know their audience).

Ms. Ramirez's interpretation of Artemio's response to the second question is also that his reading comprehension is adequate to successfully complete the task, namely, that in listing four subjects who may have committed the crime in question, he is able to make inferences based on information drawn together from various parts of the text.

Nate the Great

By

Marjorie Weinman Sharmat

Monday, April 10th	pp. 7–23
Tuesday, April 11th	pp. 24–42
Wednesday, April 12th	pp. 44–55
Thursday, April 13th	pp. 56–62

Hi M. E., Carlos, and Artemio,

Welcome to your first book group! We are going to read *Nate the Great*. This is a mystery series so it is VERY important that you do not read ahead. We have to gather the clues together and solve the mystery at the same time. The reading schedule is above. Please keep up with your reading so we can talk about it together in class. Our next official meeting will be on Wednesday, April 12th. Remember to answer the questions each night after you read. Imagine that your reading log is your detective notebook and we are out to solve the mystery with Nate. Have fun!

Mysteriously yours,

Ms. Ramirez

Figure 5.11 Ms. Ramirez's Message to the Children.

Used with permission.

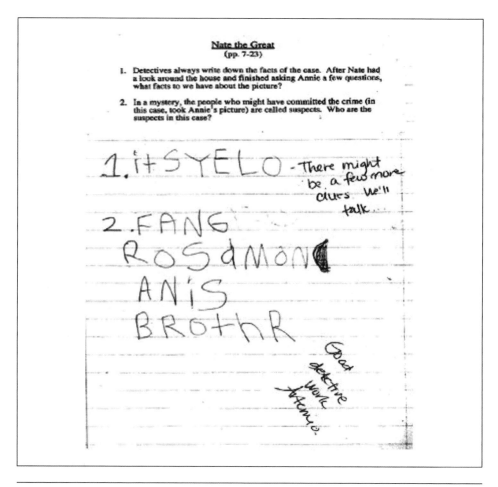

Figure 5.12 Artemio's Response.

Used with permission.

Again though, she sees a similar language pattern as she saw in the first question, where Artemio's written answers are brief and do not include all the information that he is trying to communicate, but instead he relies on the information presented in the prompting question to make his answer clear to the reader.

Ms. Ramirez has reviewed all of the students' responses in the book journals before the discussion and knows how she wants to structure the conversation. After everyone is settled on the carpet with their books in their laps, Ms. Ramirez starts the discussion by asking about their reading experience.

Ms. Ramirez: So how did it go? How are you all feeling about the book?

M.E.: It's good.

Artemio: I like it.

Carlos: I like it. I like Fang. I think he did it.

Ms. Ramirez:	Okay, so let's look at the first question. (She reads the question aloud.) After Nate had a look around the house and finished asking Annie a few questions, what facts do we have about the picture? Artemio, what did you find?
Artemio:	It's yellow.
Ms. Ramirez:	M.E., I remember you had some other things too. What were those?
M.E.:	It's a picture of a dog and it's painted on paper.
Ms. Ramirez:	Artemio, is that what you remember, too? Can you think of any more facts about the picture?
Artemio:	Well, hmmm, Rosamond painted it?
Ms. Ramirez:	Yes! Very good. Those are great facts you both found. Let's talk about question number two about the suspects who may have taken Annie's picture. Carlos, you mentioned you thought Fang did it. What makes you think that?
Carlos:	I think Fang really liked the picture because it was of a dog.
Artemio:	Yeah, but Fang couldn't have carried the picture because dogs don't have hands.
M.E.:	He could have used his mouth, that's what my dog does when she needs to carry something like her toys.
Ms. Ramirez:	M.E. that's a good point. Who do you think is a suspect in this case?
M.E.:	I think Rosamond stole the picture.
Ms. Ramirez:	Why do you think that?
M.E.:	She's Annie's close friend, so maybe she really wanted to have it.
Ms. Ramirez:	What page made you think that?
M.E.:	(She looks through the book for a minute.) On page twenty-three. (Everyone then turns their books to page twenty-three and spends some time discussing the evidence found there implicating Rosamond.)
Artemio:	I think it could have been Rosamond cause she was one of the only one's who saw it, but what about Annie?
Carlos:	Why would Annie take it? That doesn't make any sense. It was hers in the first place.
Artemio:	What if she lost it and forgot about it?
Ms. Ramirez:	Those are all good speculations.

The discussion then continues for a while longer as they discuss the feasibility of the various suspects. Several times, they refer back to the text to either confirm or discard the evidence that makes them suspects. Then they list a set of potential suspects that they can agree upon.

Ms. Ramirez sums up the discussion with some comments on how to use the reading comprehension strategies she modeled during the discussion when they read independently in the mystery genre (i.e., writing up a list of suspects and looking for evidence in the text to support their speculations).

Ms. Ramirez: A good thing readers of mystery do is to keep adding to the suspect list as they read along in the book. Also, as they read, if they discover that someone is off the hook for the crime, they cross them off their list. Remember too, that during our discussion, we always checked the text for evidence to back up our ideas about suspects. That is another strategy good readers of mystery use.

During the discussion with students, Ms. Ramirez carefully scaffolded students' thinking through her questions and enabled students to share and build ideas among themselves. For example, she asked M.E. to describe additional facts about the picture after Artemio had stated his one fact. She prompted the children to look for evidence to support their points and discuss the merits of the evidence.

Of course, the entire discussion was not only an instructional strategy, but also a formative assessment strategy. During the interaction, Ms. Ramirez could gather information about students' ability to self-select turns and to expand on or counter each others' assertions, in addition to discovering how well the children were able to draw inferences from the text. All this information will feed into the next steps of instruction.

Ms. Clark's and Ms. Ramirez's Knowledge and Skills

Earlier in the chapter, we saw how Ms. Thompson used the knowledge and skills that we show in our model for formative assessment (Figure 5.6). Both Ms. Clark and Ms. Ramirez drew on the same set of knowledge and skills in their formative assessment practices.

Both teachers used their domain knowledge and pedagogical knowledge to decide what to teach, how to teach it, and what to assess. Ms. Clark was focusing on tracking and decoding skills with her student, and Ms. Ramirez was supporting her students' inferential comprehension and academic language acquisition. They were both building on prior knowledge of their students to differentiate instruction, and both used an instructional activity as a formative assessment strategy. Ms. Clark used the read-aloud to assess skills, and Ms. Ramirez used the students' responses to the reading journal for both instruction and assessment. They were able to interpret their respective student responses in light of their knowledge about Stage 2, and because they had clear criteria for success based on their Stage 2 knowledge, they were able to give students clear feedback to help them move forward in their learning. Recall that Ms. Clark gave Marco feedback about how he was sounding out letters and then blending them together in reverse order and also made an instructional intervention there and then to help him blend the letters in the correct order. Ms. Ramirez gave the children feedback about what a reader does when reading a mystery and modeled the strategy for them and made plans to provide a mini lesson for the group of students on how to use appropriate academic language in their written responses. Finally, the two teachers use the assessment information for immediate instruction and also to inform future plans.

Stage 3

By Stage 3, children have already acquired a considerable amount of word, sentence, and text level knowledge and skills to build on. Recognizing and reading words with more complex suffixes, increasing knowledge of how to transform words by changing tenses, and changing verbs to nouns, are all part of Stage 3 word level work.

Vocabulary in Stage 3 continues to grow through the same means as in Stage 2, and students also become aware of and understand an increasing range of idioms.

Grammatical awareness becomes much more sophisticated at Stage 3. Students' ability to understand and produce sentences with subordinate clauses and in active and passive voice increases, as does their ability to understand and use connective and adverbial phrases in constructing an argument. Punctuation knowledge also increases so that by the end of Stage 3 they are able to recognize most functions of punctuation and use them to make meaning when reading.

At the Stage 3 text level, understanding of text becomes much more detailed and ranges from understanding the elements of narrative, to how paragraphs are structured for different types of text, to the function of text connectives. Knowledge of genre is also extended, and by the end of Stage 3, students should have a working knowledge of most text genres. Students are able to use their more detailed text knowledge and their knowledge of grammar to support comprehension. By the end of Stage 3, students are equipped with the knowledge and skills needed for

---

Stage 3: Word Level

Word Analysis

- Understand the ways in which nouns and adjectives can be made into verbs by use of suffixes (e.g., simple, simplify)
- Recognize the suffixes, -ible, -able, -ive, -tion, -sion
- Recognize words with common letter strings but different pronunciations (e.g., tough, through, trough)
- Distinguish between homophones
- Identify root words and derivations (e.g., sign, signal, signature)
- Transform words by changing tenses (e.g., -ed, -ing) negation (e.g., -un, -im, -il), making comparatives (e.g., -er, -est, -ish), changing verbs to nouns (e.g., -ion, -ism, -ology) and nouns to verbs (e.g., -ify, -en, -ize)

Vocabulary

- Increase vocabulary associated with subject matter content
- Increase vocabulary through reading and being read to
- Increase vocabulary associated with grammar, print, reading content, and figurative language (e.g., clause, semicolon, preposition, metaphor, alliteration, homophone, persuasion, cause and effect)
- Develop knowledge of idioms (e.g., beat about the bush, par for the course)

Figure 5.13   Stage 3: Learning Progression for Word Level Knowledge

---

Stage 3: Sentence Level

Grammatical Awareness

- Aware of how tense relates to the purpose and structure of the text
- Understand the use of adverbs in sentences and how adverbs can be formed with common -ly suffix
- Understand the significance of word order (e.g., some reordering of words can destroy meaning, some make sense but change meanings)
- Understand how the grammar of a sentence alters when the sentence type alters (e.g., when a positive statement is made negative)
- Understand the use of connective and adverbial phrases in structuring an argument (e.g., if . . . then, finally, so)
- Recognize prepositions and understand their effect on meaning
- Understand the difference between direct and reported speech
- Identify the imperative form

(Continued)

(Continued)

- Recognize the first, second, and third person
- Understand active and passive voice and how changing the voice affects the word order of a sentence
- Understand how points are connected in different types of text (e.g., besides, therefore, first, second)
- Understand independent and dependent clauses
- Understand that clauses work together to elaborate ideas and information
- Understand how meaning is affected by the sequence and structure of clauses
- Understand the role of conditionals in deduction, speculation, and supposition
- Understand how clauses can be manipulated in complex sentences to achieve different effects
- Understand the use of more sophisticated figurative language (e.g., metaphor, personification)

Punctuation

- Identify possessive apostrophes in reading and know to whom or what they refer
- Distinguish between the use of apostrophes for possession and contraction
- Recognize how commas and periods can join separate clauses
- Recognize semicolons, colons, parenthesis, dashes, hyphens, quotation marks and respond to them when reading

---

Figure 5.14 Stage 3: Learning Progression for Sentence Level Knowledge

reading to learn. Their knowledge and skills should also contribute to feelings of self-efficacy and success in reading, leading to a desire to read for pleasure, too.

A Formative Assessment Story: Stage 3

Our next story about formative assessment strategies linked to Stage 3 takes place in Ms. West's fifth grade classroom at Mozart Elementary, located in West Los Angeles. This school, situated in a middle-class neighborhood, has an equal balance of English language learner students and English-only students. The reading curriculum is an integration of a prescriptive, school-wide, phonics-oriented program with a readers' workshop approach.

In this formative assessment example, Ms. West is working with her students to understand expository text in the context of a social studies unit on early nineteenth century America. In an activity that integrates learning and assessment, she asks students to read the beginning of a chapter on the Lewis and Clark expedition. She also asks students to fill out a reading log as they are reading. The reading log has an evidence

Stage 3: Text Level

Understanding of Text

- Understand how settings influence characters and events in narratives
- Understand that characters are created through dialogue
- Understand the settings, plot, and characters associated with different forms of narrative (e.g., fantasy, thriller)
- Understand that the first sentence of a paragraph is a topic sentence
- Understand how paragraphs are structured differently on different text types
- Recognize how arguments are presented and how graphics can be used to support argument
- Recognize persuasive writing and understand how vocabulary and style contribute to persuasion
- Recognize myths, fables, legends, science fiction, adventure, mystery, biography, autobiography, and detective/thriller
- Recognize how logical relations are built through the use of text connectives to clarify, compare, contrast, and sequence and to indicate time or cause and effect
- Recognize how authors use a range of figurative language (e.g., idioms, analogy, allusions)

Comprehension Skills

- Use a range of context cues (e.g., restatement, author's summary)
- Identify different types of text in terms of content, structure, layout, vocabulary, and purpose and use to support comprehension
- Use knowledge of grammar and vocabulary to support comprehension (e.g., connectives, passive voice, technical vocabulary, persuasive devices)
- Take account of a viewpoint in a novel
- Use skills of skimming and scanning and efficient reading in research

Figure 5.15 Stage 3: Learning Progression for Text Level Knowledge

column on the left where students record what they "saw/heard/read in the text" and a column to the right where they record their interpretations, such as what they wondered, made connections to, and thought. This task is intended to help students keep track of new information they come across while they are reading, as well as activate their metacognitive processes to help them synthesize that information, with the final goal for students to create new, usable knowledge.

Based on past assessments of students' reading of expository texts, Ms. West believes that reading this text will represent somewhat of a challenge for most of her students. She knows that the topic of the reading material itself is difficult for the students to conceptualize, that is, that there could be large areas of land discussed in the text that are unfamiliar—not thoroughly understood, documented, and/or fairly inaccessible.

Also, the text the students have been exposed to over the previous years has been primarily narratives, even in the content areas of social studies and sciences, and as such, has followed a predictable generic structure of complication, rising action, and resolution. Expository text (in this case, an explanation that provides detailed historical information) has its own text structure specific for its purpose. In this example, the text being used is structured temporally into a series of sequential stages related to the Lewis and Clark expedition that are set in the context of specific significant historical categories (e.g., types of animals inhabiting various terrains, variations in Native American tribal cultures, and political tensions between tribes and the U.S. government). Each stage has a similar tone and is organized around concepts as much as time sequence. This different organizational structure of the text could be confusing for students who might try to overlay their expectations of a narrative text structure onto an expository one.

At the sentence level, this text could represent an extra challenge because expository text tends to include more complex sentences in which students are required to keep closer track of references and linking words. For example, in the sentence, "Clark had no trouble charting the expedition's course until the Corps came to a fork in the river that none of their Indian advisors had mentioned (near present-day Loma, Montana)," students need to follow the logic of the string of clauses to understand that the relative clause "that none of their Indian advisors had mentioned" modifies the noun phrase "a fork in the river," and that this concept feeds back to contradict the original clause that "Clark had no trouble charting the expedition's course." Finally, understanding the meaning of the whole sentence hinges on catching the important conjunction *until* that describes the key relationship between the various ideas (i.e., Clark had no trouble before coming to the river, but had trouble after).

Ms. West's desire to expose her students to this type of text rests on her knowledge that it contains a rich source of information for them, and because she knows it will figure increasingly in their schooling as they begin to study subjects such as biology and U.S. history in the future.

In using the reading logs in conjunction with the text, she wants to (1) determine which aspects of the text present the greatest problems for students' reading comprehension, (2) determine students' strengths and weaknesses in their application of reading strategies, and (3) find any gaps that may exist for particular students in their reading comprehension processes. She hopes to then use this information to better focus future reading comprehension instruction for the class as a whole, for small groups, and for individual students.

Looking at the example of Octavia's reading log (Figure 5.16), we see what inferences Ms. West drew about the student's reading comprehension.

Octavia is a primary English speaking student who, according to the school's informal reading inventory, reads at grade level. Ms. West can learn more from the information she has gathered from the text in the left-hand "evidence" column. Octavia mentions many of the "big ideas" from the passage and is not overly distracted by details in her reading. Ms. West notes that Octavia records facts about the expedition, the big rivers, the map, the West, trade, Indians, and Thomas Jefferson. Yet, she also sees clearly that Octavia does not quite understand the larger significance of these concepts in relation to one another.

For example, she accurately mentions that, "There is an e[x]pedition into lands outside of U.S.A." and "The Mississippi, Columbia and Missouri would act as one waterway" but Octavia does not link the two

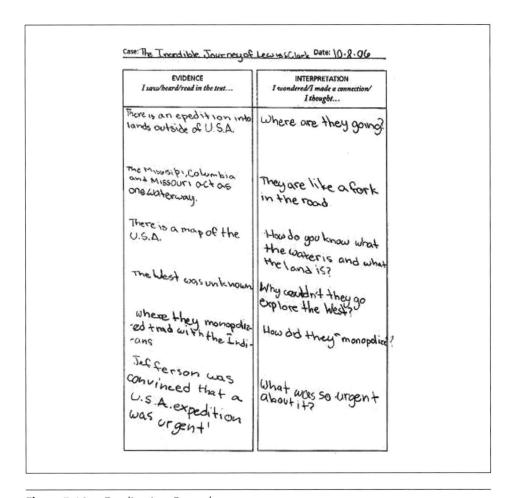

Figure 5.16   Reading Log Example

ideas together conceptually (i.e., that people will need to *cross* these rivers during their expedition).

Ms. West decides that while Octavia is positively focusing her attention during reading on noun phrases in the text (e.g., words that describe people, places, things, and ideas), she is not placing enough attention on the action verbs in the text that can show the links between ideas she is reading about.

In considering Octavia's interpretations of the facts in the right-hand column of the reading log, Ms. West is impressed that she has activated her metacognitive processes by asking several questions of the text. These questions are related to fundamental ideas of *where*, *what*, *why*, and *how*. These question types also lead Ms. West to believe that Octavia needs more background knowledge to understand the context of Lewis and Clark's journey. Ms. West finds this trend in other students' work and decides that she will address this issue during whole group instruction where she plans to provide students with additional background information on the topic. She also decides to give the students opportunities to share their reading log questions with each other in the context of small group discussions, sharing their knowledge and insights, as well as using the text *The Incredible Journey of Lewis and Clark* (Blumberg, 1987) and others as resources to find answers to their questions.

In one instance in the reading log, Octavia uses a simile to help her make a connection between new information and her prior knowledge when she describes the idea of converging rivers as being, "like a fork in the road." This lets Ms. West know that Octavia is applying another reading comprehension strategy during her reading practice (i.e., connections between prior knowledge and new information).

To give Octavia feedback and help her with her reading processes, Ms. West decides to talk to Octavia about the role of action verbs in text and how she can go about looking for them in her next reading assignment.

Ms. West: What did you think of the book, *The Incredible Journey of Lewis & Clark?*

Octavia: I didn't really like it that much.

Ms. West: Oh no? How come?

Octavia: It was hard to tell what was going on.

Ms West: Well, let's talk a look at your book log and see what you *were* able to figure out. Okay, I see that you understood that the book was about an expedition. There were waterways and a map. The West was unknown and someone was trying to

	monopolize trade with the Indians. That's a lot! Do you know what monopolize means?
Octavia:	To take over?
Ms. West:	That's right, very good. It means to have complete control over something and not let others have any control at all.
Octavia:	Sort of like what my brother tries to do with the TV remote.
Ms. West:	Very similar. Do you have a sense of what these things you wrote about had to do with each other? For example, the expedition, the waterways, and the West?
Octavia:	Not really.
Ms. West:	That's alright, I was thinking of a strategy that might help you. It's a strategy that readers of history often do to help them understand what they are reading. They pay special attention to the action verbs in the text. Do you remember what action verbs are?
Octavia:	Yes, I remember, we had to find them in that chapter in *Island of the Blue Dolphins*.
Ms. West:	Exactly. Action verbs often can tell a reader what things and people do and how they are connected together. Let's take a quick look at the action verbs in the Lewis and Clark book and see if we can figure out how these ideas you wrote about in your reading log relate to one other. (Octavia opens book to the right pages.)
Octavia:	Okay, here it is.
Ms. West:	Can you find the part where they talk about the expedition and the waterways?
Octavia:	It's right here. (Octavia points to the section in the text.)
Ms. West:	Great, read to me some of the action verbs you find there.
Octavia:	cross, paddle, row, sail. . . .
Ms. West:	Great. Do these words give you any hint about what the waterways had to do with the expedition?
Octavia:	Well, maybe they had to get beyond them, to cross them in the expedition.

Ms. West: I think so too! Very good, I think you may have a strategy that can work for you. Now, let's take a look for a minute also at your interpretations. I really liked how you asked a lot of questions in this section. This tells me you are checking your understanding while you're reading. Also, I love your comparison between the rivers and the fork in the road. Good readers often take new information and put it in terms they can understand better. You did a very good job!

At this point, Ms. West goes on to explain to Octavia that in her next reading assignment she should underline the action verbs that give her information about "what is going on" in the text before completing her reading log. Ms. West also provides Octavia with a copy of the Lewis and Clark expedition chapter that is consumable so that she can write directly on it.

In this chapter, we have seen how teachers can use a continuum of skills needed for reading comprehension as a road map for instruction and assessment. They used different formative assessment strategies, some involving short cycles (e.g., Ms. Clarke when she made an immediate instructional response) and some that were medium cycles in length (e.g., Ms. Ramirez reviewed the student responses to decide how she would structure the group discussion and made plans for a future mini-lesson). We have also seen how children's developing knowledge of words, sentences, and text contributes to their abilities to comprehend text and that language and reading skills are both equally important for making meaning of text.

In the next chapter, we will see how children develop reading skills into middle school and how their writing becomes a means for assessing reading comprehension.

REFLECTION QUESTIONS

1. How will you be able to use the learning progression for reading comprehension laid out in this chapter?

2. The teachers described in this chapter had organized their classrooms so that they were able to spend some time with individuals and small groups each day for formative assessment. How well is your classroom organized for formative assessment? What changes

could you make to increase opportunities of individual and small group assessment?

3. Think about the different formative assessment strategies that the teachers in this chapter used to collect evidence of their students' reading development. Do you use any of these strategies in your classroom? Are there other strategies that you use that you did not see in the chapter?

4. In this chapter, we saw teachers systematically blending assessment and instruction in one activity. How well do you think you do this in your classroom? Are there ways in which you can increase opportunities to assess and instruct in one activity?

5. Teachers in this chapter gave feedback to their students that helped them understand their own learning. What kind of feedback do you give to students? Does it help students move forward in their learning? How could you improve the feedback to students?

REFERENCES

Anderson, R. C., & Pearson, P. D. (1984). A schema-thematic view of basic processes in reading comprehension. In P. D. Pearson, R. Barr, M. L. Kamil, & P. Mosenthal, (Eds.), *Handbook of reading research* (pp. 255–291). New York: Longman.

Billmeyer, R. (2001). *Capturing all of the reader through the Reading Assessment System*. Omaha, NE: Dayspring Printing.

Blumberg, R. (1987). *The incredible journey of Lewis & Clark*. New York: Lothrop, Lee & Shepard Books.

Borkowski, J. G. (1992). Metacognitive theory: A framework for teaching literacy, writing and math skills. *Journal of Learning Disabilities, 25,* 253–257.

Chan, L. K. S. (1994). Relationship of motivation, strategic learning, and reading achievement in Grades 5, 7, and 9. *Journal of Experiential Education, 62,* 319–339.

Chaney, C. (1992). Language development, metalinguistic skills, and print awareness in 3-year-old children. *Applied Psycholinguistics, 13*(4), 485–514.

Dickson, S. C., Collins, V. L., Simmons, D. C., & Kameenui, E. J. (1998). Metacognitive strategies: Research bases. In D. C. Simmons & E. J. Kameenui (Eds.), *What reading research tells us about children with diverse needs.* Mahwah, NJ: Lawrence Erlbaum Associates.

Durkin, D. (1993). *Teaching them to read*. Boston: Allyn & Bacon.

Englert, C. S., & Thomas, C. C. (1987). Sensitivi text structure in reading and writing: A comparison between learning disabled and non-learning disabled students. *Learning Disability Quarterly, 10*(2), 93–105. Retrieved November 14, 2006, from http://links.jstor.org/sici?sici=0731–9487%28198721%2910%3A2%3C93%3ASTTSIR%3E2.0.CO%3B2-R

Fielding, L. G., & Pearson, P. D. (1994). Reading comprehension: What works. *Educational Leadership, 31,* 62–68.

Gibbons, P. (1998). Classroom talk and the learning of new registers in a second language. *Language and Education, 12*(2), 99–118.

Hirsch, E. D. (2003). Reading comprehension requires knowledge of words and the world. *American Educator*, Spring, 10–29.

Johnston, P. H., & Winograd, P. N. (1985). Passive failure in reading. *Journal of Reading Behavior, 17,* 279–301.

The National Council of Teachers of English. (2007). Standards for the English Language Arts. Urbana, IL: Author.

National Literacy Strategy. (1998). London: Department for Education and Employment.

National Reading Panel. (2000). *Report of the National Reading Panel: Teaching children to read.* U.S. National Institute of Child Health and Human Development, NIH Pub. No. 00–4769. Washington, DC: Government Printing Office.

National Research Council. (1998). *Preventing reading difficulties in young children.* Committee for the Prevention of Reading Difficulties in Young Children. C. E. Snow, M. S. Burns, & P. Griffin (Eds.), Washington, DC: National Academy Press.

Piaget, J. (2000). *The psychology of the child.* London: Routledge.

Pintrich, P. R., Anderman, E. M., & Klobucar, C. (1994). Intra-individual differences in motivation and cognition in students with and without learning disabilities. *Journal of Learning Disabilities, 27,* 360–370.

Pressley, M., & Afflerbach, P. (1995). *Verbal protocols of reading: The nature of constructively responsive reading.* Hillsdale, NJ: Lawrence Erlbaum Associates.

Queensland Syllabus for English. (2006). Brisbane, Queensland, Australia: Queensland Studies Authority.

RAND Reading Study Group. (2002). *Reading for understanding: Toward an R & D program in reading comprehension.* Santa Monica, CA: RAND Corporation.

Rottman, T. R., & Cross, D. R. (1990). Using informed strategies for learning to enhance the reading and thinking skills of children with learning disabilities. *Journal of Learning Disabilities, 23,* 270–278.

Schleppegrell, M. J. (2004). *The language of schooling: A functional linguistics perspective.* Mahwah, NJ: Lawrence Erlbaum Associates.

Schunk, D. H., & Rice, J. M. (1992). Influence of reading-comprehension strategy information on children's achievement outcomes. *Learning Disability Quarterly, 15,* 51–64.

Snow, C. E., Burns, M. S., and Griffin, P. (Eds.). (1998). *Preventing reading difficulties in young children.* National Research Council. Washington, DC: National Academy Press.

Tolchinsky, L. (2004). Domain-general and domain-specific processes in cognitive development. *Human Development, 47*(6), 370–375.

Turner W. E., Nesdale, A. R., & Wright, A. D. (1987). Syntactic awareness and reading acquisition. *British Journal of Developmental Psychology, 5*(1), 25–34.

Stages of Reading Comprehension Skills

STAGE 1

Word Level

Phoneme Awareness

- Compound word isolation and blending
- Syllable isolation and blending
- Onset and rime isolation and blending
- Phoneme isolation and blending

Alphabetic Principle

- Understand that letters are visual symbols that represent sounds
- Understand that letters have names as well as sounds
- Sound out and name each letter of the alphabet in lower and upper case
- Understand alphabetical order
- Understand reading a word requires the letters to be read in order

Vocabulary

- Develop vocabulary related to own environment
- Through new experiences, read alouds, and interactions, increase social and content vocabulary
- Develop vocabulary associated with grammar, print and reading content (e.g., sentence, capital letter, period, alphabet)

Sentence Level

Grammatical Awareness

- Understand that a sentence is a group of words that make sense and conveys meaning
- Know that statements provide information and questions ask about something or request information
- Understand and use simple sentence structure

Punctuation

- Know that a capital letter is used for the start of own name
- Recognize capitals and periods in print and know that they are demarcations of sentences

Text Level

Understanding of Text

- Understand that print communicates a message
- Recognize environmental print
- Understand that words can be written down to be read again for a range of purposes
- Understand and use correct terms about books and print: book, cover, beginning, end, page, line, word, letter, title
- Know that words need to be read from left to right to make sense
- Know that a line of words with spaces between can make a sentence
- Track the text in the right order, page by page, left to right, top to bottom; pointing while reading/telling a story, and making one-to-one correspondences between written and spoken words

Comprehension Skills

- Awareness of the difference between spoken and written forms
- Retells a narrative in sequence
- Awareness that some books tell stories while others give information
- Use informational language when recounting the content of expository text
- Respond to simple questions about the content of books read aloud
- Make predictions based on portions of story
- Use knowledge from own experience to make sense of and talk about text

STAGE 2

Word Level

Phonics

- Use knowledge of regular letter sound correspondences to read words
- Read regularly spelled one- and two-syllable words automatically
- Use knowledge of irregular spelling patterns diphthongs and digraphs to read words

- Use knowledge of irregular spelling patterns, diphthongs and digraphs to read words automatically
- Use knowledge of prefixes, affixes, suffixes, and inflections to read words automatically
- Identify syllabic patterns in multi-syllabic words

Sight Words

- Read on sight a range of familiar words(e.g., children's names, captions, labels, and words from favorite books)
- Read on sight an increasing range of high frequency words
- Read on sight the words from texts of appropriate difficulty

Vocabulary

- Increase vocabulary associated with subject matter content
- Increase vocabulary through reading and being read to
- Increase vocabulary associated with grammar, print, reading content, and figurative language (e.g., consonant, syllable, prefix, verb, adverbial phrase, apostrophe, antonym, simile)
- Use knowledge of prefixes, suffixes, to generate new words

Sentence Level

Grammatical Awareness

- Understand subject-verb agreements, plurals, and word order
- Understand and use simple and compound sentences
- Understand verb tense signals when an action takes place
- Use verb tenses and agreements with increasing accuracy
- Use past tense consistently for narration
- Use present tense consistently for explanation
- Know the difference between statements and questions and commands and the predictable structure of each
- Know the functions of pronouns (first, second, and third person) and conjunctions moving from simple to complex (e.g., and, then, to, though, since)
- Know the functions of nouns, verbs, adjectives, adverbs
- Know the functions of adjectival and adverbial phrases
- Understand that clauses can represent what is happening, who is taking part and the circumstances surrounding the activity
- Know that vocabulary choice is influenced by text type, topic, and the function of the word

- Know that the beginning part of a sentence carries the key information (theme position)
- Understand the role of simple figurative language (e.g., simile)

Punctuation

- Know common uses of capitalization – people, places
- Progressively know the functions of and recognize in print commas, question marks, exclamation points, apostrophes, and speech marks

Text Level

Understanding of Text

- Understand that texts can be produced for different audiences
- Know that texts are constructed differently for different audiences (e.g., letters, recipes, stories, instructions)
- Know that a topic can be maintained through related pages or sections
- Understand that in narrative the sequencing of events builds up to a high point and ends with a resolution
- Understand that main ideas in narrative are developed through connections among plot, setting, characters, and events
- Recognize the range of text types within genres (e.g., narratives, expository, procedures, reports, poetry)
- Understand how paragraphs and chapters are used to order text
- Understand that chapters are subdivisions of whole text
- Recognize that in expository text main ideas are developed by elaborating on ideas and information with supporting details
- Know that chapters, paragraphs, headings, subheadings, and hyperlinks can be used to link ideas and information in text
- Understand that text can convey meanings that are not directly stated

Comprehension Skills

- Determine the purpose of reading
- Self-monitor while reading
- Use grammar and grapho-phonic knowledge to predict and check the meanings of unfamiliar words and to make sense of what is being read
- Use definition/explanation context cues
- Identify main topic, key events, and supporting details of a text and recall key events in sequence
- Summarize a paragraph by identifying the most important elements
- Summarize a chapter by identifying the most important elements

- Activate prior knowledge and combine it with information in the text to make sense of the text
- Make inferences from information that is closely related to the text
- Make inferences from information that is not directly stated
- Understand how punctuation shapes meaning and use the cues of punctuation to gain meaning
- Use intonation, pauses, and emphasis when reading aloud to signal understanding of meaningful grammatical units
- Focus on large chunks of text

STAGE 3

Word Level

Word Analysis

- Understand the ways in which nouns and adjectives can be made into verbs by use of suffixes (e.g., simple, simplify)
- Recognize the suffixes, -ible, -able, -ive, -tion, -sion
- Recognize words with common letter strings but different pronunciations (e.g., tough, through, trough)
- Distinguish between homophones,
- Identify root words and derivations (e.g., sign, signal, signature)
- Transform words by changing tenses (e.g., -ed – ing) negation (e.g., -un –im, -il), making comparatives (e.g., -er, -est, -ish), changing verbs to nouns (e.g., -ion, ism, -ology) and nouns to verbs (e.g., -ify, -en, -ize)

Vocabulary

- Increase vocabulary associated with subject matter content
- Increase vocabulary through reading and being read to
- Increase vocabulary associated with grammar, print, reading content, and figurative language (e.g., clause, semicolon, preposition, metaphor, alliteration, homophone, persuasion, cause and effect)
- Develop knowledge of idioms (e.g., beat about the bush, par for the course)

Sentence Level

Grammatical Awareness

- Aware of how tense relates to the purpose and structure of the text
- Understand the use of adverbs in sentences and how adverbs can be formed with common –ly suffix

- Understand the significance of word order (e.g., some reordering of words can destroy meaning, some make sense but change meanings)
- Understand how the grammar of a sentence alters when the sentence type alters (e.g., when a positive statement is made negative)
- Understand the use of connective and adverbial phrases in structuring an argument (e.g., if. . . then, finally, so)
- Recognize prepositions and understand their effect on meaning
- Understand the difference between direct and reported speech
- Identify the imperative form
- Recognize the first, second, and third person
- Understand active and passive voice and how changing the voice affects the word order of a sentence
- Understand how points are connected in different types of text (e.g., besides, therefore, first, second)
- Understand independent and dependent clauses
- Understand that clauses work together to elaborate ideas and information
- Understand how meaning is affected by the sequence and structure of clauses
- Understand the role of conditionals in deduction, speculation, and supposition
- Understand how clauses can be manipulated in complex sentences to achieve different effects
- Understand the use of more sophisticated figurative language (e.g., metaphor, personification)

Punctuation

- Identify possessive apostrophes in reading and know to whom or what they refer
- Distinguish between the use of apostrophes for possession and contraction
- Recognize how commas and periods can join separate clauses
- Recognize semicolons, colons, parenthesis, dashes, hyphens, quotation marks and respond to them when reading

Text Level

Understanding of Text

- Understand how settings influence characters and events in narratives
- Understand that characters are created through dialogue
- Understand the settings, plot, and characters associated with different forms of narrative (e.g., fantasy, thriller)

- Understand that the first sentence of a paragraph is a topic sentence
- Understand how paragraphs are structured differently on different text types
- Recognize how arguments are presented and how graphics can be used to support argument
- Recognize persuasive writing and understand how vocabulary and style contribute to persuasion
- Recognize myths, fables, legends, science fiction, adventure, mystery, biography, autobiography, and detective/thriller
- Recognize how logical relations are built through the use of text connectives to clarify, compare, contrast, sequence, and to indicate time or cause and effect
- Recognize how authors use a range of figurative language (e.g., idioms, analogy, illusions)

Comprehension Skills

- Use a range of context cues (e.g., restatement, contact, author's summary)
- Identify different types of text in terms of content, structure, layout, vocabulary, and purpose and use to support comprehension
- Use knowledge of grammar and vocabulary to support comprehension (e.g., connectives, passive voice, technical vocabulary, persuasive devices)
- Take account of a viewpoint in a novel
- Use skills of skimming and scanning and efficient reading in research

6

Assessing Reading Through Writing

Science Journals

Michelle Bravo

magma chamber

Rocks and Minerals Unit

Used with permission.

Our first story in this chapter takes place in Ms. Perlmutter's sixth grade class at University Elementary School in Los Angeles. For the past two weeks, the focus of her literature teaching has been to examine the effects of authors' use of literary devices in a range of genres from short stories to essays to poetry. In her most recent lessons, she has focused on four poems by Langston Hughes: "Dreams," "Dream Deferred," "I, Too, Sing America," and "Let America be America Again." Class discussions of Hughes's poems have centered on the organizational structure of his work and the significance of metaphor in his poetry. In particular, Ms. Perlmutter's students have thought about how Hughes uses metaphor, establishing a comparison of unlike things with just a few words to create new meanings to powerfully convey feelings and experience.

After several discussions, Ms. Perlmutter gives her student the following assignment, "Take something from one of his [Hughes's] poems, either a word, a line, an idea, or an image, and write from that line or have the line in the writing." She tells the students that they can respond in any form of writing. In Figure 6.1, we see how one of the students, Jordan, a native speaker of English, decides to write her poem in response to a single line in Hughes's poem, "I, Too, Sing America."

Jordan selected the line "but I laugh" from Hughes's poem to be the stimulus and starting point for her writing. By using this line as the title, she implies, as Hughes does with his title "I, Too, Sing America," that this

But I laugh

They call me names,
They make faces at me,
They put me down,
But I laugh,
Because one day
I will fly on silver wings,
Singing to myself.
Singing the songs of
Freedom,
Joy,
Laughter,
And love.
Sure, they might try to bring me down,
But I will only laugh.
For my feet will never touch the ground.
And they will only watch me fly away.
By flapping my wings I will shake off
The names,
And the faces,
And forever more, I will be no place but up.
— Jorda Joh...

Figure 6.1 Jordan's Poem

Used with permission.

is a response to someone. As the poem develops we see that she is responding to those who have taunted her. Her inclusion of the word "I" in the title mirrors Hughes's use of the first person pronoun, making emphatic that she is the subject of the title and the poem's content. Hughes's poem uses the metaphor of tomorrow to represent the future—a future in which all people are valued equally. Jordan uses the metaphor of flying to signal a future world in which she will be able to shake off the taunts she experiences today. In Hughes's poem, he uses the line "but I laugh" to suggest his feelings toward the treatment meted out to him. Jordan does the same, using the line a second time in the poem to reinforce that she will not be "brought down," instead she will rise above the names, the faces, and the put-downs. Clearly, Hughes's poem has resonated strongly with Jordan, and the relevance to her personal experience is powerfully expressed.

What Does Jordan's Writing Say About Her Reading?

From her reading of Jordan's poem, Ms. Perlmutter infers that she has a deep understanding of the message that Hughes is conveying in his work. She has brought her own experience to her reading of the text. She is aware of the effects of metaphor as a literary device and the impact of Hughes's word choice. She is familiar with poetic form and has appropriated poetry conventions in her writing. From this assessment of Jordan's writing, Ms. Perlmutter decides that her next steps in reading will be to introduce her to poetry and prose that use other literary devices (e.g., allegory), to read and discuss books which present points of view (she infers that Jordan has understood Hughes's point of view and wants to develop this notion of perspective in other genres), and to have her compare and contrast points of view represented in the books and speculate about the authors' motivations.

Ms. Perlmutter has used her assessment of Jordan's writing to inform how she will continue to support her reading development. With the overlap in knowledge areas between reading and writing, she can take advantage of her students' writing as formative assessment, not only to decide what writing skills have developed and what to teach next, but also as a complement to reading assessments in order to determine what children know about language and text to provide insights into reading development.

Now we will consider the links between reading and writing skills at a more general level and describe how these unfold across the three stages of the reading learning progression. Subsequently, we show how the kinds of information that we can obtain from various kinds of students' writing can add to the knowledge gained from the formative assessment strategies that we discussed in prior chapters.

LINKING READING AND WRITING SKILLS

Reading and writing are both communication activities. Readers access other people's ideas, knowledge, and points of view from print, and writers communicate their ideas, knowledge, and points of view to others in written language. Reading supports writing and vice versa, and readers and writers share knowledge about communication in print forms (Berninger, Cartwright, Yates, Swanson, & Abbott, 1994). Studying student writing for what it can reveal about student reading can be used as an important part of the battery of formative assessment strategies a teacher has in order to place students along the reading comprehension learning progression.

As class sizes tend to increase by the later elementary grades and teachers come to rely on student writing to reveal their learning across all areas of the curriculum, assessing reading *through* writing makes a lot of sense. Student writing is something teachers can contemplate in a quiet moment, perhaps away from the classroom, especially if they feel they missed the opportunity to carry out other less tangible formative assessments during a busy school day.

Shared Knowledge in Reading and Writing

Research on the knowledge that readers and writers share can be categorized into four types (Fitzgerald & Shanahan, 2000):

- *Metacognitive knowledge:* knowing about the purpose and functions of reading and writing, monitoring meaning-making, word identification or word production strategies, and one's own knowledge
- *Content knowledge:* prior knowledge that the reader brings to text, knowledge that can result from a reading or writing interaction, knowledge of word meanings and the meanings that are constructed through connected text
- *Text attribute knowledge:* letter and word identification and generation (including phonological awareness, letter-sound correspondences, and morphology), knowledge of the rules of grammar and of the use of punctuation, knowledge of text structure (e.g., informational, narrative), and of the organization of text (e.g., paragraphs, headings, relations between pictures and print)
- *Procedural knowledge:* knowing how to access, use, and generate knowledge in any of the above areas

What the Experts Say About Reading-Writing Links

According to the New Standards Primary Literacy Committee (1999/2004), "When students read like writers—that is, when they bring their own knowledge about craft and genre to text—they become more discriminating about written language. They also use this discrimination to guide their own writing. They write like enlightened readers."

Reading and writing are interactive processes. There is a dynamic relationship between reading and writing and each one influences the development of the other, with well-developed reading skills exposing children to larger print vocabularies, spelling, and models of good writing on which to draw for their own writing (Heck & Crislip, 2001; Shanahan & Lomax, 1986).

Reading and writing share some of the same cognitive processes (e.g., orthographic and phonological processing), and students employ many of the same strategies for making meaning, be that extracting meaning from the texts they read or creating meaning with the texts they write (e.g., activating prior knowledge, making predictions, monitoring comprehension) (Berninger, Cartwright, Yates, Swanson, & Abbott, 1994; Olson, 2003). Readers and writers develop insights about how communication works by being both the receivers and senders of communication activities (Nelson & Calfee, 1998).

WHAT CAN WE LEARN ABOUT READING THROUGH ASSESSING WRITING?

Although, historically in the United States, reading and writing have been treated as separate entities with teaching writing only occurring after reading skills were well established (Nelson & Calfee, 1998), more recently reading and writing are taught hand-in-hand from the earliest grades (e.g., Calkins, 1994). Very young children engage in mark making of different kinds as a clear indication of communication even before they have knowledge letter-sound correspondences. Over the school years, students' writing develops, leading to the production of a wide variety of different types of writing for different purposes, with increasing levels of sophistication of vocabulary, syntax, and stylistic features.

Recall that in Chapter 5 we presented a learning progression that comprises three stages of reading development organized around word, sentence, and text level knowledge and skills. As students are acquiring the skills at each stage of the reading continuum, we can expect to see these skills represented in their writing. As Nell Duke and David Pearson (2002) have so nicely summarized the connection between reading and writing, the students who learn to write for others "write like a reader and read like a writer" (p. 208).

Let us now take a closer look at what we mean by thinking about how *word, sentence,* and *text* knowledge at each stage of the reading progression can be paralleled in students' writing. The connections that we highlight here have been informed by both the research and, at Stage 3, by the New Standards English Language Arts Performance Standards (1998).

WORD LEVEL

At Stage 1 of our learning progression for reading, children are developing phoneme awareness and knowledge of the alphabetic principle. This knowledge shows up in their very first attempts at writing in the form of scribbles and pictures. These are replaced first by random letters and then by letters that actually correspond to the phonemes that the child hears in the word that she or he wants to write. At this stage, children often use one letter to represent all the phonemes or write the initial consonant they hear to stand for the entire word.

At Stage 2, when children are acquiring a sight vocabulary, grapheme-phoneme knowledge, and decoding skills, they will reproduce this knowledge in their writing. Sight vocabulary words appear in their writing, as do their attempts to put all the letters in a word for the sounds they hear. At the early stages, children write the letters as they hear them, for example, *favrit* for the word *favorite.* As their grapheme-phoneme knowledge increases during this stage it is reflected in their writing, which comes to include more irregular spelling patterns (e.g. diphthongs and digraphs), prefixes, affixes, suffixes, inflections, and multi-syllabic words.

During Stage 3, students' word level knowledge becomes more sophisticated, including recognizing words with common letter strings but different pronunciations (e.g., *tough, through, trough*), recognizing the suffixes -ible, -able, -ive, -tion, -sion; understanding the ways in which nouns and adjectives can be made into verbs by use of suffixes (e.g., *simple, simplify*); and recognizing homophones. Again, students' writing can provide teachers with opportunities to assess how well these more sophisticated forms of written language are being produced by their students and cross-reference this information with what they acquire from their formative assessments of students' reading.

Of course, during the three stages, children's vocabulary knowledge is also growing. In early writing, children's vocabulary will reflect their oral language vocabulary. As content and reading knowledge increase, so does the size and richness of children's vocabulary. With an expansion of children's lexicon, we can expect to see written vocabulary appearing that may not be part of a student's everyday speech, but it has been selected for a specific purpose, for example, to describe a concept in a science report or a personal attribute in a biographical account from research.

SENTENCE LEVEL

We saw in Chapter 2 how the language of text is different from oral language, and that children become aware of this as they get more experience as readers. This holds for writing, too. Young children's writing is essentially their speech written down. As they increasingly become aware of the differences between spoken and written language, and their knowledge of grammar grows, these aspects are reflected in their writing. For example, children typically construct simple chained clauses with the use of the conjunction word *and* (Kress, 1994). As their language experience grows, children's writing takes on the cadence of academic writing with increased use of more complex syntax, for example, the incorporation of dependent clauses, variations in sentence structure, different clause combining strategies, and increases in the use of adjectives and adverbs.

> ### KEY TERMINOLOGY
>
> **Personification:** A figure of speech (i.e., nonliteral use of language) that gives non-humans and objects human traits and qualities.
>
> **Alliteration:** The reiteration of a sound at the beginning of two consecutive or slightly separated words (e.g., *splish, splash, splosh*).
>
> **Nominalization:** In order to make a process the topic of the sentence, what is commonly expressed in verb form when speaking or in informal writing is expressed in noun form (e.g., the processes of *evaporate* and *precipitate* expressed by the nominalizations *evaporation* and *precipitation*).

As students become more familiar with literary devices that authors use, these too will be incorporated into their writing. For young children, the simple device "once upon a time" can be a favorite opening to a narrative. In Stage 2, students begin to use literary devices such as *personification* and *alliteration*. The device of *nominalization,* commonly used in academic and scientific texts, characterizes the most mature writing (Schleppegrell, 2004).

In our reading progression in Chapter 5, we saw how children's knowledge of punctuation as an aid to reading comprehension develops over the elementary school years. In Stage 1, children learn to write a capital letter for the start of their name and learn that periods are demarcations of sentences. At this stage, many young writers who are producing only a few words of text will embellish their writing with periods (New Standards Primary Literacy Committee, 1999/2004). During Stage 2, students learn common uses of capitalization and the functions of commas, question marks, exclamation points, apostrophes, and speech marks. They experiment with these forms of punctuation in their writing, progressively incorporating them accurately.

In Stage 3, students' knowledge of punctuation becomes more sophisticated and includes, for example, distinguishing between the use of apostrophes for possession and contraction, recognizing how commas and periods can join separate clauses and knowing how semicolons, colons, parenthesis, dashes, hyphens, and quotation marks are used to support meaning. Increasingly, we see these conventions appearing in students' writing.

TEXT LEVEL

Text level knowledge in Stage 1 ranges from an awareness that words can be written down to be read again for a range of purposes, to tracking the text in the right order, page by page, left to right, top to bottom, to pointing while reading/telling a story, and to making one-to-one correspondences between written and spoken words. Beginning writers may not yet have developed the concept of a word or know that text goes from left to right. Their early attempts at writing may be limited to a string of letters, which they will "read" as a story. As understanding of text develops, the kinds of skills needed for reading in Stage 1 are reflected in their writing: words (even though they may include a few letters that stand for all the phonemes the child hears) are separated by a space and they are written from left to right on the page.

In Stage 1, children also develop an awareness of the difference between spoken and written forms and understand that some books tell stories while others give information. In writing, they experiment with these forms of language and their awareness of different genres begins to develop.

During Stage 2, students become much more knowledgeable about genres and genre elements. For example, they come to understand that main ideas in narrative are developed through connections among plot, setting, characters, and events, and that in expository text main ideas are developed by elaborating on ideas and information with supporting details. This knowledge assists students when they read and is reflected in their writing—they are able to write in a range of genres for different audiences from their first contact with formal instruction in writing. Indeed, young students can produce writing for different purposes from very early on, for example, producing lists and dialogues along with chronological texts used to convey narrative information, and "centered texts" used to convey hierarchical information (Chapman, 1994). However, the link to reading is not without some complexities regarding the role of genres. Writing narratives seems to improve reading comprehension for the narrative genre only, whereas writing expository texts improves reading in both expository and narrative genres (Carver, 1998). In terms of text organization and format, children learn that chapters, paragraphs, headings, subheadings, and hyperlinks can be used to link ideas and information in text, and these features also become apparent in their writing. Increasingly, at this stage in reading, they understand how punctuation shapes meaning and use the cues of punctuation to gain meaning. Control over punctuation develops in the students' writing and is used to support their audiences' understanding of what they have written.

In Stage 3, students' understanding of genre increases. For example, they understand the settings, plot, and characters associated with different forms of narrative and how settings influence characters and events in narratives. Their awareness of how authors use figurative language grows with their own creative writing explorations using first *simile* and then *metaphor* to create novel comparisons and connections between objects, people, and abstract concepts.

> ## KEY TERMINOLOGY
>
> **Metaphor:** A figure of speech in which the qualities of one object or abstract concept are given to another object or abstract concept to make an implicit comparison about their resemblance. The use of metaphor allows the writer to equate two seeming disparate things as the same thing (e.g., "Lily, my daughter, is the light of my life").
>
> **Simile:** A figure of speech in which two unlike objects or things are explicitly compared (e.g., "Tomas wandered around like a lost puppy").

Knowledge of the structure of informational and analytical writing increases, and children learn how logical relations are built through the use of text connectives to clarify, compare, contrast, sequence, and indicate time or cause and effect. They recognize persuasive writing and understand how vocabulary and style contribute to persuasion. As their understanding of genre for reading becomes more sophisticated, their writing takes on these forms and they are able to move from one genre to another with relative ease. At this stage, they are also able to order their writing in paragraphs and chapters and they know how to use graphics effectively to support text.

A Role for Later Developments in Oral Language

While the focus of this chapter is on connections between reading and writing, we should not forget that children's oral language skills continue to develop as they enter middle school. Later developments include the gradual increase in accuracy of English inflectional morphology (e.g., agent+*er; driver, snake-charmer*), although some inflectional processes are not successfully mastered until high school or even adulthood (e.g., adverb+*ly*; *disastrously, funnily*) (Derwing & Baker, 1979). Older children also use phonological information such as the placement of stress on syllables to determine word meaning in the case of words that differ by their part of speech (e.g., *prod*uce = noun versus pro*duce* = verb). At the discourse level, by age 9, children use far more anaphoric references to create cohesive ties in their narratives (e.g., pronominalizations substituting *he* for *the man* once *man* has been introduced) (Karmiloff-Smith, 1986). Children's conversational skills also continue to develop, and teachers should see a qualitative shift in the sophistication of the types of questions students can pose about their reading and about their content learning. Teachers can help increase the complexity of question formation by reframing questions for their students in a variety of ways, including asking for questions to be posed from a particular point of view, questions to include a request for explanation, or questions couched as formal hypotheses (Clarke, 2005). Important for the development of creative writing, as we have already seen with Jordan's poetry, figurative uses of language, such as metaphor and simile, are also developing by the late elementary and middle school years, with many children mastering a mature, nonliteral understanding of metaphor by about fourteen-years-old (Winner, Rosensteil, & Gardner, 1976).

Now we will examine more examples of writing used as formative assessment of reading.

Example of Formative Assessment at Stage 1 Reading-Writing Links

Responding to Expository Text Through Writing

When students respond to text, they make a judgment about the text they have heard or read. This judgment can be evaluative or interpretive and often requires them to refer back to the text to support their evaluation or interpretation (New Standards Primary Literacy Committee, 1999/2004). Recall that we encountered children doing this in Ms. Ramirez's group in Chapter 5. Responding to text is a demanding skill, and examining responses as formative assessments can provide insights into how well students comprehend the text, as well as how well they are able to use evidence from the text to support their evaluations and interpretations.

The following is an example of second grader Melanie's science journal writing produced in response to reading expository texts and materials in Ms. Cardenas's class at Para Los Niños (PLN) Charter Elementary School. Melanie is bilingual in Spanish and English in the oral domain. She is being taught Spanish language literacy skills, but has yet to be formally taught to read and write in English.

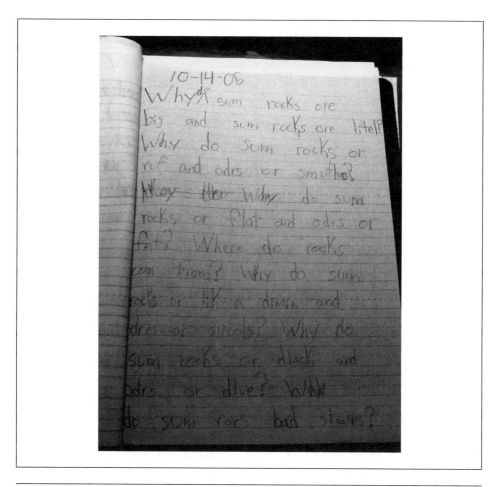

Figure 6.2 Melanie's Science Journal Writing

Used with permission.

We discussed, in Chapter 4, how journal writing also took place after oral discussions of science concepts and ideas. This was used by Ms. Cardenas as part of her formative assessment strategy for gauging how well students were comprehending the discussions. Analysis of journal writing in this instance provides Ms. Cardenas with information about how well Melanie has comprehended the expository texts she has been reading. She was asked to write down, in her science journal, the questions that she thought the text was attempting to answer as she was reading.

Melanie's writing appears to be at the early stage of the reading-writing link for many reasons. Her writing includes approximations of many different, often high frequency, words (e.g., *sum* for *some*, *ore* for *are*, *litel* for *little*, and *dlack* for *black*). These approximations show she is using phonemic knowledge, which is a positive aspect she can build on. She makes errors in grammatical structure, such as question formation, "Why do *sum* rocks *ore* big and *sum* rocks *ore litel*?" Many of the questions appear to be declarative statements, perhaps simply taken directly from the text of the book. It appears that she made an attempt to self-correct here. That is, she appears to transform the declarative forms into the syntactic form of questions in English with the insertion of the auxiliary (or helping) verb *do*. This shows her knowledge of English grammar whereby many questions are formed with this auxiliary verb. However, in some cases, Melanie overextends this strategy and renders the sentences ungrammatical with the insertion of *do* (e.g., when used with the verb *to be*).

Ms. Cardenas is pleased to see that Melanie has appropriated challenging vocabulary for the texts, namely *dimin* and *sircols* for *diamond* and *circles*. Assessing these invented spellings tells Ms. Cardenas about the influence of Spanish literacy on Melanie's English literacy skills. For example, final word sounds /t/ and /d/ are rare in many languages, including Spanish. It is likely that Melanie does not perceive the final /d/ sound in the word *diamond*, and this influences her spelling of this word. Similarly, she writes *odrs* for *others* reflecting her substitution of the sound /th/ for /d/.

At the level of the text, the organization of the writing and expression of ideas are simple, with repetitive use and perhaps an overreliance on the same sentence structure. "*Sum* rocks *ore* . . . and *sum* rocks *ore* . . ." is the frame used for five of the seven sentences that Melanie writes.

What Does Melanie's Writing Say About Her Reading?

From her analysis of Melanie's science journal writing, Ms. Cardenas notes that Melanie's writing reflects her oral language usage rather than the stylistic devices more commonly found in written language. Specifically, she decides to provide direct instruction of some key reading skills, as well as design reading experiences for Melanie to expose her to texts that provide her with a variety of sentence structures. In word level work, Ms. Cardenas will need to build on Melanie's approximations of spellings, including the final /d/ sound in English. Also at the word level, she notes she needs to help Melanie work on high frequency words, and to do this, she will provide Melanie with decodable books that she can read independently to practice decoding the words that she is working on with Ms. Cardenas. At the sentence and text levels, she guides Melanie in selecting reading materials for shared reading that are a little more challenging than those she might read alone, with more varied and complex sentence structures (e.g., embedded clauses such as relative clauses) and greater diversity in their organization and use of expository literary devices (e.g., explicit contrasts, exemplars).

Examples of Formative Assessment at Stage 2 Reading-Writing Links

Example 1: Writing Composition

Ana is a bilingual second grade student in Ms. Lozano's class at PLN. Her teacher has followed an oral discussion of what the students did over the summer break with a writing activity. In this activity, Ms. Lozano has asked the students in the class to write about a specific moment from their summer vacations. First, the students jot down a few sentences to capture their ideas and she provides feedback as they read their writing aloud to her during individual conferences. Next, she asks them to write their stories. The final versions are pinned up around the classroom with the earlier drafts attached to a piece of cardboard overlaid with the finalized versions of the stories and accompanied by pictures or other decorative illustrations.

While this example of writing is still not linked to a particular text that the class may have read, Ana's writing and that of her peers still tells Ms. Lozano much about their understanding of print and the genre of stories. Her analysis of Ana's work reveals some interesting features of Ana's learning. In particular, it illuminates Ana's transfer of her knowledge of Spanish literacy to that of English.

Remember that most of the students at PLN begin to learn to read and write in Spanish. They acquire their English language and literacy skills in the content areas of math, science, and social studies. When they have reached proficiency in Spanish reading, they transition into English reading. Ana's written work in English shows the process of her taking her literacy skills in Spanish and applying them, first, to her oral English for discussion of the task, and then applying them to printed English.

Ana's writing predominantly displays Stage 2 level skills (see her writing sample below). At the word level, her writing shows Ms. Lozano two interesting influences of Spanish on English. First, her spelling of the word *fieldtrip* is revealing. As we saw in Melanie's writing in Example 1 above, it is likely that Ana does not perceive the /d/ in the word *field* and this influences her spelling of the word *fieldtrip*. Ana's rendition is *filtrip*. Ana is also reproducing her Spanish grapheme-phoneme knowledge and decoding skills in her English writing. For example, Ana writes *faund* for *found*, *faik* for *fake*, and *mein* for *mean*. The approximations of the English vowel digraph /ou/ in *found* and the vowel followed by the consonant and the silent "e" in *fake* show the influence of Spanish grapheme-phoneme knowledge.

Ana's vocabulary is varied. Ms. Lozano notices in particular that she uses a variety of verbs and does not just rely on *is* or *was* exclusively. However, she is still very much influenced by her oral language rather

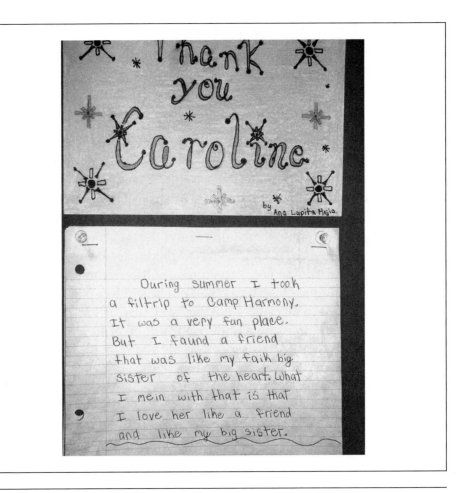

Text in the image:

Thank you Caroline
by Ana Lupita Mejia.

During summer I took
a filtrip to Camp Harmony.
It was a very fun place.
But I faund a friend
that was like my faih big
sister of the heart. What
I mein with that is that
I love her like a friend
and like my big sister.

Figure 6.3   Ana's Personal Story

Used with permission.

than printed language, with few of the words she uses suggesting any strong literary influence yet. Given Ana was composing a personal story rather than responding to a piece of writing she had read this seems appropriate. Ms. Lozano will pay attention to how Ana's knowledge of more literary, or reading influenced, vocabulary develops over time.

At the sentence level, however, Ana clearly exhibits knowledge of written language from her reading, as it stylistically differs from oral language. For example, her use of the prepositional phrase "During summer . . ." in sentence initial position, rather than the use of simple *subject+verb+object* sentence order shows a sensitivity to more complex and interesting grammatical structures often to be found in print. Ana also uses relative clauses, and in her last sentence a multiple embedded clause (" . . . with that is that . . .") which, while not very elegant English, is grammatically correct and contains a complex idea she is trying to clarify for the reader. Ms. Lozano is prepared to let Ana work out these complex thoughts in the message she wants to convey in this awkward but accurate way—for now.

At the text level, Ana has organized her short story in a logical, chronological way, much as written stories are temporally ordered within classic (Western) narrative structure. She tells us where she has been, that she liked it, and that the most salient thing for her was the meeting with her *"faik* big sister of the heart." Notice that her use of the clause connector *but* between the second and third sentences, "It was a very fun place. But I faund a friend . . ." suggests a misunderstanding of the meaning of this disjunctive form. The disjunctive is meant to convey contrast or something counter to what has gone previously. In this instance, Ana's use of *but* to link these two pieces of information clauses does not seem semantically logical. Through either oral language or further exposure to written texts, Ana will come to know the meaning of *but* and *and* as well as other discourse connectors that convey relations between clauses. However, Ms. Lozano makes a note of this on her graphic organizer for Ana and decides she will deliberately check to see whether Ana is using simple clause connectors accurately in both her oral language and in other written productions. She also makes a note to check if Ana comprehends them correctly when she encounters them in the speech of others and in her reading comprehension of new texts.

What Does Ana's Writing Say About Her Reading?

Ms. Lozano's analysis of Ana's personal story leads her to decide on direct instruction of some reading skills, as well as putting together a new collection of texts for Ana's independent reading during Readers' Workshop. Ms. Lozano will also pay closer attention to the material she chooses to read to the class. Because she knows reading and writing share many of the same types of print skills and knowledge, Ms. Lozano decides that she can combine activities in Readers' Workshop with those in W*riters' Workshop* to help Ana develop both her writing and her reading comprehension. The two methods of teaching share many of the same components so Ms. Lozano can frequently use the same activities to foster both reading and writing abilities.

Specifically, at the word level, Ms. Lozano decides that in the future she will need to explicitly teach English vowel spellings to Ana, particularly vowel digraphs (e.g., *ou, ai*) and spelling rules with silent *e* (e.g., *cake,*

> **KEY TERMINOLOGY**
>
> **Writers' Workshop:** A method for teaching writing that builds fluency by daily exposure to the *process* of writing. Students choose their own writing topics and learn to plan, revise, incorporate peer or teacher feedback, and share or "publish" their work by reading it aloud to the class.

take). At the sentence and text levels, she selects reading materials for Ana that have repeated use of simple clause connectors, and during the independent time in Writers' Workshop she reminds Ana to pay attention to how she links her sentences in her journal writing. During sharing time in Writers' Workshop, Ms. Lozano suggests Ana solicit feedback from her peers about how well her sentences are now connected. Finally, Ms. Lozano decides that she will begin to build the next step in Ana's development by exposing Ana and her classmates to more complex clause connectors (*however, while*) and more complex syntactic structures (e.g., subordinate clauses) when Ms. Lozano next reads aloud to the class.

Example 2: Writing Composition

The example in Figure 6.4 was sent in an e-mail to one of the authors from her native-English-speaking niece, Emily, a few months before her eighth birthday and is reproduced exactly as it was sent.

We can immediately see from Emily's e-mail that she clearly understands the structure of chronological narratives, using the past tense consistently, and that she can write an account for an audience that was not present at the event. She organizes a chronology of events very well, and strongly signals sequence through her use of time cue words throughout the narrative—*next, after, then, later.* Her writing provides much detail that helps the reader create mental images. For example, when describing the desert camel ride she writes, "It had a gear stick which you have to pull down to go flying up in the air and you had to let go if you wanted it to go down." This gives the reader a picture of what the ride was like, and when she says that she went on the roller coaster "millions of times" it is clear that this is something that she enjoyed.

Emily also signals her reaction to events, for example when she says, "I was enjoying myself more than I could." Her use of the verb *forced* clearly indicates her reluctance to go on the ride that Olivia wanted her to.

Emily understands the difference between spoken and written language. Her vocabulary choices show that she is picking up words in her reading and using them in a way that is different from the spoken language of a child of her age. She uses the synonyms *tiny* and *mini* for the word *little;* she chooses the word *entered* rather than *went in,* and she nicely explains the rides she could not go on with the word *except.*

Although many of her sentences have several clauses, she is still at the stage of linking clauses through the use of the word *and.* For example, "It started raining and we put our hoods up and Mommy got a bag of candy while I went on the roller coaster caterpillar ride and Olivia went on these little boats with real water in the tub." However, she has a good basis on which to develop different clause combining strategies, and she will likely

From: Emily
Subject: How are you?
Date: May 24, 2006 11:20 am
To: A.M.

Well, I better tell you what I did at southport funfair . . .

When we got to Pleasureland (the funfair bit) we first had to get something called a wristband so you can go on certain rides. Me and Olivia had to have a junior wristband but you cannot go on all the rides. There was also a wristband called all day wristband and you could go on every ride exept 3 little kids rides. When we had got our wristbands, we entered the park and first we went on the gallopers (merry-go round). I went on a horse, Olivia went on a carriage. Next, we went on the little train. After, we looked at the ride called caterpillar (it was closed) and Mommy told us what it did. Then we went on a new ride called desert camels. It had a gear stick which you have to pull down to go flying up in the air and you had to let go if you wanted it to go down. Next, we went on a mini ferris wheel of course you know what ferris wheels do. After, we went on another merry go round with tiny cars and it was very hard to stay in (well it was for me) and I was forced by Olivia to go on the ride. Later, we split up and I went on a caterpillar rollar-coaster ride and you can have your photo taken on the ride. Olivia went on the little train again because the roler coaster was too fast for her and also to scary. It was brilliant and was enjoying myself more than I could! Then the ride stopped and me and Mommy brought a photo of me on the roller coaster in a photo frame. We could have had a key fob or a magnet. I wanted to go on it again and this time Olivia watched me. Then I had a look at the next set of photos. We didn't buy one though. Next, we both went on a ride with land rovers and you ride on a little track. It started raining and we put our hoods up and Mommy got a bag of candy while I went on the roller coaster caterpillar ride and Oliviawent on these little boats with real water in the tub. They go round and round. After, we want to Mommy and had a little walk round sharing the candy. Then we both went on the camel ride again (the flying one). After that, I straight away yet again went on the roller coaster caterpillar ride (I went on this millions of times) while Olivia went on the land rover ride again. Then Olivia wanted something to eat. So we went to the cafe. By the way, it was still raining. We got an ice cream and then I went on the caterpillar rollercoaster twice and Olivia watched me. The final ride was going on the little train. I wanted to go on one more ride but Olivia wanted to go to the car. So Mommy took Olivia to the car and Daddy took me to ride one more ride. We then brought a bag of candy to share on the way home. We went to pizza hut in Southport and then set off home. We got back at 10:00 pm. That is everything almost everything!

Emily

Figure 6.4   Emily's E-mail

Used with permission.

be able to understand more complex sentence structures when they are read aloud. Emily's writing also shows that she is using stylistic devices that she has a come across in her reading, for example, "By the way it was still raining . . .," ". . . I straight away yet again went on the roller coaster . . .," and "After, we looked at the ride called caterpillar (it was closed)."

In sum, what we learn from Emily's writing is that she can imitate narrative elements from the books she has read, and she consistently uses capital letters and periods but is only beginning to correctly use other punctuation (namely, commas and explanation points), that her spelling is consistently accurate, that paragraphing is still not in place, but she can reproduce the stylistic devices found primarily in written English.

What Does Emily's Writing Say About Her Reading?

Emily's writing provides a window into her meaning-making strategies in reading. It shows that she has a good understanding of chronological text structure and knows the vocabulary that signals this structure; she knows the functions of nouns, verbs, and adjectives and will be able to use them to infer meaning; she can make mental pictures in writing and hence use this as a comprehension strategy when reading; and she can use punctuation to make sense of the text. Importantly, Emily's writing also provides a window into what her teacher's next steps will entail. In terms of text structure for reading, she needs to learn the structure of paragraphs, understanding that a topic sentence usually starts a paragraph, that the paragraph contains one main idea and that paragraphs can be used to link ideas in text. This is an important next step to support reading comprehension. Introducing Emily to simple figurative devices, similes for example, would also be appropriate given how she described flying up in the air— her sentence simply begs for a comparison to be made. Reading text with a range of clause combining strategies and directing her attention to the structure of such sentences, and focusing Emily's attention on more sophisticated uses of punctuation in text and how it can support meaning, are other areas that seem ripe for growth.

Example of Formative Assessment at Stage 3 Reading-Writing Links

At the start of this chapter, we read about Jordan's response to literary texts through her own impressive piece of creative writing. In the next two examples, we see further illustration of how we can assess reading through the writing of students who are responding to expository and literary texts.

Responding to Expository Text Through Creative Writing

This example is a rather unusual response to expository text through creative writing. Nick is a native-English-speaking sixth grader in his first year at Verde Valley Middle School. His arts and literature teacher has directed her students to research the characteristics and behaviors of an animal of their own choosing. To do this, students had science textbooks available, as well as a variety of reference books and the Internet. The twist in this task is that the students had to take the information they had previously learned about their chosen animal and create a metaphor to show how the animal was in some manner the same as something else (e.g., another animal, object, or even an abstract concept). The class had been studying simile and metaphor and had already practiced producing poetry that incorporated simile. Nick chooses to write a poem (Figure 6.5) about the sea dragon, a type of sea horse he remembers from an aquarium visit some years before.

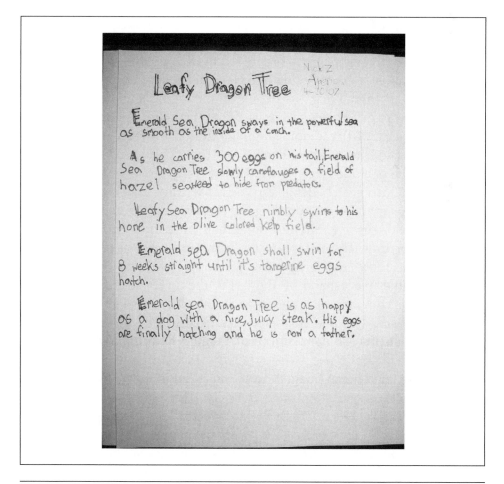

Figure 6.5   Nick's Poem

Used with permission.

Nick's writing succeeds in evoking some very vivid images using unusual adjectives for color, uncommon verbs and adverbs for movement, and interesting similes to set up two different comparisons between the sea dragon and other animals. For example, rather than the simple color orange we get *tangerine,* instead of the run-of-the-mill green or brown seaweed we get *hazel,* the kelp is *olive,* and of course the sea dragon itself is *emerald.* Movement verbs and adverbs also show Nick to have a rich vocabulary. His sea dragon *sways* and swims *nimbly* through his underwater world. Of the two similes Nick uses in the poem, one maintains the ocean theme (*sways . . . as smooth as the inside of a conch),* whereas with the second he likens the sea creature to *a dog with a nice juicy steak.* Also notable is an evocation of an eastern or Chinese sensibility to the writing, with his choice of *emerald* to describe the dragon and the omission of definite and indefinite determiners *the* and *a* in the noun phrases *Emerald Sea Dragon, Leafy Sea Dragon Tree, Emerald Sea Dragon Tree.* The absence of determiners is a grammatical feature of several Asian languages.

Nick's blank verse poem is organized by five predominantly one sentence paragraphs each conveying one main fact about the characteristics or behavior of the animal (e.g., its habitat in the kelp, the number of eggs it produces, the length of incubation, and that the father sea dragon hatches the eggs). Specialized academic language from the science content area is also appropriated from the research Nick first conducted in preparation for writing the poem (e.g., *conch, camoflauges* [sic], *predators, kelp, hatch*).

Where we can see challenges in Nick's writing is in creating a more elaborated metaphor, in maintaining the ocean theme throughout, in using other poetic devices (e.g., rhyme, alliteration), and in using more complex syntactic structures. The metaphor implicitly compares the sea dragon to a *tree* first in the title (*"Leafy Dragon Tree"*), by using *tree* in the name of the sea creature in other places, and by the use of the adjective *leafy* in its name. However, this comparison is not extended in other ways in the poem, for instance by using tree-like characteristics to describe the sea creature, or using tree-related vocabulary. The ocean theme could be maintained with a different second simile: *dog with a nice juicy steak* is an odd choice because he had maintained ocean imagery until this point in the poem.

While there is one attempt to front an adverbial phrase (*As he carries . . .*), Nick's sentence length is extended primarily by prepositional phrases (e.g., *in the olive colored kelp field*), and the use of just one (simple) clause connector *and.* In terms of mechanics and conventions of writing, there are the odd errors in spelling (*camoflauge* for *camouflage*) and punctuation (*it's* for *its,* and missing hyphenation in *olive colored kelp*). There also seems to be some confusion with the use of the verb *camouflage* as a transitive verb when Nick writes that the sea dragon *slowly camouflages a field of hazel seaweed* rather than use this as a reflexive verb with the creature camouflaging *itself* amongst the seaweed.

What Does Nick's Writing Say About His Reading?

Metaphors are powerful literary devices because they can convey in just a few words or sentences what an author most wants his or her audience to perceive in the resemblance between two objects or concepts. Ideas are rendered down to their essence in a successful metaphor. Through Nick's writing, we can determine that he needs to read many more models of successful metaphor in order to develop his understanding and his own writing. His ideas and richly-described images are a strong base from which to start, but his reading needs to include greater exposure to sophisticated uses of metaphor. Nick's choice of reading material at independent reading time and during out-of-school contexts may also not be sophisticated enough to expose him to literary uses of language and complex syntactic structures. Based on this analysis and other samples of Nick's writing, his teacher may decide to select texts (and make suggestions for self-sponsored reading outside school) at a more challenging content and readability level.

Responding to Literary Text Through Expository Writing

In this final example, students in Ms. Andrews's sixth grade class at Madison Elementary School were taught about writing responses to literature. This is a Reading/Language Arts standard for the sixth grade in California. As the New Standards English Language Arts Performance Standards (1998) points out in the introduction to its Middle School Standards:

> . . . for many people who go through school, the study of literature is the only situation in which they have the chance to explore the big ideas and the themes that emerge from social and political conflict, both in their own writing and in the writing of others. (p. 21)

Jordan's poetry at the start of this chapter was a powerful example of this connection between reading and writing. In this example, students are writing in response to *The Weaving Contest* (Wright, 2001), a story that depicts the Greek legend of Athena and Arachne. They must identify the moral of the story, or the main lesson learned by the chief protagonist, Arachne.

During class, students first discussed the story and were then taught two styles of response, an essay and an opinion piece. The essay focused on the content of the story with the typical essay format of an introduction, portrayal of the main ideas and events of the story, and a conclusion. The opinion piece had to connect the ideas of the story to the students' own personal opinions or experiences.

We examine the opinion piece of one of Ms. Andrews's students who is a native speaker of English. Figure 6.6 shows Jessie's writing in response to *The Weaving Contest*. The class had been further prepared using various process writing strategies similar to those we already described in Ana's example. First, the class planned and outlined the structure of their responses. Students then produced a rough draft of their writing for editing and a final draft for sharing.

Jessie's opening sentence captures the main idea of the story. In the remainder of the three paragraphs, he focuses mainly on recounting the events of the story and includes direct speech of Peta's warnings and the boasting of Arachne that ultimately incurs Athena's wrath. Jessie inserts his opinion of the events in the last paragraph, stating that in his mind Athena would not have appeared had Arachne not said anything.

His writing has several word level errors. For example, the misspelling of near-homonyms (*his* for *is*), compound words (*any thing* for *anything*), the use of *'s* instead of the third person singular *+s* in *ignore's*. There is inconsistency of tense with some verbs in the present tense (e.g., *learns, warns*) and some in the past tense (e.g., *said, kept, continued*) even within the same sentence. The shift to present tense with *I think*, however, is appropriate for expressing his current opinion of the story. At the sentence level, words are occasionally omitted (e.g., *then* [there was] *a distant roll of thunder*), and a simple *and* was the most favored clause connector.

Where Jessie did choose a different clause connector, *so*, this word did not logically link the sequence of events. This word functions as a conjunct, suggesting Arachne's actions followed from Peta's advice. However, in this context Jessie needed a disjunct (e.g., *but* or *however*) to more accurately show that the behavior of Arachne was contrary to Peta's advice.

What Does Jessie's Writing Say About His Reading?

Jessie's writing can inform Ms. Andrews not only about his comprehension of this particular story *The Weaving Contest*, but also about his understanding of literary genres more widely. While most students in this sixth grade class could successfully write essays that reported the events of the story, many found the opinion piece of writing much more challenging. Jessie, for example, seems to be reluctant to let go of reporting the events of the story and replacing these with a summary of main ideas. He needs to be able to link these main ideas to his own opinion or to his own comparable experiences of harmful boasting, learning lessons the hard way, etc.

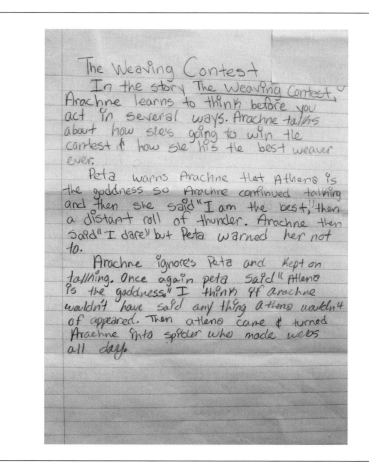

Figure 6.6 Jessie's Opinion Piece

Used with permission.

As he reads, Jessie needs to be making these connections, making evaluations, and noting his own affective reactions to the events and opinions conveyed in text. He also needs to examine the source of his opinions so he can learn to reference them in his academic writing: are they formed by this text, by his reading of other texts, or by his prior knowledge of a topic? Ms. Andrews can support this development through the kinds of books she assigns and by the level of engagement with texts she provides and models for her students. For example, assigning culturally relevant texts will allow students to read and then express their opinions on familiar topics. The creation of persona, or the use of role play, in the discussion of texts will give students the chance to "try on" others' opinions, especially the more provocative opinions that they may feel inhibited in expressing without such role play. Modeling this behavior for students is one way for

Ms. Andrews to make explicit the metacognition that goes into the writing process and scaffold the critical development of literary response as students move into the later middle school years.

In the next and final chapter, you will read about concrete actions that principals and the school systems that support them can take to make formative assessment part of a teacher's everyday instructional practice.

REFLECTION QUESTIONS

1. How often do you use your students' writing to provide a window on their reading? After reading this chapter, do you think you might evaluate writing as a formative assessment about reading?

2. How often do you use your students' writing as a formative assessment about their academic language development? Could you do this more frequently and use the information to plan for academic language instruction (e.g., building vocabulary)?

3. In this chapter, we saw several types of student writing. Do you give your students opportunities to read and to write in a range of genres?

4. How could you make the reading-writing connection more explicit in your classroom practice?

REFERENCES

Berninger, V., Cartwright, A., Yates, C., Swanson, H., & Abbott, R. (1994). Developmental skills related to writing and reading acquisition in the intermediate grades: Shared and unique functional systems. *Reading and Writing: An Interdisciplinary Journal 6*(2), 3–30.

Calkins, L. M. (1994). *The art of teaching writing.* Portsmouth, NH: Heinemann.

Carver, R. (1998). Predicting reading levels in Grades 1 to 6 from listening level and decoding level: Testing theory relevant to the simple view of reading. *Reading and Writing: An Interdisciplinary Journal, 10*(2), 121–154.

Chapman, M. L. (1994). The emergence of genres: Some findings from an examination of first-grade writing. *Written Communication, 11*(3), 348–380.

Clarke, S. (2005). *Formative assessment in the secondary classroom.* London: Hodder Murray.

Derwing, B. L., & Baker, W. J. (1979). Research on the acquisition on the acquisition of English morphology. In P. Fletcher & M. Garman (Eds.), *Language acquisition* (pp. 209–223). Cambridge, UK: Cambridge University Press.

Duke, N., & Pearson, P. D. (2002). Effective practices for developing reading comprehension. In A. Farstrup & S. Samuels (Eds.), *What research has to say about reading* (3rd ed., pp. 261–290). Newark, DE: International Reading Association.

Fitzgerald, J., & Shanahan, T. (2000). Reading and writing and their development. *Educational Psychologist, 35*(1), 39–50.

Heck, R., & Crislip, M. (2001). Direct and indirect writing assessments: Examining issues of equity and utility. *Educational Evaluation and Policy Analysis, 23*(3), 275–292.

Karmiloff-Smith, A. (1986). Some fundamental aspects of language development after age 5. In P. Fletcher & A. M. Garman (Eds.), *Language acquisition* (2nd ed., pp. 455–474). Cambridge, UK: Cambridge University Press.

Kress, G. (1994). *Learning to write.* (2nd ed.). London: Routlege.

Nelson, N., & Calfee, R. C. (1998). The reading-writing connection. In N. Nelson & R. C. Calfee (Eds.), *Ninety-seventh yearbook of the National Society for the Study of Education* (Part II, pp. 1–52). Chicago: National Society for the Study of Education.

New Standards English Language Arts Performance Standards. (1998). *New Standards Performance Standards: Volume 2 middle school.* Washington, DC: National Center on Education and the Economy and the University of Pittsburgh.

New Standards Primary Literacy Standards Committee. (1999/2004). *Reading and writing grade by grade.* Washington DC: National Center on Education and the Economy and the University of Pittsburgh.

Olson, C. (2003). *The reading/writing connection: Strategies for teaching and learning in the secondary classroom.* Boston: Allyn & Bacon.

Schleppegrell, M. J. (2004). *The language of schooling: A functional linguistics perspective.* Mahwah, NJ: Lawrence Erlbaum Associates.

Shanahan, T., & Lomax, R. G. (1986). An analysis and comparison of theoretical models of the reading-writing relationship. *Journal of Educational Psychology, 78,* 116–123.

Winner, E., Rosensteil, A. K., & Gardner, H. (1976). The development of metaphoric understanding. *Developmental Psychology, 12,* 289–297.

Wright, N. (2001). *The weaving contest.* Auckland, New Zealand: Shortland Publications.

7 Schoolwide Formative Assessment

Used with permission.

Teachers in these schools (eight schools receiving the National Award for Model Professional Development) did not walk on the moon, fight in great wars, write significant pieces of literature, discover a cure for life-threatening disease, or invent a way to end world hunger. Instead, their heroism is manifest in the success of their students. They work hard. They work outside their comfort zones. They come together and make decisions to influence the direction of the entire school. They set aside their personal interests for the benefit of their students. They support and coach one another in a community of learners. They demand the best of themselves and their colleagues. And, their efforts pay off in the only way that matters to them—increased student success.

—Joellen Killion (1999, p. 5)

Throughout this book, we have read the stories of different teachers using formative assessment practices in their classrooms. For these teachers, formative assessment is a way of life. They seamlessly integrate formative assessment and instruction, they evoke and interpret evidence of student learning on an ongoing basis, and they use this information to provide feedback to their teaching and to their students. We also saw in every instance how the teachers brought a wide range of skills and deep knowledge to the practice of formative assessment.

However, these teachers did not acquire the knowledge and skills needed to do this overnight. Nor would any of them say that they are not still learning how to be effective in evoking evidence to inform their instruction. And they would agree that evoking evidence affords them a constant source of information about students' learning, which not only helps them identify their current students' zone of proximal development to acquire language and literacy knowledge and skills, but also helps them to accumulate knowledge about how students learn.

They would also say that they are not the only teachers in their school who integrate instruction and formative assessment. They might say that the different teachers have different levels of skill in interpreting evidence, adapting instruction and providing feedback, but they would tell you that all of their colleagues value formative assessment and recognize that it is essential to teaching and learning. Like the teachers at the award winning schools that Joellen Killion describes, they have not finished learning to teach—rather, they are learning from their teaching. They accomplish this by being participants in a learning community where they work hard, support and coach one another, and engage in a process of continuous professional growth. Consequently, the practices of formative assessment are not isolated occurrences. Rather, they are practices that have been adopted schoolwide.

In this chapter, we are going to examine what it takes to establish schoolwide formative assessment practices. Specifically, we will look at some of the ways in which the teachers in our book have become skilled in formative assessment and how they have built and sustained a community of professionals who are continuously learning to teach by learning what to teach through formative assessment. But first, we will consider what we know from research about effective ways to support teachers' professional learning. Then we will look at one of our schools in particular and describe how teachers and administrators come together as a community of professionals and put into practice what the research tells us. We end on how we see the role of formative assessment expanding in the near future and some of the challenges to this that we hope the book will help overcome.

WHAT WORKS IN PROFESSIONAL DEVELOPMENT

Over the last several years, our knowledge of what works in professional development has increased considerably. One thing that we have learned is that the "one shot deal" workshops are not effective. Michael Fullan (1991) succinctly sums up the problem with this kind of professional development when he says:

> Nothing has promised so much and has been so frustratingly wasteful as the thousands of workshops and conferences that led to no significant change in practice when teachers returned to their classrooms. (p. 315)

What we have learned about effective professional development is that it needs to be:

- sustained and take place over a period of time (Cohen & Hill, 1998)
- directly connected to teachers' work with their students (Cobb, McClain, Lamberg, & Dean, 2003; Hiebert, Gallimore, & Stigler, 2002)
- directly related to content and to pedagogical strategies, deepening teachers' knowledge and understanding of how children learn (Darling-Hammond, 1998; American Educational Research Association, 2005) collaborative, involving active participation in teacher learning communities where knowledge is shared (Desimone, Porter, Garet, Yoon, & Birman, 2002)
- grounded in teachers' questions, inquiry, and experimentation as well as research
- supported by coaching and modeling (Darling-Hammond, 1997)

Two additional recommendations on professional development aimed at teachers of ELLs are provided by Diane August in the Report of the National Literacy Panel on Language-Minority Children and Youth (August & Calderón, 2006). First, given the dearth of reliable research on literacy instruction for language minority students, it is important for teachers to continue to engage in professional development that "builds on theory, effective teacher craft and close collaboration between researchers and teachers" (p. 562). Second, in order "to develop a coherent program of instruction for language minority students, it is important to involve all staff concerned with their education (i.e., bilingual and English-language specialists, learning disability specialists if called for, and classroom teachers) in the same professional development efforts" (p. 562).

If you were to visit the teachers whose practices we have described in our stories, you would find that they are involved in ongoing professional development characterized by the elements from the research that we have identified above. Our story in this chapter, however, centers on what happens at Para Los Niños Charter Elementary School (PLN), and it is to PLN that we now turn.

HOW DOES THE FORMATIVE ASSESSMENT MODEL WORK AT PLN?

Recall from the preface that PLN is located in downtown Los Angeles and serves a population of English language learners from impoverished families. The teachers at PLN regard themselves as participants in a professional community in which they all have opportunities to learn from teaching. In fact, one of the teachers left the school a year ago to work nearer to her home, but despite the length of the commute, she returned to the school this year because she so missed being a part of the professional learning community established at PLN.

The school principal, Norma Silva, places great emphasis on creating a professional learning community in which she and the teachers work collaboratively to extend their knowledge and skills to best serve the needs of their students. In Norma's view, a priority for her and the teachers is "to define what the school is. We need to be clear about our beliefs and make sure that what we do is aligned at all times to how we define ourselves." To this end, at the start of every school year, she and her teachers engage in a process of reviewing established beliefs, reaffirming many of them, and, depending on what they have learned during the previous year, making changes and modifications.

Their beliefs are not static but change or are modified according to new evidence that they accumulate. The sources of evidence are the teachers' own classroom experiences (what has worked and the challenges they have encountered), evidence of students' learning from state tests, schoolwide assessments and classroom-based formative assessments, and research findings. In line with the recommendations from the National Literacy Panel (August & Calderón, 2006) to collaborate with researchers, Norma has established a formal network of researchers from universities in California who provide her and the teachers with guidance about program planning based on current research. One of the teachers' collective beliefs is that while children should first learn to read in their primary language, academic English needs to be developed simultaneously with the content they learn in the subject areas. The teachers believe that this is necessary so their students develop strong literacy skills built on their oral language knowledge of Spanish at the same time they learn to become math or science communicators in English. This belief is drawn from a combination of knowledge of the research literature and teachers' own experiences about the best ways to support the reading and language development of language-minority students. During the process of translating this belief into practice, they asked questions that pushed them to extend their thinking, such as, "Why do we believe that children should first learn to read in their primary language? What is the basis for our belief that academic language development should start as early as kindergarten and be developed in the content areas? What evidence do we have to show that the instruction that stems from this belief is working?" Each year the teachers and administrators engage in this process and what they finally agree on becomes the touchstone that guides their work and by which they evaluate what they do.

Revisiting established beliefs each year also provides teachers who are new to the school with the chance to learn more about the context in which they will be teaching. They learn about the beliefs that have been established prior to their arrival. Their experience and knowledge will also be important contributors to the process of challenging beliefs, examining evidence, and collectively determining the consensus beliefs that will be the backdrop for their classroom practice.

In each chapter, we have stressed the importance of teacher knowledge to formative assessment: domain knowledge (knowledge of both reading and academic language); knowledge of students (specifically, their zone of proximal development for acquiring new knowledge and skills); pedagogical content knowledge; and knowledge of formative assessment strategies. At PLN, all teachers are involved in increasing their knowledge for teaching and for assessment.

We will now look at some of the ways in which Ms. Silva supports the development of teacher knowledge through a variety of professional development opportunities: (1) professional development institutes, (2) pupil-free days, (3) learning progression planning meetings, (4) formative assessment meetings, (5) professional library, and (6) mentoring. Each of these professional development events is carefully planned for the year to ensure that they are not a series of ad hoc events but a coordinated and complementary set of experiences that are focused on clear goals.

1. Professional Development Institutes

One of Ms. Silva's goals in professional development is to build up her own and her teachers' expertise so that they can be resources for each other. She does not expect that everyone will be an expert in everything, and, as you might expect, the school does not have the resources to make that happen. Instead, she and the teachers discuss their relative interests, the school's needs, and the resources available; they also decide who is the most appropriate person or most appropriate people to be involved in long-term professional development in specific areas. Some of the institutes that Ms. Silva and her teachers participate in take place during the summer, and others occur during the year. One thing that they all have in common is that they are not "one-shot deals"—they all extend over a period of time. Some of the institutes that teachers have been involved in are the week-long Institutes on the Teaching of Reading and Writing at Teachers College, Columbia University, a week-long institute attended by Ms. Silva to learn about the Reggio Emilia teaching philosophy and techniques firsthand in Italy, and closer to home, a six-day institute that occurred over a period of several months at University Elementary School, UCLA.

Ms. Silva guards against the all too common practice of teachers attending quality professional development, returning to their classrooms, and not having the opportunity to share their newly acquired expertise with anyone except perhaps their grade level colleagues. She implements specific mechanisms through which the distributed knowledge among the teachers can become shared knowledge strategically throughout the school year.

2. Pupil-Free Days

One of the ways Ms. Silva supports the development of new domain knowledge is by providing opportunities throughout the year for the teachers to share what they know and what they have recently learned. This process begins before the start of school for the school year during pupil-free days. Teachers who have been involved in professional development during the summer make presentations about what they have learned, and collectively they discuss how the content adds to their knowledge and what changes in practice they will make because of it. Twice each quarter, the institute participants lead meetings at which their colleagues share some of the practices they have been implementing in their classrooms, and subsequently discuss successes and challenges.

3. Learning Progression Planning Meetings

In addition to the pupil-free days, before the start of school when teachers meet, Ms. Silva has established structures in the school to enable teachers to come together and develop their expertise throughout the year. The school has implemented a system of "banked time" in which students have longer days on Mondays, Wednesdays, and Fridays, and shorter days on Tuesdays and Thursdays, freeing up time for teachers to meet during the afternoon. The content of these meetings always relates to teaching and learning. The "nuts and bolts" aspects of school life are dealt with outside the context of these meetings in shorter after-school meetings on an as-needed basis.

During these meetings, the teachers focus on the different aspects of formative assessment practices across the whole curriculum. While teachers at PLN know that it is crucial to focus on reading and academic language in all the content areas, they also know that their formative assessment practices need to address conceptual and skill development in the content areas too.

At PLN, learning progressions are clearly established to provide coherence and continuity across the school's curriculum so that what happens in one grade level is built on in the next. However, they are not set in stone. Teachers regularly review and refine the learning progressions in each subject area in light of their experience to ensure that they are really representative of a trajectory of learning and that they are useful for instruction and assessment. They also create and review learning progressions for the corresponding academic language (curriculum content language) in a particular subject area. In this way, teachers can discuss how their teaching of language and literacy supports acquisition of math, science, and social studies knowledge and skills. For example, what language structures and vocabulary or specific reading and writing demands will be necessary for comprehension of new concepts and display of new learning in a subject area?

4. Formative Assessment Meetings

Remember from earlier chapters that these learning progressions are essential to formative assessment. They provide interpretive frameworks for formative assessment by enabling teachers to locate students' current learning status on a continuum along which students are expected to progress. Learning progressions also enable teachers to know what to teach next. At their weekly meetings, sometimes as an entire faculty and sometimes in grade level groups, they use the interpretive framework that the progression provides to discuss evidence of student learning. They examine students' work and students' responses to tasks, including oral language and written responses. They discuss the strategies they used to collect evidence of learning. Sometimes they focus on specific questions (e.g., questions designed to generate specific oral language structures in the students' responses), and other times they look at certain tasks (e.g., activating prior knowledge and combining it with information in the text). The result of these conversations is that all teachers increase their knowledge of formative assessment strategies and how they can be integrated with instruction. They also increase their interpretive skills, which are pivotal to the effective use of formative assessment. Teachers' skills in this area can continue to grow throughout their professional life. Collaborating with other teachers to discuss what the evidence from formative assessment strategies means about what students know, understand, and can do provides just the right opportunity for the growth of interpretive skills.

Based on their interpretations of the evidence, they discuss what the next set of instructional goals for students will be, and develop success criteria against which they will be able to judge student performance. They have found that one of the most challenging aspects of formative assessment is providing quality feedback to students. Recall that quality feedback is descriptive, is criterion referenced, and helps students understand how they can move forward in their learning. They work on putting this kind of feedback into child-friendly language which they will provide to students in either oral or written forms.

Only when they have reached this point in the process do they consider what their teaching strategies will be. We think that it is worth noting that the whole process is driven by a focus on learning—what have students learned and what do they need to learn next. This stands in contrast to a planning process that concentrates on what children will do (i.e., the activity). Decisions about the learning activity come after learning goals have been established.

To decide on the next instructional plan, the teachers pool their pedagogical content knowledge to come up with what they think will be the most effective way to support students' next steps in learning, a process that also helps to increase their repertoire of teaching strategies. They also make an assessment plan. This consists of determining when and how they will elicit evidence of learning during instruction and ensures that formative assessment is systematic. Of course, they know that formative assessment opportunities may arise spontaneously during the course of instruction and this evidence can be used to make pedagogical adjustments there and then. However, the assessment plan ensures that they will be collecting the evidence they need to guide teaching and learning.

To summarize the key elements of the formative assessment meetings, teachers have collected evidence of learning, they jointly interpret it, and then they decide how this information will guide their future instruction. Even if the evidence they examine is not from students in their class, or even from their own grade level, all teachers are active participants in the discussion. They know that they can learn from each other, that it is important to look at evidence of learning from students who are either below or above the specific grade levels they teach, and that all of them have a responsibility to contribute their best thinking to the discussion.

5. Professional Library

Over the past several years, Ms. Silva and the teachers have been building up a professional library. The library includes practitioner books and journals about teaching as well as academic research. Often they select books that have been recommended by the professional development institutes that they have attended. Other selections depend on the particular areas that they would like to strengthen in their practice. Ms. Silva pays consistent attention to the National Research Council through its National Academies Press (NAP) Web site, which offers syntheses of research in many areas. For example, she has included core professional texts such as *How People Learn* (2000), *How Students Learn* (2005), and *Knowing What Students Know* (2001), all published by NAP.

In addition to being a resource for individual teachers, throughout the year, the teachers and Ms. Silva select for discussion research texts from the library on different aspects of learning. Of course, reading and language research feature prominently. The research extends their understanding of learning and of curriculum, teaching, and assessment. After reading and discussing research, they always ask themselves the questions "What have we learned that we didn't know before?" and "How will this new knowledge change what we do in our classrooms?"

6. Mentoring

Because of the collaborative culture established in the school, teachers feel comfortable voicing what they do not know and readily asking for support in areas where they feel less confident. Support in the form of mentoring comes from other teachers and from the principal. More experienced teachers pair with less experienced ones and act as mentors. They plan instruction together, and teachers also have opportunities to observe each other teaching and provide constructive feedback. The principal regularly visits classrooms too and also provides supportive feedback that helps teachers grow professionally.

If we return to the hallmarks of effective professional development that we described earlier in the chapter, it is easy to see how the principal's and the teachers' work at PLN reflects these criteria. Their professional learning involves every teacher, and structures are in place so that it is ongoing. It is focused directly on the teachers' work with students, deepening their knowledge of content and pedagogy. It is grounded in teachers' inquiry and in research. Furthermore, the professional learning is supported by coaching and modeling.

The principal and the teachers at PLN provide us with a clear model of teachers who have not finished learning to teach. On the contrary, they are educators who are deeply engaged in a continuous process of learning *from* teaching. Together, they are truly a professional learning community. Their heroism is manifest in their commitment to being the best teachers they can be for each of every one of their students.

We have seen in this chapter how Ms. Silva and her teachers work together to enable teachers to build their skills in implementing formative assessment seamlessly into instruction and to increase their skills in interpreting evidence. Undoubtedly, practitioners who read this chapter will be at different stages in their use of formative assessment. Some may be at the very beginning stages, thinking about questions such as, "How can we even start the process of implementing formative assessment in our school?" Others may be further along and want to know how they can increase their use of formative assessment. To assist teachers and principals to move forward with formative assessment practices, we have provided a set of reflection questions at the end of this chapter. These questions are specifically designed to focus schoolwide thinking and planning on the following topics: (1) teacher beliefs, (2) structural supports, (3) building expertise, (4) process and content of formative assessment, and (5) additional professional support.

Final Words on the Role of Formative Assessment

Dispelling Myths

School principals and their teaching staff would be forgiven for thinking that the efforts described here to plan and effectively carry out formative assessment are beyond the time constraints of many, if not most, contemporary elementary schools. Given the pressures of administering mandated statewide standards-based assessments coupled with a potential myriad of district-level assessment demands, principals and their staff may conclude that adding further assessment activities into the mix would indeed require them to become superhuman, if not Killion's heroes!

Educators everywhere would also be forgiven for thinking that formative assessment is in opposition to the current nationwide assessment initiative to test if students have met the academic standards set by their state. Formative assessments are thought to be unable to do what large-scale summative assessments can (i.e., provide valid and reliable evidence of yearly gain in a subject area). Indeed, formative assessments typically cannot meet established criteria for technical quality in terms of validity and reliability in the traditional sense (e.g., statistical evidence based on field testing and norming studies).

On both counts, in terms of being time consuming and being in compliance with current educational policy, we hope we can assure principals and teachers that these concerns are unfounded. First, the formative assessment model we have developed and illustrated in this book integrates formative assessment with everyday instructional activity. It should take no more time to implement formative assessment as part of regular instruction than it would teaching students inefficiently because you did not know until much later (say during an end of unit summative quiz) where student levels of understanding really were. Formative assessment is not another "add on" for teachers to have to work into their busy schedules and their students' burgeoning curricular demands. Rather, using formative assessment for instruction augments what teachers learn from summative assessments. Most often it will tell them where student strengths and weaknesses reside, well in advance of the annual summative assessments, so that their teaching can be modified to support ongoing needs.

Second, it is important to remember that formative assessment gives teachers the information for teaching and learning that they need on a daily basis, which by their nature, large-scale, summative assessments (e.g., the federally mandated state-wide standards-based) cannot. Recall that the formative assessment model takes account of state content standards in the creation of learning progressions along which formative assessments are anchored. Moreover, state-wide standards-based assessments cannot assess every standard. A sampling of the standards is made due to time constraints on testing. In contrast, formative assessment for instruction can focus on the full complement of content standards over the course of a school year.

Thinking About Constructs and Skills, Not Tests

Formative assessment, while it yields information about what next to teach, can be aggregated across students and across time to also yield comparative and summative information for a teacher at the classroom level or for a principal at the school level. This can be achieved if we make a shift from thinking about assessment as a specific test to thinking about the constructs or specific skills being tested. For example, we can take a skill such as the ability to blend onsets and rimes, and if we have a good sense of the development of this skill on a continuum much as we laid out in Chapter 5, it should be possible to systematically capture this knowledge with a range of different probes for each of our students (calling on them during instruction, while students read aloud, and so on). Each student's performance along the learning progression can be duly recorded to monitor progress in this skill area. It is of lesser consequence that the students were measured with the same test or probe than whether the different tests all measure the *same underlying skill.*

With this shift in focus, as long as the formative assessments clearly target a specific construct or skill, a teacher or principal can compare a student's performance at different points in time, compare overall class performance over time, or even compare different classes in the same grade. By making these comparisons, a principal will not only get a regular snapshot of student performance in this way, but she or he will also learn about the range of formative assessment approaches a teacher is employing in his or her classroom and will be able to tailor professional development meetings to further expand teacher knowledge of formative assessments practices if necessary.

The Investment

Putting into place the formative assessment practices that we have described in this book will undoubtedly require a considerable investment of time and effort on the part of principals and teachers. Some teachers will be closer to the model we have presented than others, but wherever teachers are in relation to the model, an investment of professional resources to develop and refine formative assessment practices in the classroom will be needed. We hope that you believe, as we do, that the benefits to teaching and learning must surely be worth it.

REFLECTION QUESTIONS

Beliefs

1. What are our core beliefs about how students learn?

2. What is the evidence base that supports these beliefs?

3. How will we come to a consensus about core beliefs that define the school?

Structures

4. What structures do we have in our school to support teacher collaboration?

5. Are there ways in which these structures could be improved to increase opportunities for collaboration? (for example, time for regular teacher meetings, mentoring opportunities)

6. Do we ensure that teacher meetings always focus on teaching and learning rather than "nuts and bolts?"

Building Expertise

7. How do we build in-house expertise so that our teachers can become experts in different areas?

8. How do we create learning progressions for reading, academic language, and the other content areas?

Process and Content

9. Have we defined a progression of learning in each subject area with a corresponding progression for academic language?

10. Do the progressions provide sufficient continuity of skill and concept development across the school?

11. How do we/will we modify the progressions in light of experience?

12. Have we made an inventory of formative assessment strategies? How effectively do we use these strategies in our classrooms?

13. Do we meet together regularly to focus on interpreting evidence from formative assessment to increase our interpretive skills?

14. Are we effective at identifying learning goals from our evidence and deriving criteria for success?

15. How well developed are our skills in providing feedback to students? Is this an area where we need to focus?

16. Do we pool our pedagogical content knowledge to come up with the most effective strategies for moving student learning forward?

Additional Professional Support

17. Do we have access to researchers and other experts who can help us increase our knowledge about student learning?

18. Do we have a professional library?

19. What kind of opportunities do we have to go beyond the school for in-depth professional development?

REFERENCES

American Educational Research Association. (2005). Teaching teachers: Professional development to improved student achievement. In L. B. Resnick (Ed.), *Research points: Essential information for education policy*. Washington, DC: American Educational Research Association.

August, D., & Calderón, M. (2006). Teacher beliefs and professional development. In D. August & T. Shanahan (Eds.), *Developing literacy in second-language learners: Report of the National Literacy Panel on language minority children and youth*. Mahwah, NJ: Lawrence Erlbaum Associates.

Cobb, P., McClain, K., Lamberg, T. D. S., & Dean, C. (2003). Situating teachers' instructional practices in the institutional setting of the school and district. *Educational Researcher, 32*(6), 13–24.

Cohen, D. K., & Hill, H. C. (1998). *State policy and classroom performance: Mathematics reform in California*. Philadelphia: University of Pennsylvania Consortium for Policy Research in Education.

Darling-Hammond, L. (1998). Teacher learning that supports student learning. *Educational Leadership, 55*, 6–11.

Darling-Hammond, L. (1997). *What matters most: Investing in quality teaching*. New York: National Commission on Teaching and America's Future.

Desimone, L., Porter, A. C., Garet, M. S., Yoon, K. S., & Birman, B. F. (2002). Effects of professional development on teachers instruction: Results from a three-year longitudinal study. *Educational Evaluation and Policy Analysis, 24*(2), 81–112.

Fullan, M. (1991). *The new meaning of educational change*. London: Cassell.

Hiebert, J., Gallimore, R., & Stigler, J. (2002). A knowledge base for the teaching profession: What would it look like and how can we get one? *Educational Researcher, 31*(5), 3–5.

Killion, J. (1999). *Islands of hope in a sea of dreams: A research report on eight schools that received the national award for model professional development.* Arvada, CO: National Staff Development Council for U.S. Department of Education and San Francisco, CA: WestEd. Retrieved October 27, 2006, from http://www .wested.org/wested/pubs/online/PDawards/PDAward Report Draft1299 .pdf

McKay, P. (2006). Assessing young language learners. Cambridge, UK: Cambridge University Press.

National Research Council. (2000). *How people learn: Brain, mind, experience, and school* (Expanded ed.). Committee on Developments in the Science of Learning, and Committee on Learning Research and Educational Practice, Commission on Behavioral and Social Sciences and Education. J. D. Bransford, A. L. Brown, and R. R. Cocking (Eds.). Washington, DC: National Academies Press.

National Research Council. (2001). *Knowing what students know: The science and design of educational assessment.* Committee on the Foundations of Assessment. J. Pellegrino, N. Chudowsky, & R. Glaser (Eds.). Washington, DC: National Academies Press.

National Research Council. (2005). *How students learn: History, mathematics and science in the classroom.* Committee on How People Learn. M. S. Donovan & J. D. Bransford (Eds.). Washington, DC: National Academies Press.

Index

CORWIN PRESS